Innovation Policies, Business Creation and Economic Development

For other titles published in this series, go to
http://www.springer.com/Series/6149

INTERNATIONAL STUDIES IN ENTREPRENEURSHIP

Series Editors:
Zoltan J. Acs
George Mason University
Fairfax, VA, USA

David B. Audretsch
Indiana University
Bloomington, IN, USA

Max Planck
Institute of Economics
Jena, Germany

Neslihan Aydogan

Editor

Innovation Policies, Business Creation and Economic Development

A Comparative Approach

Springer

Editor
Neslihan Aydogan
Cankaya University
Department of Economics
Ögretmenler Cad. 14
06530 Ankara, Baglica Campus
Turkey
aydongan@cankaya.edu.tr

Series Editors
Zoltan J. Acs
George Mason University
Fairfax, VA, USA

David B. Audretsch
Indiana University
Bloomington, IN, USA

Max Planck
Institute of Economics
Jena, Germany

ISBN: 978-0-387-79975-9   e-ISBN: 978-0-387-79976-6
DOI 10.1007/978-0-387-79976-6

Library of Congress Control Number: 2008940693

Printed on acid-free paper

springer.com

Contents

Part II Company Innovativeness and Growth

Part III Small and Medium-Sized Enterprises and Growth

Contributors

Belgin Akçay
Ankara University
Ankara, Turkey

Erdal Akdeve
Department of Management
Ankara University
Ankara, Turkey

Ahenk Aktan
Izmir University of Economics
Balcova Izmir, Turkey

Gulem Atabay
Izmir University of Economics
Balcova Izmir, Turkey

Dumitru Baleanu
Department of Mathematics
   and Computer Sciences
Çankaya University
Ankara, Turkey

Ismail Bakan
Department of Management
Kahramanmaras Sutcu
   Imam University
Kahramanmaras, Turkey

Yüksel Birinci
Turkish Patent Institute
Ankara, Turkey

James B. Burnham
Donahue Graduate School
   of Business
Duquesne University
Pittsburgh, PA, USA

Gökhan Çapoğlu
Atilim University
Ankara, Türkiye

Şirin Elçi
Technopolis Group Turkey
Ankara, Turkey

Lale Gumusluoglu
Faculty of Business
   Administration
Bilkent University
Ankara, Turkey

Gonca Gunay
Izmir University of Economics
Balcova Izmir, Turkey

Burcu Guneri
Izmir University of Economics
Balcova Izmir, Turkey

Klaus Jurgens
Faculty of Business
    Administration
Bilkent University
Ankara, Turkey

Alev Katrinli
Izmir University of Economics
Balcova Izmir, Turkey

Ali Riza Köker
Turkish Patent Institute
Ankara, Turkey

Lance B. Kurke
Carnegie Mellon University
Pittsburgh, PA, USA

Tolga Omay
Çankaya Vocational School
Çankaya University
Ankara, Turkey

Özlem Özkanli
Department of Management
Ankara University
Ankara, Turkey

A. Orçun Sakarya
Administrative Sciences
    Department of Management
Cankaya University
Ankara, Turkey

N. Aydan Sat
Department of City
    and Regional Planning

Gazi University
Ankara, Turkey

Başak Söylemez
Turkish Industrialists' and
    Businessmen's Association
Ankara, Turkey

Asli Gurel Ucer
Department of City
    and Regional Planning
Gazi University
Ankara, Turkey

A. Kadir Varoğlu
Baskent University
Ankara, Turkey

Cigdem Varol
Department of City
    and Regional Planning
Gazi University
Ankara, Turkey

Bulent Yildiz
Department of Management
Kahramanmaras Sutcu
    Imam University
Kahramanmaras, Turkey

Gulsen Yilmaz
Department of City
    and Regional Planning
Gazi University
Ankara, Turkey

Uğur Zel
uzel@ugurzel.com

Introduction

It is now apparent to many scholars and practitioners that research and development activities and innovation are the pathways to sustainable economic growth. One also recognizes that delving into a topic as such is rather challenging as it is a multidimensional task. We have learned quite a bit on the innovation-growth relationship of the developed countries based on the extensive research on the topic. However, we are yet to understand the very same process for the developing countries where the challenges are expected to be paramount. There obviously is few empirical and theoretical discussion on this topic. This book dares to provide a succinct discussion on a wide array of issues on the innovation and growth relationship for the developing countries.

The book starts off by providing the reader with a promising alternative to endogenous growth models that entails understanding the effect of variables, such as technological change on growth in considerable detail. The next step in the book involves a thorough analysis of economic growth models and how the investment climate affects innovation and entrepreneurship and hence economic growth. Against this background is examined the context of the telecommunications industry in Turkey. Following this, we delve into understanding the radical versus incremental innovation activities, where it is argued that developing nations are more likely to engage in radical innovation, whereas developing nations are engaged in incremental innovation. This argument is important as innovations that produce new products are more likely to occur in developed nations because of the need for larger budgets and the increased uncertainty involved. Moreover, in order to engage in product innovations, an obvious pre-requisite is the ability to claim ownership and hence the existence of intellectual property rights. This has obvious implications on the level, which countries have the ability to leap forward in the development game.

The book moves forward, comparing and contrasting the European Union countries with Turkey in their respective ability to compete by engaging in innovation. As it is discussed in the previous piece, a thorough empirical analysis proves that patent applications and expenses on per capita research and development increases the competitive ability of countries through their ability to innovate. Further to this observation, we focus on the effective use of intellectual property rights in promoting innovative activity via increased incentives, but enabling the diffusion of knowledge nevertheless.

Concluding the first part, the importance of institutional structure in promoting innovation and questions that are related to Turkey's ability to pick up pace are discussed. The implications of the study are applicable to all developing nations that are struggling to move ahead.

In the next part, diverging from the first part's macro analysis, beliefs and ability to change them in relation to creativity and leadership are discussed. Innovation is very much a change process that requires ability to foster that change; understanding how easily one can move from inefficient stagnant thinking to innovation is a great recipe for understanding what promotes great leaders and entrepreneurs. Following on this very note, the part delves more into understanding the value system and the leadership style of the entrepreneur in connection with a company's ability to innovate. The next step in the analysis is to move to a rather significant concept for entrepreneurship that is the technology development zones and their ability to promote innovative activity. Several Turkish (in particular Ankara) technology development zones are compared and contrasted for their regional innovation systems and their resulting ability to innovate. In relation to this, a particular technology development zone, Ankara-Ivedik technology zone, is empirically analyzed to investigate the ability of small and medium-sized enterprises to benefit from the networks of such dense areas that large firms do not have access to.

The following part focuses on small and medium-sized enterprises. It starts off with a detailed empirical investigation of the small and medium-sized enterprises in the Gaziantep and Kahramanmaras regions in Turkey, analyzing product, process, organizational, and marketing innovations. Next, the advantages and disadvantages of the

Turkish small and medium-sized enterprises in terms of their ability to innovate are compared and contrasted with that of the European Union. Once small and medium-sized enterprises are considered, the financial challenges of the Turkish SME's are also discussed where there is little access to risk capital and consequences of such reality are analyzed.

The part next moves onto explaining the continuous improvement and reengineering activities of the SME's in relation to innovation. Finally, the part tries to reconcile the paradoxical observation of high demand for product innovation and a seemingly low level of innovation in Turkey by laying out in detail the changes in the national innovation system in the country.

Overall, the book provides the reader with a wide array of empirical and theoretical discussion on the very topics of innovation from a perspective of the developing world, often employing Turkish and European Union data. Such work is rather scarce despite its obvious importance. Closing the gap between the developed and developing world is possible only if we understand the challenges of the developing world. We believe that this book provides eclectic pieces that form congruent parts to understand the developing world in the innovation game. We hope that it encourages further work in this area.

Part I
Growth and Innovation

1 Solving Technological Change Model by Using Fractional Calculus

Tolga Omay and Dumitru Baleanu

Abstract

Fractional calculus is a generalization of classical calculus, which is a generalization of ordinary differentiation and integration to arbitrary order, and has recently been used in various fields like physics, engineering, biology, and finance. By applying fractional calculus to Romer's Technological Change Model, we introduce this new method to the field of economics and obtain a generalized solution for the model.

1.1 Introduction

1.1.1 Motivation and Contribution to the Literature

Economic growth theory has been the focus of economics literature for a long time. From the classic Ramsey (1928) growth model to the neoclassical growth model of Cass (1965) and Romer's (1990) growth model with endogenous technological progress, one observes a progressive refinement of technological change within an analytical growth framework (Chiang, 1992). In addition to the progressive economic formulation of technological change, the literature also witnessed several improvements in the mathematical methods used to solve the aforementioned economic models. Our aim is to contribute to this literature by introducing a mathematical method that has never been used by the previous economic growth theory.

To the authors' knowledge, Ramsey (1928) is the first to apply dynamic optimization methods to economic growth model dealing

N. Aydogan (ed.), *Innovation Policies, Business Creation and Economic Development*, International Studies in Entrepreneurship 21, DOI 10.1007/978-0-387-79976-6_1, © Springer Science+Business Media, LLC 2009

with technological change. The model was solved by the "calculus of variation," which is one of the earliest dynamic optimization techniques. On the other hand, to tackle the problem of dynamic optimization, "calculus of variation" is only one of the three major approaches in mathematics. The other two are dynamic programming by Belmann (1958)[1] and the modern generalization of variational calculus under the name of optimal control theory founded by Potrayagin et al. (1962).[2] In this study, we apply an improved version of optimal control theory, namely fractional Hamiltonians, to the economic growth model by Romer (1990).

In its simplest form, fractional calculus is the generalization of classical calculus; hence, the fractional Hamiltonian is a generalization of classical Hamiltonian. Our application to economic growth, on the other hand, is the first application of this novel mathematical technique to the field of economics. We have chosen a relatively early endogenous growth model with technological change as it is free of complicated secondary assumptions.[3]

1.1.2 A Short Overview of Economic Growth Literature

The neoclassical growth theory by Solow (1956) and Swan (1956) treated technological change as exogenous. On the other hand, later models by Arrow (1962), Uzawa (1965), and Rebello (1991) did not involve technological change. One striking feature of these models is the possibility of infinite growth rate since that newly accumulated capital is not subject to the law of diminishing returns. In the late 1980s, economic growth literature experienced a major forward move with the help of endogenous growth theory by Romer (1986) and Lucas (1988). In the endogenous growth theory, the long-run growth rate depends on many factors, including but not limited to fiscal policy, procurement of legal framework, protection of property rights, regulation of international trade, and regulation of financial markets.

---

[1] See Sargent (1987) for comprehensive discussion.

[2] See Chiang (1992) for comprehensive discussion.

[3] The models of Peretto and Smulders (2002), Klette and Kortum (2004), and Aghion and Howitt (2005) are among more recent endogenous growth models with technological change.

Moreover, the new endogenous growth theory made technological change as one of the endogenous factors determining the steady-state growth rate, and highlighted the importance of research and development (R&D) and imperfect competition in the growth process. Based on those models, Grossman and Helpman (1991) and Agion and Howitt (1992) argued that the use of R&D could bring ex post monopolistic power and might lead to the disappearance of "Pareto Optimality" due to the distortions that occurred by the formation of new goods and new methods of production.

As technology became more and more important in growth theory, the spread of technology became one of the key questions in the literature. Some recent studies considered the possibility that technological knowledge developed by a "leader" country can be imitated by a follower country (Grossman and Helpman, 1991). Since imitation is less costly than inventing or innovating, conditional convergence in this group of models is handled similar to the neoclassical approach.

1.1.3 A Short Overview of Fractional Calculus

Fractional calculus is an emerging field and, during the last decade, has provided an alternative tool to solve several problems from various fields (Kilbas et al., 2006; Podlubny, 1999). Of late, fractional variational principles have been developed and applied to fractional optimal control problems by Baleanu and Muslih (2005), Rabei et al. (2007), and Heymans and Podlubny (2006). Moreover, based on a series of examples from the field of viscoelasticty, Heymans and Podlubny (2006) have demonstrated that it is possible to assign a physical interpretation meaning in terms of Riemann–Liouville fractional derivatives. In spite of various efforts over the recent years, the fractional Lagrangian and Hamiltonian formulations of both discrete and continuous systems are only at the beginning of their development. Although the fractional variational principles were being investigated, the appropriate physical interpretation of fractional derivatives creates problems in physical interpretation of the obtained equations. The existence of various fractional derivatives leads to several Hamiltonian formulations for a given dynamical system. By construction, the fractional Lagrangian and fractional Hamiltonian contain as a particular case the classical counterparts. Hence, we can use this approach to dynamical economic system in order to obtain generalization of classical solution.

Rest of the chapter is organized as follows: In Section 1.2 we give the basic definitions, in Section 1.3 we provide generalization of the technological change model by using fractional calculus, and Section 1.4 concludes with our findings.

1.2 Basic Definitions

There are many similar definitions for the fractional derivative. In this work, we employ the left Caputo fractional derivative that is given by

$$\prescript{C}{0}{D}^{\alpha}_t f(t) = \frac{1}{\Gamma(n-\alpha)} \int_0^t (t-\tau)^{n-\alpha-1} \left(\frac{d}{dt}\right)^n f(\tau)d\tau \qquad (1.1)$$

Since we will restrict the order alpha of our derivative to the range of zero to one, this definition can be simplified as

$$\prescript{C}{0}{D}^{\alpha}_t f(t) = \frac{1}{\Gamma(1-\alpha)} \int_0^t (t-\tau)^{-\alpha} \left(\frac{d}{dt}\right) f(\tau)d\tau \qquad (1.2)$$

The Caputo derivative of a constant is zero but the Leibniz rule for the αth order derivative is given below

$$\prescript{C}{0}{D}^{\alpha}_t [\phi(t)f(t)] = \sum_{k=0}^{\infty} \binom{\alpha}{k} \phi^{(k)}(t) \prescript{C}{0}{D}^{\alpha-k}_t f(t),$$

$$\text{where } \binom{\alpha}{k} = \frac{\Gamma(\alpha+1)}{k!\Gamma(\alpha-k+1)}. \qquad (1.3)$$

This is valid provided that both $f(t)$ and $\phi(t)$ and all their derivatives are continuous on the interval $[0, t]$ (Podlubny, 1999).

In the following, we construct the Hamiltonian formulation within Caputo's fractional derivatives. Let us consider the fractional Lagrangian as given by Rabei et al. (2007).

$$L\left(q, \prescript{C}{a}{D}^{\alpha}_t q, t\right), 0 < \alpha, \beta < 1 \qquad (1.4)$$

By using equation (1.1), we define the canonical momenta p_α and p_β as follows:

$$p_\alpha = \frac{\partial L}{\partial_a^C D_t^\alpha q} \tag{1.5}$$

We define the fractional canonical Hamiltonian as

$$H = p_{\alpha a}^{D} D_t^\alpha q - L \tag{1.6}$$

Taking total differential of equation (1.3) and by using equation (1.2) we obtain

$$dH = dp_{\alpha a}^{D} D_t^\alpha q - \frac{\partial L}{\partial q} dq - \frac{\partial L}{\partial t} dt \tag{1.7}$$

Taking into account the fractional Euler–Lagrange equations we obtain

$$dH = dp_{\alpha a}^{D} D_t^\alpha q - (_t D_b^\alpha p_\alpha) dq - \frac{\partial L}{\partial t} dt \tag{1.8}$$

Finally, after some simple manipulations the fractional Hamiltonian equations are obtained as follows

$$\frac{\partial H}{\partial t} = -\frac{\partial L}{\partial t} dt, \, \frac{\partial H}{\partial p_\alpha} = {}_a^C D_t^\alpha q, \, \frac{\partial H}{\partial q} = {}_t D_b^\alpha p_\alpha \tag{1.9}$$

1.3 Theoretical Model and Solution by Fractional Calculus

1.3.1 The Classical Solution of Technological Change Model by a Hamiltonian

In the formal setup, a Hamiltonian is solved by several steps: First, one starts with an objective function (utility in this specific case):

$$U = \int_0^\infty \frac{c_t^{1-\sigma} - 1}{1 - \sigma} e^{-\rho t} .dt \tag{1.10}$$

that is maximized subject to several constraints.

$$\dot{K} = Y - C \tag{1.11}$$

$$A = \delta H_A A \tag{1.12}$$

$$H_y = H - H_A \tag{1.13}$$

Equation (1.11) is capital accumulation. Equation (1.12) is the research and development accumulation constraint, and equation (1.13) is a necessary condition on the optimization problem.[4] Then we have to give production function as in equation (1.14):

$$Y = H y^\alpha L^\beta \int_0^A \bar{x}^{1-\alpha-\beta} di \tag{1.14}$$

$$K = \eta A \bar{x} \tag{1.15}$$

$$Y = (H - H_A)^\alpha A^{\alpha+\beta} L^\beta K^{1-\alpha-\beta} \eta^{\alpha+\beta-1} \tag{1.16}$$

Then we can construct the Hamiltonian for dynamic optimization as below:

$$H = e^{-\rho t} \frac{(c^{1-\sigma} - 1)}{1 - \sigma} + \lambda \big[(H - H_A)^\alpha A^{\alpha+\beta} L^\beta K^{1-\alpha-\beta} \eta^{\alpha+\beta-1} - c \big] \\ + \mu \left[\delta H_A . A \right] \tag{1.17}$$

From the Hamiltonian, one can obtain the first-order conditions as:

$$\frac{\partial H}{\partial C} = 0, \ \frac{\partial H}{\partial H_A} = 0, \ \frac{\partial H}{\partial K} = -\dot{\lambda}, \ \frac{\partial H}{\partial A} = -\dot{\mu} \tag{1.18}$$

1.3.2 Fractional Calculus Solution of Technological Change Model

Furthermore, we have a similar objective function, this time in fractional form:

$$F(c, t) = e^{-\rho t} \frac{(c^{1-\sigma} - 1)}{1 - \sigma} . dt \tag{1.19}$$

---

[4] The definitions of the variables and the equation can be obtained from Romer (1990).

Now we are getting the constraints in fractional derivatives. These constraints are the counterpart of the classical case that is derived by fractional calculus.

$$_aD_t^\alpha A = \sigma S_A A \tag{1.20}$$

$$_aD_t^\alpha K = \gamma^{\alpha+\beta-1} A^{\alpha+\beta}(S_o - S_A)^\alpha L_o^\beta K^{1-\alpha-\beta} - c \tag{1.21}$$

We have to define the Δ in order to use in simplification of the notation

$$\Delta = \gamma^{\alpha+\beta-1} A^{\alpha+\beta}(S_o - S_A)^\alpha L_o^\beta K^{1-\alpha-\beta} \tag{1.22}$$

Therefore, the equations (1.20) and (1.21) can be written in short notation

$$_aD_t^\alpha A = \sigma S_A A \tag{1.23}$$

$$_aD_t^\alpha K = (\Delta - c) \tag{1.24}$$

Then we can construct the dynamic optimization by fractional calculus for a general case:

$$\bar{J} = \int_a^b e^{-\rho t} \frac{(c^{1-\sigma} - 1)}{1 - \sigma} + \lambda_1 \left[_aD_t^\alpha A + \sigma S_A A \right] + \lambda_2 \left[\Delta - c - _aD_t^\alpha K \right] dt \tag{1.25}$$

The equations are as follows:

$$_aD_t^\alpha A = \sigma S_A A \tag{1.26}$$

$$_aD_t^\alpha K = (\Delta - c) \tag{1.27}$$

$$_bD_t^\alpha \lambda_1 = \lambda_1 \sigma S_A + \lambda_2 (A^{\alpha+\beta-1}) X \gamma^{\alpha+\beta-1} A^{\alpha+\beta-1}(S_o - S_A)^\alpha L_o^\beta K^{1-\alpha-\beta} \tag{1.28}$$

$$_bD_t^\alpha \lambda_2 = \lambda_2 (1 - \alpha - \beta) X \gamma^{\alpha+\beta-1} A^{\alpha+\beta}(S_o - S_A)^\alpha L_o^\beta K^{1-\alpha-\beta} \tag{1.29}$$

From the fractional optimization, one can obtain the first-order conditions:

$$\frac{\partial F}{\partial c} + \lambda_1 \frac{\partial G_1}{\partial c} + \lambda_2 \frac{\partial G_2}{\partial c} = 0 \tag{1.30}$$

$$\frac{\partial F}{\partial S_A} + \lambda_2 \frac{\partial G_1}{\partial S_A} + \lambda_2 \frac{\partial G_2}{\partial S_A} = 0 \tag{1.31}$$

$$c^{-\sigma} e^{-\rho t} + \lambda_1 . 0 - \lambda_2 = 0 \tag{1.32}$$

$$0 + \lambda_1 \sigma A - \lambda_2 \alpha \left[\gamma^{\alpha+\beta-1} A^{\alpha+\beta} (S_o - S_A)^\alpha L_o^\beta K^{1-\alpha-\beta} - c \right] = 0 \tag{1.33}$$

$$\lambda_2 = c^{-\sigma} e^{-\rho t} \tag{1.34}$$

$$\Delta = \frac{\lambda_1 \sigma A}{\lambda_2 \alpha} (S_o - S_A) \tag{1.35}$$

$$_a D_t^\alpha A = \sigma S_A A \tag{1.36}$$

$$_a D_t^\alpha K = (\Delta - c) \tag{1.37}$$

$$_b D_t^\alpha \lambda_1 = \lambda_1 \sigma S_A + \lambda_2 (A^{\alpha+\beta-1}) X \gamma^{\alpha+\beta-1} A^{\alpha+\beta-1} (S_o - S_A)^\alpha L_o^\beta K^{1-\alpha-\beta} \tag{1.38}$$

$$_b D_t^\alpha \lambda_2 = \lambda_2 (1 - \alpha - \beta) X \gamma^{\alpha+\beta-1} A^{\alpha+\beta} (S_o - S_A)^\alpha L_o^\beta K^{1-\alpha-\beta} \tag{1.39}$$

$$\Delta = \gamma^{\alpha+\beta-1} A^{\alpha+\beta} (S_o - S_A)^\alpha L_o^\beta K^{1-\alpha-\beta} \tag{1.40}$$

After these simple manipulations, we obtain the generalized results given as:

$$_b D_t^\alpha \lambda_1 = \lambda_1 \sigma S_A + \lambda_2 (\alpha + \beta) A^{-1} . \Delta \tag{1.41}$$

$$_b D_t^\alpha \lambda_2 = \lambda_2 (1 - \alpha - \beta) K^{-1} . \Delta \tag{1.42}$$

Therefore, the growth paths that are obtained from this generalized formulation will have memories and detailed information in their nature for understanding the growth process that is obtained from endogenous technological change.

1.4 Concluding Remarks

For a long time, there has been no substantial theoretical paradigm change in growth literature related to model building and mathematical instruments. By providing a more general solution for the endogenous growth model by Romer (1990), we take another small step in this direction. Our new approach to solving growth models might enhance not only the theoretical model building, but also empirical studies in the future by providing a number of testable hypotheses. This is due to the fact that fractional calculus solutions to growth models yield a different kind of information set. Fractional derivative has a memory that shows the growth paths of variables in detail, which enables researchers to understand the effects of a number of variables, including technical change on growth process in greater depth. Further avenues for research include application of fractional optimization to a different set of economic models as well as testing economic models by using Real-World data.

References

Agion, P., Howitt, P. (1992). A model of growth: creative destruction. *Econometrica*, 60(2), 323–351.

Arrow, K. J. (1962). The economic implications of learning by doing. *Review of Economic Studies*, 29(6), 155–173.

Baleanu, D. (2006). Fractional Hamiltonian analysis of irregular systems. *Signal Processing*, 86(10), 2632–2636.

Baleanu, D., Muslih, S. I. (2005). Formulation of Hamiltonian equations for fractional variational problems. *Czech. J. Phys.*, 55(6), 633–642.

Bellman, R. E. (1957). *Dynamic programming*. Princeton, NJ: Princeton University Press.

Cass, D. (1965). Optimum growth in an aggregate model of accumulation. *Review of Economic Studies*, 32(8), 233–240.

Chiang, A. (1992). *Elements of dynamic optimization*. New York: McGraw-Hill

Grossman, G., Helpman, E. (1991). *Innovation and growth in the global economy*. Cambridge, MA: MIT Press.

Heymans, N., Podlubny, I. (2006). Physical interpretation of initial conditions for fractional differential equations with Rieman-Liouville fractional derivatives. *Rheol. Acta*, 45, 765, 771.

Kilbas, A. A., Srivastava, H. M., Trujillo, J. J. (2006) *Theory and applications of fractional differential equations*. Amsterdam: Elsevier.

Lucas, R. E. (1988). On the mechanics of economic development. *Journal of Monetary Economics*, 22(1), 3–42.

Podlubny, I. (1999). *Fractional differential equations*. San Diego CA: Academic Press.

Pontryagin, L. S. (1962). *The mathematical theory of optimal process*. New York: Interscience (translated by K.N. Trirogoff).

Rabei, E. M., Nawafleh, K. I., Hijjawi, R. S., Muslih, S. I., Baleanu, D. (2007). The Hamiltonian formalism with fractional derivatives. *Journal of Mathematical Analysis and Applications*, 327, 891–897.

Ramsey, F. (1928). A mathematical theory of saving. *Economic Journal*, 38(11), 543–559.

Rebello, S. (1991). Long-run policy analysis and long-run growth. *Journal of Political Economy*, 99(3), 500–521.

Romer, P. M. (1986). Increasing returns and long-run growth. *Journal of Political Economy*, 94(5), 1002–1037.

Romer, P. M. (1987). Growth based on increasing returns due to specialization. *American Economic Review*, 77(2), 56–62.

Romer, P. M. (1990). Endogenous technological change. *Journal of Political Economy*, 98(5), 71–102.

Sargent, T. (1987). *Advance macroeconomics*.

Solow, R. (1956). A contribution to the theory of economic growth. *Quarterly Journal of Economics,* 1(2), 65–94.

Swan, T. W. (1956). Economic growth and capital accumulation. *Economic Record,* 32(11), 334–361.

Uzawa, H. (1965). Optimal technical change in an aggregative model of economic growth. *International Economic Review*, 6(1), 18–31.

2 Economic Growth, Entrepreneurship, and the Deployment of Technology

James B. Burnham

Abstract

This paper analyzes the development of our understanding of the causal links between economic growth, the climate for innovation and entrepreneurship, and the deployment of technology, with specific reference to telecommunications. Particular attention is paid to the (mis)use of the Harrod–Domar model by The World Bank and other development agencies, and to the more recent appreciation for "the investment climate," which finds substantial support in the work by Parente and Prescott. The importance of an institutional framework supportive of innovation ("experimentation") and entrepreneurship is underscored by economic historians, such as Rosenberg and Birdzell, and North.

The role of telecommunications technology in modern economies and its contribution to total factor productivity is reviewed, as are the obstacles to the technology's effective deployment. Some of these obstacles are inherent in the technology itself, but many are the result of government legislative and regulatory decisions that constrain entrepreneurial initiatives, as recent experience in Turkey demonstrates. The paper concludes with a discussion of policy choices that governments face in influencing the climate for market-driven investment in telecommunications services and infrastructure.

2.1 Introduction

This chapter seeks to address "the micro and macro issues of innovation and growth at the developing country scale." I intend to do this by describing the causal links between economic growth, the climate for

N. Aydogan (ed.), *Innovation Policies, Business Creation and Economic Development*, International Studies in Entrepreneurship 21, DOI 10.1007/978-0-387-79976-6_2, © Springer Science+Business Media, LLC 2009

innovation and entrepreneurship, and the deployment of technology (broadly defined) with particular reference to the contemporary role played by telecommunications technology in Turkey.[1]

Because of the historical importance of economic growth theory in influencing public policy, particularly in the multilateral development agencies, the first section of the paper will trace the evolution of growth theory and its practical application in recent decades. The second section will discuss the role of telecommunications technology investment on economic growth and the conditions for its effective deployment. The concluding section discusses telecommunications regulatory issues and the design of effective policy for the sector.

2.2 The Mystery of Economic Growth

Interest in the sources of long-term economic growth is long-standing. The early Adam Smith had a very succinct explanation: "little else is required to carry a state to the highest degree of affluence from the lowest barbarism but peace, easy taxes, and a tolerable administration of justice; all the rest being brought about by the natural course of things. . ."[2] Smith was to add somewhat to his minimalist requirements by the time he published *The Wealth of Nations*. However, the emphasis on "the invisible hand" of the marketplace as the primary engine of development (in a peaceful setting maintained by a competent, minimalist government) remained.

For many years, following Smith's landmark contribution, economists (with the important exception of Ricardo) tended to neglect the issue of long-term economic growth. However, in the past several decades, interest has surged.

Two driving forces behind this renewed interest have been paramount. First, efforts to estimate economic growth rates over the past 2,000 years resulted in a general consensus that, in the period up to 1800, there was little sustained improvement in the average standard

---

[1] The author thanks participants in the Boğaziçi University's Economics Department 2005 seminar for their encouragement and suggestions on an earlier draft of this paper while he was a Fulbright Senior Researcher in residence.

[2] Quoted in Rae (1895), p. 62.

of living in the world's major population centers (Western Europe and China). Extended economic growth, in other words, was a nonevent.

However, over the past 200 years, significant and sustained increases in per capita income have been achieved in a number of countries, most notably in North America, Western Europe, and Japan; notable "growth spurts" have taken place in East Asia and, more recently, China and India. As a result, whereas at the beginning of this period the difference between the richest and the poorest countries was on the order of 2:1, more recently it has grown to 25:1.[3] Over the past 50 years, however, the gap between two major groupings of countries (Western Europe and its offshoots—"the West"—and East Asia plus the Indian subcontinent—"the East") has narrowed significantly, thanks to the individual East Asia members' growth spurts.[4]

Why, after such a long period of stagnation, should some countries experience such a marked advance in living standards? And why should some countries remain mired in stagnation? Certainly an economic question of the first order.

A second impetus to renewed attention to sustained economic growth was the post-World War II political scene. The political and proxy war struggle between the NATO countries and the Soviet bloc was also seen as a test of economic systems—market-driven capitalism versus comprehensive state planning and investment. Economic growth in the parties directly concerned as well as in the "Third World" countries, particularly those that emerged from Western colonial empires in the 1950s, became a matter of international concern. Higher growth rates would create a middle class with property interests that would be hostile to political instability in general and Soviet expansionism in particular. This political consideration was reflected most clearly in the formation and operations of The World Bank and the other multilateral development institutions.

The attempts to "solve" the mystery of economic growth took two rather distinct paths. The academics focused on trying to understand the issue by hypothesizing and then decomposing the variables

---

[3] Lucas (2002), p. 109.

[4] The "West" v. "East" per capita income ratios went from 2.1 in 1820 to 7.5 in 1950 and back down to 4.3 by 1992. (Parente and Prescott (2002), citing Maddison's work, p. 15.)

associated with growth. They then constructed models that were tested with increasing degrees of confidence against a growing database. The "practitioners"—chiefly government policymakers and the economists working inside the multilateral development banks and foreign aid agencies—bowed to bureaucratic and political pressure for immediate action (e.g. disbursing financial resources). They used whatever models were immediately at hand and convenient to use to help them allocate (or justify) their lending programs and capital requests.

2.3 Economic Growth for Practitioners: The Harrod–Domar Model

Perhaps the most succinct critique of the practitioners' solution to their problems can be found in Easterly's 1997 essay, "The Ghost of Financing Gap—How the Harrod–Domar Growth Model Still Haunts Development Economics." Even though the model was originally designed to deal with short-term business cycle problems it was taken up with enthusiasm by development economists in lending institutions and aid agencies. (After they did so, Harrod disavowed its use for such purposes.[5])

The attraction of the Harrod–Domar model was that it reduced the growth mystery to one simple, manageable variable: investment. Next year's growth is a function of last year's investment:

$$\Delta Y_{t+1} = \alpha(I_t/Y_t)$$

The change in output next year is a function of the ratio of this year's investment to this year's output. Since it is not a constraint, labor does not appear in the equation. It is assumed that there is always "surplus" labor, an assumption supported (originally) by the work of Arthur Lewis and others. Given α, the incremental capital output ratio (ICOR), growth next year is determined by the volume of investment this year. If domestic savings is less than some desired level of I, we can "fill the gap" with external resources to the extent that private capital (foreign or domestic) is unavailable or prohibited (e.g. in major sectors such as energy), and external assistance can make up

---

[5] Easterly, p. 2.

the difference. Somewhat ironically, as Easterly points out, Russian economists of the 1920s used this same approach in projecting Soviet growth during that period.[6]

Despite its disavowal by the principal author, the use of the Harrod–Domar model and its linear descendants lasted well into the 1990s in most development banks' work. This occurred even though many economists inside and outside these institutions began to shift their attention to *how* capital was allocated, rather than the sheer volume made available. But the fact that the Harrod–Domar model was useful in facilitating lending program design, organizational planning, budgeting, and financing made it a mainstay in forecasting efforts for years.

Even when some World Bank studies in the early 1980s showed *negative* returns to capital investment in sub-Saharan Africa (presumably new aid programs were displacing scarce, high-level indigenous personnel from more productive activities) the "bubble machine" could not be turned off. All this despite, in Easterly's words (after extensive testing of the model against data for 88 countries for over 30 years), "there is no theoretical or empirical justification for assuming a short-run proportional relationship between growth and 'investment requirements.' There is no theoretical or empirical justification for the assumption that filling a 'financing gap' determined by 'investment requirements' will raise investment or growth in the short run."[7]

2.4 Progress in Academia

Although the practitioners continued to utilize various versions of the Harrod–Domar model, academic researchers were puzzling over the bothersome large residuals in their equations for modeling economic growth. As independent variables, the quantity of labor and capital, as traditionally measured, left a lot of explaining to do. Led by Robert Solow's modeling, which used historical data from the United States to test hypotheses, researchers pointed to the importance of the *productivity* of factors ("technical change") in economic growth, not

---

[6] Easterly, p. 5.
[7] Easterly (1999), p. 17.

just the quantity of factor inputs. The productivity of labor, it was pointed out, can depend partly on investment in education, including on-the-job training. The productivity of fixed capital can be heavily influenced by innovations, which in turn may be stimulated by investment in research and development.

By Solow's calculations, 87 percent of the increase in gross output per man-hour in the United States, from 1909 to 1949, resulted from technical change rather than increased use of capital.[8] Using a different approach and time period, Dennison found that the contribution of greater inputs of labor and capital in the 60-year period, from 1929 to 1982, accounted for roughly half of the annual 2.90 percent growth in GNP. Education and "advances in knowledge" accounted for nearly as much, 1.22 percent.[9] Despite the substantial difference in the two studies' estimates, the importance of "technical change" (now typically referred to as "total factor productivity" or TFP) in economic growth in the United States was conclusively established.[10]

2.5 Total Factor Productivity: A Case Study

At this point it may be instructive to provide a micro/entrepreneurial example of a shift in total factor productivity from an actual case study of innovation in the organization of production.[11]

In the early 1970s, Lantech Corporation invented a machine to stretch-wrap goods on pallets with plastic sheets for shipping purposes. Eventually, competitors entered the market and threatened to drive it out of business by the early 1990s. Management tried a variety of new strategies to reduce costs ("total quality management," team-based organization, "data empowerment," etc.), to no avail and continuing losses. Finally, a last-ditch, radical shift in the organization of processes for manufacturing, engineering, and order handling was

---

[8] Robert M. Solow (1957).

[9] Dennison (1985).

[10] Throughout this chapter, the terms "technical change" and "new technology" are used to refer to changes in the organization of work processes as well as the use of new "hard" technology.

[11] Womack and Jones (1996).

Table 2.1 Lantech cost savings

	Old Process	New Process
	(Batch and Queue)	(Continuous Flow)
Man-hours per Machine	160	80
Space per Machine	100 sq. ft.	55 sq. ft
Average Defects per Machine	8	0.8
Inventory on hand	US$ 2.6 million	US$ 1.9 million
Product Delivery Lead Time	4–20 weeks	1–4 weeks
Production Throughput Time	16 weeks	14 hours–5 days

Source: Womack and Jones, "Beyond Toyota: How to Root Out Waste and Pursue Perfection."

undertaken. The traditional "batch and queue" model for all processes was replaced with a "continuous flow" approach.

The measured outcomes of the shift in the manufacturing paradigm are listed in Table 2.1. No new equipment was required. The financial investment was "virtually zero" or negative, if you consider the working capital released due to lower inventories. In other words, outside of management time and a modest retraining of the workforce, no significant inputs of capital or labor were required for a roughly 50 percent increase in productivity. This is a shift in essentially unallocatable "total factor productivity" with a vengeance.[12] There has been no net investment at all, simply the implementation of an idea—"total factor productivity" with a vengeance.

2.6 Differences in Income Levels Between Countries

It is one thing to use traditional growth models to analyze a single country's economic performance. But it is considerably more difficult to engage in comparative analysis *unless it is assumed that TFP is the same in all countries*—as most studies have traditionally done. Consequently, differences in income levels follow from variations in

---

[12] This type of productivity increase is clearly different from the impressive increases that can be obtained from "learning by doing," such as the Liberty Ship construction efficiencies discussed in Lucas (2002), pp. 82–83.

measurable inputs (e.g. investment in human capital, research and development, and savings rates). At any point in time it is assumed that the "technology" available for use is common for all countries. If these assumptions are made (as they generally are), attention is focused on defining and measuring various forms of "capital" and "labor."[13] Lucas and others have also attempted to make population growth or technical change endogenous in their modeling efforts.[14]

Broadly defined, a critically weak assumption in the above models concerns technology. Just because technology (e.g. "continuous flow" organization of manufacturing as in the Lantech case or new telecommunications systems) is available does not mean that it will be used, even if the economic returns to doing so are highly attractive.

The failure to adopt new technology as a critical element in a country's economic performance is a point first emphasized strongly by historians such as Rosenberg and Birdzell (1986), North (1990), and Landes (1998).

Consider two examples of failures to adopt new technology, broadly defined. The first Turkish–Arabic publishing house in the Ottoman Empire was not permitted to adopt new technology until 1727, over 250 years after the invention of the printing press; the first Turkish-Arabic newspaper did not appear until 1831.[15] This resistance to facilitating the spread of new ideas (technology?) surely must have been a factor in the empire's weakened economic position in its later years. In a more recent example from the United States, union work rules at integrated steel plants in the United States played a major role in reducing the industry's global competitiveness—and opening the door to imports and new domestic competitors.[16] In both cases, innovations that held substantial promise for total factor productivity gains were resisted, one by the monarchs and the other by workers. Both parties

---

[13] "Endogenous" growth theory posits that productivity can be influenced by government investment in human capital and R&D, but this seems to be equivalent to redefining "capital"—and, in some cases, rationalizing increased government expenditures in sectors close to the academy.

[14] See Lucas (2002).

[15] Koloğlu (2004), p. 28. The non-Muslim communities within the Ottoman Empire had been permitted to establish printing presses and newspapers well before these dates.

[16] Burnham (1993).

feared, perhaps rightly, the disruptive consequences of new ways of doing things.

Rosenberg and Birdzell emphasized the importance of a society's political process in permitting or encouraging "seeking out behavior" on the part of individual economic agents, e.g. permitting easy entry into business, and a legal system that reduces the risk of discretionary actions by authorities. Rosenberg has summarized his position by pointing to the necessity for society to permit "the freedom to experiment" and learn from failures in all channels of economic activity if sustained economic development is to occur.[17] Nobel Prize winner Edmund Phelps has made a similar argument in contrasting the economic systems of Western Continental Europe (characterized by a lack of economic dynamism) and the United States/Canada/United Kingdom models, with their high rates of commercially successful innovation, thanks to an entrepreneurial culture.[18]

An example of "restrictive institutions" hampering the adoption of technology as an explanation for prolonged poor economic performance comes from Kuran (2004). He looks at the impact on Middle Eastern development of Islamic inheritance laws, the lack of a concept of a corporation in Islam, and the Islamic trust (*waqf*). The author finds that these institutions, which were designed to advance laudable economic objectives such as efficiency and equity "did not pose economic disadvantages at the time of their emergence." However, their inability to adapt over time has created "continuing obstacles to economic development" in the region.[19]

An extremely influential work that measured typical entrepreneurial "barriers to experimentation" is DeSoto (1989). His work points toward the critical importance of small and new firms—"entrepreneurship"—in transferring technology, new ideas, and competitive stimulus into an economy. More generally, as Audretsch puts it, entrepreneurs act as "an engine of growth by providing a vital conduit for the spillover and commercialization of new ideas"[20]—but, I would emphasize, only when permitted by existing institutions and laws.

---

[17] Rosenberg (1986), pp. 108 ff.
[18] Phelps (2006) and (2007).
[19] Kuran, pp. 71–72.
[20] Audretsch (2006), p. 33.

DeSoto documented the numerous regulatory and administrative obstacles, in terms of time as well as money, needed to establish a small garment workshop in Lima, Peru. Doing everything "by the book," it took him 289 days and 31 times the monthly minimum wage to comply with government regulatory hurdles.

This work had a major impact on the "practitioners," in the development banks, as is evident in the very large World Bank research and publication program compiling the obstacles to doing business in over 100 countries. The development of individual country indices facilitates comparative analysis and generates substantial peer group pressure on poor performers—an excellent example of how to improve total factor productivity at very low cost.

2.7 Restrictions on Deployment of Technology and Economic Growth

Perhaps the most persuasive integration of neoclassical growth theory (with the objective of understanding relative income *levels*, not relative growth rates) and economic history has been achieved by Parente and Prescott (2000). Holding TFP constant and using a national income approach to measure output, they investigate the impact of changes in savings rates, broadened definitions of "capital investment," and assumptions regarding reasonable values for the return on capital (variously defined) to determine income levels. They find none of these approaches yield plausible answers.[21] They then relax the traditional assumption regarding identical TFP across countries and show that with plausible values for the share of capital (broadly defined), differences in TFP across countries need not vary widely (on the order of 2.3) to generate income differences as large as those observed today (up to 27 times).[22]

After demonstrating how modest restrictions on individual firms' use of technology will impact TFP (e.g. the amount of extra resources needed to adopt new technology when restrictions are present), they conclude that differences in TFP arise from countries' largely

---

[21] This would include Young's (1995) paper on East Asian growth rates.

[22] Ibid., p. 68.

self-imposed constraints. These include protection for existing vested interests against new competitors, restrictions in adopting readily available technologies, and government support for workers' resistance to efficient work practices.[23] This answers what Parente and Prescott consider to be the critical question in the economics of growth: "Why don't poor countries use the existing stock of useable knowledge more efficiently?"[24]

In addition to the plausibility of their model's assumptions and parameters as well as the specific industry examples, Parente and Prescott cite numerous historical episodes as being consistent with their theory. These include England's early industrialization (relative to the European continent), Japan's growth spurt at the end of World War II, and why fourteenth-century China failed to experience sustained economic growth despite knowledge of the most advanced technology of the time.

In short, the Parente and Prescott growth model, taken in conjunction with the works of Rosenberg and Birdzell, Kuran, and DeSoto, argues strongly for the conclusion that self-imposed "barriers to experimentation" are perhaps the single most important constraint on economic growth in developing countries. Dismantling these barriers, they suggest, somewhat provocatively, means that there would be "no reason why the whole world should not be as rich as the leading industrial country."[25]

2.8 Total Factor Productivity and Communications Technology

How do advances in deployed telecommunications technology affect the TFP and economic growth? A frequent approach is to look at this question from the perspective of the economics of transactions costs. Table 2.2 summarizes significant forms of economic transaction activity that will be impacted by a decline in communications costs.

---

[23] Ibid., p. 141.

[24] Parente and Prescott, p. 5.

[25] p. 145.

Table 2.2 Total factor productivity impacts of advances in telecommunications technology

Activity	Examples	Illustrative implications
#1 Decision-making involved in allocating resources with a given amount of information	Substitution of phone call/conference call/ video-conferencing for face-to-face meetings	Reduction in cost and cycle time in decision-making
#2 Collection of information	Remote real-time scanning; online product/service search	Deterrence of criminal activity; prediction of flood crests; equipment monitoring
#3 Distribution of information	Online data banks; vendor web sites	Ability to make marginally better decisions with more information; transformation of uncertainty into risk; reduced cycle time
#4 Financial market arbitrage	Global financial markets	Reduction in cost of capital and improved liquidity in markets
#5 Substitution of information for fixed capital	Ability to single track railways; reduce inventories	Reduced capital investment
#6 Creation of value-added services	Off-shore software development; processing and analysis of financial and medical data; remote operating control	Lower cost of service activities; shifts in location of value-added activity

In a broad sense, all activities involve either (1) the substitution of information for other factor inputs into goods- and service-producing activities or (2) the reduction of value to a form that permits it to be transported nearly instantaneously at near zero cost.

Specific examples of the impact of the telegraphy are especially instructive. With respect to transaction cost implication #3, the comment cited by Garbade and Silber (1978) from an 1865 trade magazine is instructive:

> The products of the world, which, if left free to move naturally, would be attracted to the most profitable markets, are frequently impelled towards unprofitable ones because the knowledge of which are the best ones becomes known in most cases only after the product has been shipped to an unprofitable one. All this source of mercantile loss and embarrassment ceases when the telegraph is established.[26]

Garbade and Silber proceed to demonstrate how the timely distribution of information and financial arbitrage (implications #3 and #4) impacted financial markets. Using historical price data, they show that the establishment of telegraph lines by American entrepreneurs between key financial centers in the United States in the 1840s and the trans-Atlantic cable in the 1860s sharply reduced intermarket price differentials in such instruments as foreign exchange, US Treasury bonds, and corporate securities.

All of the listed activities are also affected by a sharp reduction in the amount of time it takes for information and ideas to be transmitted to individuals, firms, and societies at large. This may well be the broadest and most powerful externality and stimulus of all—the potential for acceleration in economic activity, including experimentation.

Estimates of the economic impact of such activity at both the macro and sector level are available. At the industry level, one extremely revealing historical study is by Field (1992). He investigates the cost savings as of 1890 associated with having 73 percent of the US railway system single-tracked instead of double-tracked. This was in contrast with the almost universal use of double tracking in Great Britain. With use of the telegraph, dispatchers with single-track systems could schedule trains to avoid overtaking and head-on crashes. Field estimates that the savings from single tracking were equivalent to two-and-a-half times the US steel production in 1890[27] (activity #5). Reliable telegraphic information also made possible the movement

---

[26] Hunt's Merchant Magazine, July 1865, p. 18.

[27] Ibid., p. 108. Field also points out that the labor force and capital investment in the telegraph industry was a small fraction of that in railroading.

of fresh meat, fruits, and vegetables in refrigerated railroad cars, thus spurring demand for each industry's products[28] (activity #3).

Activity #6 is probably the most recent and fastest growing manifestation of the impact of low-cost telecommunications. In effect, any value-added activity that can be reduced to electronic digital form is capable of being performed at any location in the world, given a satisfactory telecommunications infrastructure. Of course, whether or not such an activity is economically performed at such a location depends on a variety of other factors, including labor force characteristics, investment climate, and, in many activities, time zone considerations.

One way of looking at all six types of activity is to recognize that with the exception of #5 (substitution for capital), they all imply, in effect, an extension of markets—either for suppliers or producers—thus permitting greater specialization and economies of scale. At the same time, firms are subject to increased competition as previously isolated markets are integrated into a more global one. More generally, the network externalities of more widely deployed communications systems generate substantial increasing returns to users while increased competition promotes a more efficient allocation of resources.

2.9 Impact Studies of Telecommunications Investment

At the more macro level, estimates based on country cross-section and time series samples generally provide evidence of a positive and significant impact from telecommunications investment. Norton (1992) controls for reverse causality[29] and provides fairly robust evidence based on samples of 47 and 124 countries, which in economic development "a telecommunications infrastructure ... must be viewed as at least as important as conventional economic forces such as stable money growth, low inflation and an open economy."[30]

---

[28] Ibid., p. 110.

[29] To eliminate the effect of economic growth on the demand for telecommunications services, as opposed to the impact on growth of the telecommunications infrastructure.

[30] Norton, p. 192

More recently, Roller and Waverman (2001) used a four-equation structural model that also controls for reverse causality. They found that one-third of the economic growth in a group of 21 OECD countries over the 20-year period, 1970–1990, could be attributed to the telecommunications sector.[31] They also suggest their findings support the proposition that increasing returns to telecommunications investment appear to be more in evidence as the penetration rate of telecommunications rises (e.g. the number of mainline phones per 1,000 population), providing further evidence of network externalities.

An additional piece of evidence is this author's study of the Republic of Ireland's remarkable acceleration of growth in the 1990s.[32] This research concluded that that country's substantial and timely investment in telecommunications in the mid-1980s played a crucial role in transforming it into the fastest growing European Union member in the 1990s.

A recent paper funded by Vodafone (Waverman et al., 2005) examined the impact of mobile telephony in 92 developing countries using data through 2003. The authors conclude that differences in the rate at which developing countries adopt this technology significantly impact their economic growth rates. Finally, the extraordinary global spread of mobile telephony, which in less than 20 years has seen the number of mobile phone users (over 1.3 billion) surpass the number of fixed line users, provides powerful evidence of telecommunications economic value.

The six types of activity summarized in Table 2.2, along with the evidence from economic historians, econometric models, and more descriptive analyses of recent growth "spurts," provide good reason for concluding that the effective deployment of telecommunications technology plays an important role in contemporary economic development.

How does this role manifest itself in measured aggregate economic activity? First, there is the investment activity and income originating in the telecommunications sectors. Beyond this are the reductions in inputs and cycle times in production in other sectors, as well as the expansions in markets made feasible by activities of

---

[31] Ibid., p. 919.
[32] Burnham (2003).

the kind detailed in Table 2.2. Combined with the inherent network externalities associated with communications networks (e.g. the social returns exceed private returns), these types of productivity-enhancing changes in individual and organizational processes are of increasing importance. As Roller and Waverman point out, the importance of such factors increases as the information intensity of the production process increases,[33] as is generally assumed to be the case today.

2.10 Regulation and the Deployment of Telecommunications Technology

Given the critical role that modern telecommunications technology can play in accelerating economic growth rates, particularly in developing countries, and the importance that the investment environment for entrepreneurial "experimentation" plays in facilitating the deployment of technology generally, what are the implications for the public policy with respect to telecommunications? (The distinction between technology *development* and technology *deployment* should be borne in mind throughout this discussion; as Parente and Prescott emphasize, "firms in poor countries can adopt better technologies which are developed elsewhere in the world without having to make any large, non-firm specific investments."[34])

In arriving at useful answers to this question, we need to recognize that "network externalities" and the desire to achieve "universal service" have been the primary historical justifications for substantial government intervention in the sector.[35] Additional rationales for intervention have included the need for technical compatibility in equipment and difficulties in allocating property rights for over-the-air bandwidth. Combined with national security concerns, it is not surprising that many countries originally established government monopoly carriers.

---

[33] Roller and Waverman, p. 910.

[34] Parente and Prescott (1999), p. 217.

[35] See Economides (2005) for an excellent review of the general issues, as well as the situation in the United States in particular.

The chief issue arising out of "network externalities" in an unregulated telecommunications market is that larger service providers will make it difficult or impossible for smaller (e.g. new entrants) to interconnect, since the benefit to the smaller firm is substantially greater than the benefit to the larger one. The result is a tendency for monopolies to emerge as the largest carrier drives competitors out of business or acquires them and eventually is able to prevent them from entering the market. The history of Western Union and AT&T in the United States illustrates this phenomenon—and the resulting reluctance of the near-monopolist to introduce new products, services, and cost-reducing technology. AT&T was initially successful in denying MCI entrance to the switched long distance service market simply by opposing its licensing by the Federal Communication Commission.[36] Eventually, however, MCI was able to deploy new technology (microwave transmission) and low-cost pricing to acquire a significant portion of the market.

Thirty years ago, when policymakers and most economists assumed that telecommunications services were "natural" monopolies, the policy prescriptions affecting the sector were markedly different than today. Furthermore, at that time the technology was moving relatively slowly. Thus, Ireland and Turkey, both with state-owned monopoly fixed line telephone companies, made successful (although very belated) efforts to bring the cost and reliability benefits of digital switching to their customers in the 1980s.

The development of the cell phone provided an opportunity to create a much larger and more competitive marketplace for voice calling by permitting the entrance of new companies to deploy this particular technology. In Turkey, by 1987 the backlog of requests for fixed line service exceeded two million would-be subscribers.[37] Not until 1994 did the government authorize two private companies to provide mobile services under a revenue sharing agreement with Turk Telkom (TTK), the state-owned fixed line monopoly. In 1998, the two companies received licenses in their own right and became fully independent of TTK.[38] By 2002, the waiting list for service had declined to less

---

[36] Economides, p. 53.

[37] Burnham (2006), p. ??.

[38] Atiyas (2005).

than 150,000 and the number of mobile phones in use exceeded fixed line numbers.[39] Similarly, the extremely rapid deployment of mobile telephony in most countries of the world, including (most recently) sub-Saharan Africa and India, owes much to the reduction in barriers facing entrepreneurial private sector operators.

Deployment of the Internet is another example of how the absence of restrictions on entrepreneurial initiative facilitates deployment of technology. Although the technical origins of the Internet lie in US government-sponsored research, its rapid commercial deployment was aggressively facilitated by a deliberate "hands-off" policy formulated by the Clinton Administration in 1997.[40] This was contained in the 1997 White House policy document "*A Framework for Global Electronic Commerce,*" which played no small role in the rapid commercialization of this technology in the United States and, perhaps, other countries:

> For electronic commerce to flourish, the private sector must continue to lead. Innovation, expanded services, broader participation, and lower prices will arise in a market-driven arena, not in an environment that operates as a regulated industry ... business models must evolve rapidly to keep pace with the break-neck speed of change in the technology; government attempts to regulate are likely to be outmoded by the time they are finally enacted, especially to the extent such regulations are technology-specific ... accordingly, governments should refrain from imposing new and unnecessary regulations, bureaucratic procedures, or taxes and tariffs on commercial activities that take place via the Internet.[41]

The central point that emerges from the past 30 years of telecommunications history is that out-of-date regulatory frameworks intended

---

[39] International Telecommunications Union *ICT Indicators* database.

[40] "Innovation, expanded services, broader participation, and lower prices will arise in a market-driven arena, not in an environment that operates as a regulated industry," (*The Framework for Global Electronic Commerce*, The White House, July 1, 1997).

[41] http://www.technology.gov/digeconomy/framewrk.htm

to protect consumers from monopolistic practices tend to protect monopolistic market structures as entrepreneurial newcomers (large and small) seek to introduce new technology, services, and business models.

However, exactly how to structure telecommunications regulation to stimulate innovation and investment is not clear in many situations. If interconnection to existing systems is mandated, charges for doing so must be negotiated or imposed. But interconnection mandates and regulated charges may deter additional infrastructure investment by the dominant provider. They may also reduce the likelihood of a new entrant investment in an alternative infrastructure (e.g. Internet, cable, or satellite systems). Should telephone numbers belong to individuals and thus be portable between competing carriers, or should they be system-specific? Should technology standards be market-based or mandated by the government?

In the case of cell phone technology, the European Union mandated a single standard (GSM) for all carriers, which simplified customer switching between competing carriers and was a boon to suppliers. In the United States, carriers were permitted to adopt different standards, facilitating competition between technological alternatives, but creating barriers for customers trying to switch between alternative providers. The danger in the single standard approach is that the optimal technology may not be chosen, as some observers fear may be the case with the latest EU "G3" standard.[42]

There is greater agreement on the optimal policy for allocating scarce bandwidth. Governments are a logical organizer of the allocation process, particularly since they typically reserve specific frequencies for their own uses. Traditionally, spectrum allocations and licenses for private operators were determined by government authorities on the basis of the public's "convenience and needs." However, in many countries today, the government runs an auction when private demand emerges for specific sections of spectrum and thus establishes some degree of private property rights to this resource. In this manner, higher valued uses tend to receive the desired bandwidth, if the auction process is designed properly.[43]

---

[42] Gandal et al. (2003).

[43] Governments' desire to maximize revenue from the auction may result in a less-than-optimal number of licenses being issued.

In addition to the impact of regulatory policy on the deployment of telecommunications technology, excessive taxation can restrict its benefits. For decades, many governments looked to their government-owned telecommunications companies' cash flow as an important source of revenue. With most such firms now privatized, taxes have replaced dividends as a source of government income. Not surprisingly, excise taxes on voice telephony have risen to substantial levels in a number of countries. For example, in the case of Turkey, in addition to an 18 percent VAT rate on mobile communications, an additional 25 percent excise tax is imposed. Studies suggest that such a burden has a substantial deterrent effect on mobile phone usage.[44]

2.11 Implications for Policy

Ideally, in shaping public policy, conflicting objectives are clearly identified and difficult trade-offs understood. When choices (and compromises) are to be made by government, their costs should be acknowledged. Telecommunications policy is no stranger to these challenges.

This chapter has sought to establish the economic benefits that are inherent in the rapid deployment of telecommunications technology through entrepreneurial activity. But such a strategy frequently threatens the viability of existing firms—particularly the previously state-sanctioned or state-owned monopoly provider of fixed line and other services. To what extent does the state want to protect such firms (and, in the case of state-owned companies, its own revenue stream)?

A related issue is the extent to which increased competition generated by new entrants is to be encouraged. Certainly many of the new entrants will fail, but so will incumbent firms—maybe even the previous monopoly carrier, as was the case with the original AT&T in the United States—and its initially successful chief rival, MCI.

Are governments willing to see "profitless prosperity," if policies that lead to this result in faster deployment and greater public use of the technology than would be the case otherwise?

---

[44] Waverman, Meschi, and Fuss (2005), found a price elasticity of -1.5 for mobile phone usage for a sample of 38 developing countries.

A clear understanding of what is meant by "universal access" and how it is to be financed also needs to be articulated. Can access to voice telephony for everyone now be assumed, thanks to the availability of calling cards for fixed and mobile phones? To what extent do governments wish to include the Internet as part of a universal access commitment?

At what point does the tax burden on telecommunications providers and users start to conflict with government's objective regarding the speed of deployment of the technology?

Given clear guidance by governments on these and closely related issues, the design of specific implementing policies is made considerably easier. Decisions regarding whether licenses are required, how many are to be issued, what fees should be charged, wavelength allocation policies, interconnection access and fees, telephone number portability, levels of taxation, and a host of similar issues are much easier to resolve when guidance is clear. Furthermore, if basic policies are clearly laid out and understood by all concerned (including any appeals authority), implementing decisions will generate far fewer appeals from those who dislike a particular outcome.

2.12 Conclusion

This chapter has sought to link the impact of modern telecommunications to economic growth. I have started with an overview of recent economic growth theory and a brief survey of recent quantitative studies of the impact of telecommunications. This was done in order to emphasize the broad base of research—both theoretical and applied—that exists for the proposition that, for countries which currently do not enjoy the full benefits of this technology, it is literally there for the asking. Given the proper policy environment, private capital, from domestic as well as foreign sources, is generally available, as the mobile phone revolution so graphically demonstrates.

If the primary objective of government policy is to encourage the deployment of productivity-enhancing advances in telecommunications technology, the challenge for regulatory authorities is to strive for an investment climate that attracts new entrants with new technology. This means that entrepreneurs and firms have the freedom to experiment with new technology and business models designed to bring that new technology to users. It also means that competition will drive some firms, new and old, out of business.

Such an environment cannot be achieved overnight, but to the extent that existing firms and government authorities are successful in delaying progress toward this objective, the economy as a whole will be denied the full benefits of modern telecommunications technology and all that flows from it.

References

Atiyas, I. (2005), Competition and Regulation in the Turkish Telecommunications Industry. Sabanci University Discussion Papers in Economics Series 2005–05.

Bloom, D., Canning, D., and Sevilla, J. (2002) *Conditional Convergence, and Economic Growth*. NBER Working Paper No. 8713.

Burnham, J. (1993), *Changes and Challenges: The Transformation of the U.S. Steel Industry*. Policy Study Number 115. St. Louis: Center for the Study of American Business, Washington University.

Burnham, J. (2003), "Why Ireland Boomed." *The Independent Review*, Spring, 7(4).

DeSoto, H. (1989), *The Other Path: The Invisible Revolution in the Third World*. New York: Harper & Row.

Dennison, E. (1985), *Trends in American Economic Growth, 1929–1982*, Washington: Brookings Institution.

Easterly, W. (1999), "The Ghost of Financing Gap". *Journal of Development Economics*, December, 60(2).

Economides, N. (2005), "Telecommunications Regulation: An Introduction," in Richard R. Nelson (ed.) *The Limits and Complexity of Organizations*. New York: Russell Sage Foundation Press.

Field, A.J. (1992), "The Magnetic Telegraphy, Price and Quantity Data, and the New Management of Capital." *Journal of Economic History*. 52(2).

Gandal, N., Salant, D., and Waverman, L. (2003); "Standards in Wireless Telephone Networks." [Electronic version]. *Telecommunications Policy*. 27(5,6), 325.

Garbade, K.D. and Silber, W.L. (1978), "Technology, Communication and the Performance of Financial Markets: 1840–1975." *The Journal of Finance*. 33(3), 819–832.

Hall, R.E. and Jones, C.I. (1999), "Why Do Some Countries Produce So Much More than Others?" *Quarterly Journal of Economics*. February, 114(1).

Koloğlu, O. (2004),"The Printing Press and Journalism in the Ottoman State." *Boğaziçi Journal*. 18(1–2).

Kuran, T. (2004), "Why the Middle East is Economically Underdeveloped: Historical Mechanisms of Institutional Stagnation." *The Journal of Economic Perspectives*. Summer, 71–90.

Landes, D.S. (1998), *The Wealth and Poverty of Nations: Why are Some So Rich and Others So Poor?* New York: W.W. Norton.

Lucas, R.E. (2002), *Lectures on Economic Growth.* Cambridge, Massachusetts: Harvard University Press.

North, D. (1990), *Institutions, Institutional Change and Economic Performance.* Cambridge: Cambridge University Press.

Norton, S.W. (1992), "Transactions Cost, Telecommunications, and the Microeconomics of Macroeconomic Growth." *Economic Development and Cultural Change.* October. 41(1).

Parente, S. and Prescott, E. (1994), "Barriers to Technology Adoption and Development," *Journal of Political Economy.* April. 102, 298–321.

Parente, S. and Prescott, E. (1999), "Monopoly Rights: A Barrier to Riches," *American Economic Review.* 89, 1216–1233.

Parente, S. and Prescott, E. (2000), *Barriers to Riches.* Cambridge, Massachusetts: The MIT Press.

Phelps, E.S. (2006), "Dynamic Capitalism." *The Wall Street Journal*, October 10.

Phelps, E.S. (2007), "Entrepreneurial Culture." *The Wall Street Journal*, February 12.

Rae, J. (1895), *Life of Adam Smith.* Reprinted by August M. Kelly, New York. 1965.

Roller, L.H. and Waverman, L. (2001), "Telecommunications Infrastructure and Economic Development: A Simultaneous Approach." *American Economic Review.* 91(4), 909–923.

Rosenberg, N. (1994), *Exploring the Black Box.* New York: Cambridge University Press.

Rosenberg, N. and Birdzell, L.E. (1986), *How the West Grew Rich.* New York: Basic Books.

Solow, R. (1957), "Technical Change and the Aggregate Production Function," *Review of Economics and Statistics*, August, 39, 312–327.

Young, A. (1995), "The Tyranny of Numbers: Confronting the East Asian Growth Experience." *Quarterly Journal of Economics.* August, 10(3), 641–680.

Waverman, L., Meschi, M., and Fuss, M. (2005), "The Impact of Telecoms on Economic Growth in Developing Countries," in *Africa: The Impact of Mobile Phones.* Vodafone Policy Paper Series #2, March.

Womack, J.P. and Jones, D. (1996), "Beyond Toyota: How to Root Out Waste and Pursue Perfection." *Harvard Business Review*, September/October, 74(5).

3 The Relationship Between the Degree of Innovation and the Development Level of a Country

A. Kadir Varoğlu and Ali Rıza Köker

3.1 Introduction

In the current globalization scene, nations are aiming to provide sustainable and long-term economic welfare. As the competitiveness is related to rapid technological changes, many firms are positioning knowledge-based technological products and services on their core business (Verhaeghe and Kfir 2002). Innovation is a necessity for the firms that compete in environments where change is pervasive, unpredictable, and continuous. In order to achieve competitive success in an economic sense, it is necessary to create value. Innovations, as a way of creating value, are the source of economic growth (Wijnberg 2004). Therefore, interest on innovation for gaining competitive advantage in global markets is increasing (Hoffman and Hegarty 1993).

Research on the innovation term has progressed along a variety of courses rather than a single one; it encompasses diverse types of varying in scope, depth, and objective. The concept of innovation has been established in the business literature a long time ago, starting with Schumpeter's proposal (1934) of firms that survive and grow through innovations—the creation of temporary monopolies by creating new products and processes, creating new markets, new supply sources, and new types of industry organization. This was later extended to include other areas of innovation such as innovation in finance, organization, and management (Manimala et al. 2005). Parallel to these views, innovation is conceptualized in many different ways and studied with different perspectives. Therefore, it is possible to see various definitions in the literature. However, as the chapter is aimed toward

N. Aydogan (ed.), *Innovation Policies, Business Creation and Economic Development*,
International Studies in Entrepreneurship 21, DOI 10.1007/978-0-387-79976-6_3,

relating the innovation with Intellectual Property (IP) rights in this study, technical innovations will be the focus of work.

Innovations are efficient devices for gaining share in both mature and new markets by founding creative synergy that provides welfare (Dougherty and Heller 1994). Although it is possible to make innovations within times, the major difficulty is making it continuously and to guarantee sustainability. According to Koberg et al. (2003), some innovations are simply built on what is already there, requiring modifications to existing functions and practices; but some innovations change the entire order of things, making the old ways obsolete. The literature on innovation has made a useful distinction between radical and incremental innovation according to its importance or degree (McDermott and O'Connor 2002; Wijnberg 2004). Though scholars identified the organizational or environmental dynamics affecting each degree of innovation, we believe that the countries' development level is an important determinant for the degree of innovation. In this article, our aim is to discuss the relationship between countries' development level and degree of innovation by relating the degree of innovation with IP Rights.

In the first part of this study, an introduction about innovation and the different innovation degrees—radical and incremental—is mentioned. Then we try to relate these degrees with IP rights. Finally, we give some earlier research examples to answer the question whether the degree of innovation is related with countries' development level.

3.2 The Definition and Degree of Innovation: Radical–Incremental

Although many studies have been performed about innovation, it is hard to find a commonly accepted definition. In an epistemological meaning, innovation can be described as doing something new (Medina et al. 2005).

Since the subject is related to technical innovations, it is something new for the market (Hoffman and Hegarty 1993). According to Schmookler (1966), if a company develops a new product or service, uses new techniques or inputs, it means that company achieves a technical change. This company would be accepted as a performer of a new thing, and this action is regarded as innovation (Cumming 1998).

For Udwadia (1990), innovation is creation and development of new products and processes. In another definition, innovation can be regarded as a "process of using new ideas in new product development" (Galbraith 1982:6).

Most innovations simply build on what is already available, requiring modification to existing functions and practices, but some innovations change the entire order of things, making obsolete the old ways (Van de Ven et al. 1999). In the literature on innovation, it is possible to see the distinction between radical and incremental innovation according to its importance or degree (Dewar and Dutton 1986; Henderson and Clark 1990; McDermott and O'Connor 2002; Wijnberg 2004). However, differentiating the incremental and radical innovation is not always that clear-cut (Henderson and Clark 1990).

Radical innovations are said to involve revolutionary departures from existing technologies and practices (Manimala et al. 2005). According to Lee et al. (2003), radicalism can be described as the degree of departure from existing products. Some studies show that both radical and incremental innovations are important to the economic sustainability in industries that are dependent on competitive research and development for long-term survival (Koberg et al. 2003). As radical innovations are important for gaining competitive advantage, it is said to contribute to development and profitability (Veryzer 1998).

Although radical innovations have a potential to yield much, they may have higher project costs and a higher risk of failure (Abetti 2000). On the other hand, incremental innovations can be described as products in the existing market or technology, which have improvements and advantages thereof (Song and Montoya-Weiss 1998). According to Henderson and Clark, incremental innovations are minor changes on existing products (1990:9). Incremental innovations are related with minor changes in existing technology and as a result they contain lower ambiguity (Manimala et al. 2005).

3.3 The Degree of Innovation and IP Rights

Economic growth depends on the production of new ideas, but competitive markets do not provide enough and appropriate incentives for the production of new ideas, which may turn into technology production. Indeed, it is impossible to expect development of domestic technology production, without encouraging invention activities and protecting them, which is essential for the technological development. IP rights are efficient tools for protecting the technological innovations. In general definition, IP rights are defined as legally enforceable rights related to the creations of the mind. These may include inventions, literary and artistic works, symbols, names, images, and designs used in commerce.

If the subject is technical innovations, suitable protection devices are patents and utility models. A patent is an exclusive right granted for the invention of a product or a process that provides, in general, a new way of doing something, or offer a new technical solution to a problem. In order to be protected by a patent, an invention must, in general, fulfill some conditions. It must be of practical use; it must show an element of novelty, that is, some new characteristic not known in the body of existing knowledge (called as prior art) in its technical field. And the invention must show an inventive step that cannot be deduced by a person with an average knowledge of the technical field.

In addition, inventions could be protected by utility models, also known as "petty patents" or "utility innovations." A utility model is an exclusive right granted for an invention for a limited period of time, which bars others from commercially using the protected invention without the inventors' authorization. The requirements for acquiring a utility model are less stringent than that for patents. While the requirement of novelty is always to be met, that of inventive step or nonobviousness may be much lower or absent altogether. In practice, protection for utility models is often sought for innovations of a rather incremental character that may not meet the patentability criteria. It is also possible that utility models are considered particularly suited for minor improvements and adaptations of existing products.

From these definitions, it can be said that patents are suitable protection for radical innovations, while utility models are suitable for incremental ones. Considering this match up, we can use patent numbers as the indicator of radical innovation indicator and utility model numbers as the indicator of incremental innovation.

3.4 Linking Development Level of Country with the Degree of Innovation

New products are the source of economic growth. Therefore, it is important to give priority to innovation and the development of new products. This process is subject to a high degree of uncertainty in terms of the low probability of success and high costs for the research process. Indeed it is possible to say that there is a mutual relationship between development level and new product innovation. As the development level increases, the welfare of the country increases, and more sources become available for R&D that is supportive of new product innovations. Considering the fact that developing countries are unable to save enough capital to create and maintain their own technological base, it would be difficult to expect radical innovations originated from such countries due to its risky and costly nature. A more suitable way is to absorb technologies and develop them, which is exactly suitable for the scope of incremental innovations.

According to Rapp and Rozek (1990), IP system is positively related with economic development. Scientific and technological actions may turn to inventions and innovations, and then contribute to the economic development and growth. IP rights are important at this point as they have a strong effect on individual economic actions, thinking that the cumulative economic actions are accumulation of such individual actions. If outcomes of creative activities have no returns for the creators, motivation for taking part in such activities will reduce. So, the creators will avoid spending their efforts, money, and time on such activities that may give rise to the loss in productivity and efficiency. With these thoughts, the developed countries have a view that patents are essential to international economic development as they provide a means to guarantee the return on invested time and capital in R&D.

Both in micro and macro perspectives, it is possible to find some evidence to support this relationship. Manimala et al. (2005) developed a study for a better understanding of incremental innovations, especially in the context of a developing economy. In this study, innovation is seen as the cause of further innovations, and the accumulated impact of incremental innovations would eventually develop a culture of innovation, generate access to key resources, and create a competitive orientation, which would in turn lead to the creation of radical innovations. Moreover, incremental innovations are shown as an important source of change in developing economies, as such innovations are easier to implement within the resource availability as well as operational constraints (Manimala et al. 2005). In other researches, Gluck (1985) has found that many established organizations achieve improved performance through continuous, small, and incremental innovations. Moreover, incremental innovations are preferred by most established organizations as these are easier to implement within the operational constraints of the organization (Mezias and Glynn 1993). According to Banbury and Mitchell (1995) incremental innovations bring more than incremental returns and large market share.

The major factors in the development of developing countries are production of new technologies, application of these technologies in industry, and selling them to other countries. Two main variables can be seen as an indicator of such technological development, namely: R&D expenditures and patent application numbers (Crosby 2000). However, due to difficulties in measuring exact R&D expenditures, patent numbers have priority in using this indicator. According to Lehman (1999), welfare of the country and patent numbers are in mutual relation. Clearly, increase in economic welfare in the country gives rise to increase in importance of patent protection, and the reverse is also true. Thinking in macro perspective, it is possible to see that developed countries in economical sense have huge numbers of patents, and this trend is increasing. Figure 3.1 shows this trend in the United States, Japan, Korea, Germany, and United Kingdom as technological leaders.

In Fig. 3.2 GDP per capita is given as an indicator of welfare and economic growth. In all the selected countries seen in Fig. 3.2, there exist a positive trend in the GDP per capita parallel to a number of patent applications that can be taken as an indicator of radical innovations.

However, in developing countries, since the resource allocated for such a risky process is low, innovations are not exceeding the level of incremental and therefore can not be patented. Consequently, they are in the range of imitating or incremental innovations. Turkey is a good example of the developing countries. Figure 3.3 shows the patent and utility model applications within the period 1981–2006 in Turkey. It

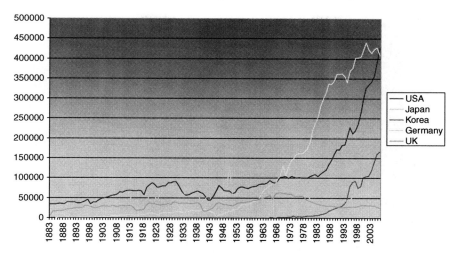

Fig. 3.1 Number of patents in selected countries (Adapted from WIPO Statistics)

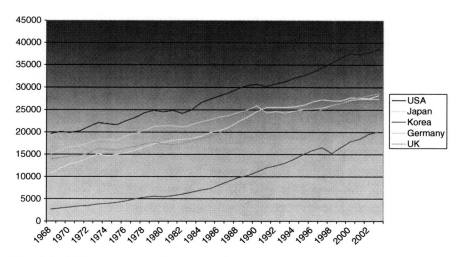

Fig. 3.2 GDP per capita for selected countries (Adapted from http://www. demographia.com/db-ppp60+.htm)

is important to note that utility model application data existed after 1995, as no such protection was available in Turkey before that year. Figure 3.3 also shows that Turkey has an increasing trend in both patent and utility model numbers. However, it is also clear that the difference between patent and utility model number is very high. Com-

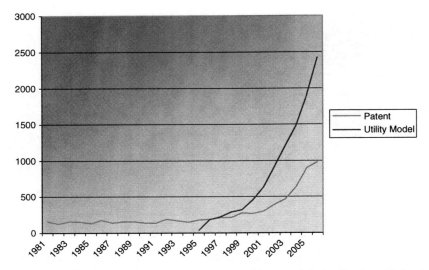

Fig. 3.3 Number of domestic patents and utility models in Turkey (Adapted from TPI statistics)

pared to the developed countries, the R&D expenditures are very low in Turkey,[1] which restricts resources available for radical innovations. Instead of radical innovations, some incremental improvements on the existing products are preferable as they require less R&D costs and involve fewer risks.

At this point, we believe that there should be a transition point from incremental to radical innovations like the case of transition from the developing to the developed countries. Since Japan may be shown as the best example for this status, we will focus on the Japanese development process. In one study, it has been demonstrated econometrically that Japan's system of utility models contributed positively and significantly to its postwar rise in productivity (Maskus and McDaniel 1999). Maskus and McDaniel (1999) viewed how the Japanese patent system affected postwar Japanese technical progress. The Japanese Patent System was designed to encourage incremental innovation and diffusion of technical knowledge into the economy between 1960 and 1993. The mechanisms for promoting these pro-

---

[1] Concluded from OECD statistics (http://www.oecd.org/statisticsdata/).

cesses included early disclosures and the opposition proceedings to patent applications, and an extensive system of utility models. The authors found that this system encouraged large numbers of utility model applications for incremental inventions, which were based in part on the laid-open prior applications for invention patents. As a result, utility models had a strong and positive impact on real total factor productivity growth over the period. They concluded that utility models were an important source of technical change and information diffusion in Japan, while patent applications provided both a direct and an indirect stimulus to productivity. It is interesting to note that as Japan has become a global leader in technology creation, its patent system has shifted away from encouraging diffusion and more toward protecting fundamental technologies (Maskus 2000).

Examples about this situation can be extended to several other East Asian countries such as Korea and Taiwan. Like the Japanese, Korea too gave importance to the utility model system for encouraging incremental innovations that are built on foreign technologies (Yalçıner and Kurt 2004). Korea had a view of absorption of foreign technologies as fundamental of risk-free production and growth. Within this view, it is thought that these incremental innovations and duplicative imitations of foreign technology results with great economical growth within years (1960s–1980s).

Taiwan's policy is not different from Japan's or Korea's, and therefore we take it as another example for our case. In the case of Taiwan, the government explicitly stated their growth strategy as absorption of foreign technology by imitating and reverse engineering (Yalçıner and Kurt 2004). This strategy means encouraging incremental innovations. In this way, the economies of these countries have grown and they established their own technology base.

These examples can be extended for many other developed countries. Assuming that the major source of economic growth is technological innovations, it is believed that many of these countries have experienced the same stages.

3.5 Summary and Conclusion

In this chapter, we aimed to offer a theoretical background about the relationship between countries' development level and degree of innovation by relating the degree of innovation with IP Rights.

It is a widely accepted fact that innovative products are important engines of economic growth. In the current globalization circumstances, innovation is a necessity for firms that compete in environments where change is pervasive, unpredictable, and continuous. Innovations are seen as a way of creating value and thereof a source of economic growth (Wijnberg 2004). The studies on the reasons of this relationship are diverse—varying in scope, depth, and objective—and therefore possible to find many aspects of innovation.

Related to technical innovations, there exist useful distinction between radical and incremental innovation. Moreover, these classification studies have tried to identify the organizational or environmental dynamics affecting different types of innovation. At this point we show that major determinant for each degree of innovation is the countries' development level.

On the other hand, in order to make a distinction between the degrees of innovation, we have used IP rights, which is a form of knowledge or intellectual activity embodied in various ways in the production and marketing of goods and services of an industrial, scientific, literary, or artistic nature. When the point of interest is the technical innovation, then we must consider patents and utility models. From their definitions, it can be clearly understood that while patents are indicator of radical innovations, utility models are that of incremental.

Considering that the nature of radical innovations are having a high degree of uncertainty, a low probability of success, and high costs for R&D, it is expected that such innovations come from developed countries. On the contrary, developing countries would allocate their limited resources not for developing such radical innovations, but making little improvements on existing products according to their needs, or imitating directly depending on the IP effectiveness. We have found several research results that are parallel with this thought, both in micro and macro level. The Japanese development case is a good example to illustrate this distinction. After World War II, when the economy was in shambles, Japan made a huge progress with the help of incremental innovations, which finally made Japan as one of the biggest power in world economy, and innovation degree moved from incremental to the radical.

All these relations and conclusions could be deduced with existence of IP regime in a country. The countries without IP regime are not categorized as either developed or developing countries. Such regimes determine the growth strategy by encouraging innovations either as radical or incremental. More detailed examination of the transition point from incremental to radical innovations may be a good topic for future studies.

References

Abetti, P. A. (2000). Critical success factors for radical technological innovation: a five case study. *Creativity and Innovation Management*, 9(4), 208–221.

Banbury, C. M. and Mitchell, W. (1995). The effect of introducing important incremental innovations on market share and business survival. *Strategic Management Journal*, 16, 161–182.

Camison-Zornoza, C., Alcami, R. L., Ciprés M. S. and Navarro, M. B. (2004). A Meta-analysis of innovation and organizational size. *Organization Studies*, 25(3), 331–361.

Crosby, M. (2000). Patents, innovation and growth. *The Economic Record*, 76(234), 255–262.

Cumming, B. S. (1998). Innovation overview and future challenges. *European Journal of Innovation Management*, 1(1), 21–29.

Dougherty, D. and Heller, T. (1994). The illegitimacy of successful product innovation in established firms. *Organization Science*, 5(2), 200–218.

Ettlie, J. E., Bridges, W. P. and O'Keefe, R. D. (1984). Organization strategy and structural differences for radical versus incremental innovations. *Management Science*, 30(6), 682–695.

Fidler, L. A. and Johnson, J. D. (1984). Communication and innovation implementation. *Academy of Management Review*, 9, 704–711.

Galbraith, J. (1982). Designing the innovative organization. *Organizational Dynamics*, Winter, 5–25.

Gluck, F. W. (1985). Big-bang management: creative innovation. *The McKinsey Quarterly*, 1, 49–59.

Henderson, R. M. and Clark, K. B. (1990). Architectural innovation: the reconfiguration of existing technologies and failure of established firms. *Administrative Science Quarterly*, 35(1), 9–30.

Hoffman, R. C. and Hegarty, W. H. (1993). Top management influence on innovations: effects of executive characteristics and social culture. *Journal of Management*, 19(3), 549–574.

Koberg, C. S., Detienne, D. R. and Heppard, K. A. (2003). An empirical test of environmental, organizational and process factors affecting incremental and radical innovations. *Journal of High Technology Management Research*, 14(1), 21–45.

Lee, H., Smith, K. G. and Grimm, C. M. (2003). The effect of new product radicality and scope on the extent and speed of innovation diffusion. *Journal of Management*, 29(5), 753–768.

Lehman, B. A. (1999). Industrial property as an engine of global economic growth, Presented in the Symposium on the Management of Patent and Trademark Offices in Countries in Transition, Republic of Moldova, September 1, 1–9.

Manimala, M. J., Jose, P. D., and Thomas K. R. (2005). Organizational design for enhancing the impact of incremental innovations: a qualitative analysis of innovative cases in the context of a developing economy. *Creativity and Innovation Management*, 14(4), 413–424.

Maskus, K. E. (2000). IP rights and economic development. *Case Western Reserve Journal of International Law*, 32, 471–506.

Maskus, K. E. and McDaniel, C. (1999). Impacts of the Japanese patent system on productivity growth. *Japan and the World Economy*, 11, 557–574.

McDermott, C. M. and O'Connor, G. C. (2002). Managing radical innovation: an overview of emergent strategy issues. *The Journal of Product Innovation Management*, 19(6), 424–438.

Meyer, A. D. and Goes, J. B. (1988). Organizational assimilation of innovations: a multilevel contextual analysis. *Academy of Management Journal*, 31, 897–923.

Mezias, S. J. and Glynn, M. A. (1993). The three faces of corporate renewal: institution, revolution and evolution. *Strategic Management Journal*, 14(2), 77–101.

Rapp, R. T. and Rozek, R. P. (1990). Benefits and costs of intellectual property protection in developing countries. *Journal of World Trade*, 24(5), 75–102.

Schmookler, J. (1966). *Invention and Economic Growth*. Cambridge: Harvard University Press.

Schumpeter, J. A. (1934). *The Theory of Economic Development*. Cambridge: Harvard University Pres.

Song, M. X. and Montoya-Weiss, M. M. (1998). Critical development activities for really new versus incremental products. *Journal of Product Innovation Management*, 15(2), 124–135.

Udwadia, F. E. (1990). Creativity and innovation in organizations: two models and managerial implications. *Technological Forecasting and Social Change*, 38, 65–80.

Van de Ven, A. H., Polley, D. E., Garud, R. and Venkataraman, S. (1999). *The Innovation Journey*. New York: Oxford University Press.

Verhaeghe, A. and Kfir, R. (2002). Managing innovation in a knowledge intensive technology organization. *R&D Management*, 32(5), 409–417.

Veryzer, R. W. Jr. (1998). Discontinuous innovation and the new product development process. *The Journal of Product Innovation Management*, 15, 304–321.

Wijnberg, N. M. (2004). Innovation and organization: value and competition in selection systems. *Organization Studies*, 25(8), 1413–1433.

Yalçıner, U. G. (2000). *Sinai Mülkiyet'in İlkeleri*, Ankara:Metal Ofset.

Yalçıner, U. G. and Kurt, Z. (2004). Fikri ve Sinai Mülkiyet Korumasının Ekonomik ve Teknolojik Gelişme Üzerindeki Etkileri-Tarihsel Analiz, Teknolojik ve Ekonomik Gelişme Fikri ve Sınai Mülkiyet Hakları Uluslararası Konferansı, 1–2 Ekim 2004, 1–60.

4 The Role of Effective Protection of IP Rights on Economic Growth

Yüksel Birinci

4.1 Introduction

Nowadays, economic actions are turning in to a global shape due to the increasing importance and spillover of information technologies. Almost all activities are spread worldwide with the help of information technologies. Knowledge becomes a major source of competitive advantage for both organizations. Therefore, it is impossible to realize development of social life without knowledge. Increasingly, economists are recognizing the importance of institutions like the Intellectual Property (IP) policies. In a global, knowledge-based economy, IP Rights are becoming more important and seen as the key to international competitiveness of both nations and firms. IP is now at the center of economy not only because of its value in its own right, but also because ownership of control over and access to IP are fundamental to development and use of other forms of property and capital. According to Langford (1997), IP is an institutional structure of the economy and one of the major determinants of economic growth.

IP rights have been considered a trade issue as international competition in traded goods contain a high degree of innovation (Langford 1997). In order to maintain competitiveness, an environment that safeguards IP, and thereof encourages inventors and organizations to invest resources in R&D for technological innovation is needed (Atun et al. 2006). Especially in knowledge-based economies, IP plays a fundamental role in the decisions to invest in innovation. It is well appreciated that IP rights can play an important role in codifying and diffusing knowledge, for example, by placing the underlying principles

N. Aydogan (ed.), *Innovation Policies, Business Creation and Economic Development,*
International Studies in Entrepreneurship 21, DOI 10.1007/978-0-387-79976-6_4,
© Springer Science+Business Media, LLC 2009

and operations of the innovated or invented products and processes as public domain information (Wattanapruttipaisan 2004).

The main benefit of effective IP protection is allowing innovators to appropriate a share of the benefits of their creative activities and encouraging R&D, which leads to innovation and higher long-run growth (Falvey and Foster 2006). Although developed countries argue that IP rights are essential to international economic development as they provide a means to guarantee a return on invested time and capital in R&D (Su 2000), in some studies, it has been noted that overly broad IP protection can result in anticompetitive outcomes that may adversely affect the rate of innovation and technology transfer, especially in the developing countries (Maskus 2000a). For developing countries to benefit from IP rights' advantages there is a need for balance, which we can call as effective system.

In this chapter, contribution of effective protection of IP Rights on development of innovative structure that has an impact on both economic growth and establishment in developing countries will be reviewed. In the first part of this chapter, a brief introduction to IP rights will be given. This introduction covers both the definition and types of IP rights. In the second part, key elements of effective IP protection will be discussed. Finally, I discuss the role of effective protection of IP Rights on both economic growth and establishment, especially in developing countries.

4.2 IP Rights[1]

The protection of property rights is one of the major components of a free information society, and the value of assets lies in intellectual capital rather than physical capital. In that context, IP describes products of the mind. IP is a form of knowledge or intellectual activity embodied in various ways in the production and marketing of goods and services of an industrial, scientific, literary, or artistic nature (Wattanapruttipaisan 2004). IP right is a property right not over a commodity but over capacities of production, ideas, or information.

---

[1] Definitions related to IP are adapted from World Intellectual Property Organization web page. Please check http://www.wipo.int for more information about IP Rights.

Broadly speaking, IP rights are legally enforceable rights relating to creations of the mind, which include inventions, literary and artistic works, symbols, names, images, and designs used in commerce (Atun et al. 2006). These rights can be seen as awards to inventors, artists, or institutions because they provide exclusive rights like production, using, distribution, or trade within a specified region or country. After registering, the owners of IP rights are assigned with specific rights, which prevent others from making unauthorized use of these protected goods and services for a specified limited period of time. A number of individual rights are covered by IP rights in different forms and they operate in distinct fashions. So it is misleading to group them together. IP is traditionally divided into two categories—industrial property (patents, trademarks, industrial designs, etc.), and artistic and literary property (copyrights and related rights).

Patent is an exclusive right granted for an invention, which is a product or a process that provides a new way of doing something or offers a new technical solution to a problem. For a patent protection, an invention must fulfill some conditions that are evaluated together. It must be of practical use; it must be novel, that is, some new characteristic that is not known in the body of existing knowledge, or art in its technical field. And the invention must show an inventive step that could not be deduced by a person with average knowledge of the technical field. Patents establish a protected market advantage in return for revealing technical knowledge (Maskus 2000a).

Trademarks are a type of industrial property, protected by IP rights. Trademarks are distinctive signs, used to differentiate between identical or similar goods and services offered by different producers or services providers. In contrast with the patents, trademark applications are likely to be more strongly associated with the offer to market new product varieties that are not as strikingly novel as those awarded patents. This system helps consumers identify and purchase a product or service due to its nature and quality, indicated by its unique trademark, which meets their needs. According to Maskus (2000a), trademarks encourage firms to invest in name recognition and product quality. They also induce licensees to protect the value of assets by selling goods of guaranteed quality levels. If trademarks were not protected, rival firms could pass off their lower-quality goods as legitimate versions of those produced by recognized companies. This situation would diminish incentives for maintaining quality and would raise consumer search costs (Maskus, 2000a).

Copyright is a legal term describing rights given to creators for their literary and artistic works. Copyright and related rights are legal concepts and instruments that contribute to the cultural and economic development of nations while respecting and protecting the rights of creators for their works. Copyright law fulfills a decisive role in articulating the contributions and rights of the different stakeholders taking part in the cultural industries, and the relation between them and the public. Copyright protection covers literary works such as novels, poems, computer programs, films, and musical compositions; artistic works such as paintings, drawings, photographs, and sculpture; architecture and advertisements.

An industrial design is the ornamental or aesthetic aspect of an article. The design may consist of three-dimensional features, such as the shape or surface of an article, or two-dimensional features, such as patterns, lines, or color. Industrial designs are applied to a wide variety of products from technical and medical instruments to watches, jewelry, housewares and electrical appliances, vehicles, architectural structures, textile designs, and leisure goods. To be protected by this right, an industrial design must appeal to the eye. This means that an industrial design is primarily of an aesthetic nature, and does not protect any technical features of the article to which it is applied.

An environment that safeguards IP encourages inventors and organizations to invest resources in R&D for technological innovation that is needed to maintain competitiveness (Atun et al. 2006). The protection of these rights in today's society requires flexible and informed policy-making, not only taking into account the benefits offered by IP to national and individual interests, but also the challenges faced by IP right holders. In the next section, the components of IP protection will be discussed.

4.3 Effective System of IP Protection

The importance of IP rights has gained more significance due to increase in the share of knowledge-intensive or high-technology products in total world trade. IP rights provide incentives to inventors, authors, and artists to develop innovations or create forms of artistic expression. Accordingly, over time they provide gains from the introduction of new products, information, and creative activities. Many countries now recognize the importance of creating an enabling framework for IP and the protection of IP rights, as these are seen to be critical to business innovation, competition, and economic growth (Atun et al. 2006). Stronger and broader protection of IP rights have combined with wide-ranging advances in science and technology plus the rapid globalization of trade and investment to exert a pervasive influence on the patterns and processes of human relationships across many sectors and industries (Wattanapruttipaisan 2004). A well-established IP system is a key ingredient of market economy; however, it is not a simple issue to provide such system. Developing a stable and effective IP system requires a balance to be maintained between individual rights and the public interest, so that IP rights can be used in an appropriate and sustainable manner (Keplinger 2007).

An effective IP system requires several key elements—establishment, enforcement, and exchange. Establishment is a legal framework that can establish the identity of the owner of rights as an asset. It ensures that creators have the ability to control or sell those assets. Enforcement is a system for enforcing those IP rights that ensures that those rights will be protected and those that violate them will be punished. Exchange can be defined as a mean by which those rights can be exchanged without great costs. The ability to exchange or other contracts related to assets' use ensures that a full range of market options is open to the owner (Gans et al. 2002).

Although it is possible to emphasize key elements of effective IP system, it may not be practical to develop. There may be several difficulties for implementation of these key elements. For example, transferability of IP may cause some enforcement problems for owners in tracking the use of this right. Additionally, establishment may be difficult because of nonrival nature of intellectual property and widespread use of technology that may facilitate the transfer. Moreover, exchange problems may occur due to difficulties in valuation of IP rights. As it can be seen, all these elements are required to be balanced effectively if IP rights are to work as an insurance in which an agent may realize a return or value from the right owned by him. Considering the aim of this study, I will not discuss further on these difficulties, which may be a subject for future researches, but once again I emphasize the need of structure balanced by these elements.

4.4 The Role of IP Rights on Economic Growth

The major themes of economic development are focused on issues of business, trade, competitiveness, and international and domestic economic policy. As neoclassical market fundamentalist policies failed to deliver the growth they promised, a more contemporary model took hold after the 1990s, called the new growth theory of endogenous growth. This theory is described as incorporating the necessity of technology, in addition to human and physical capital (Todaro and Smith 2003). This theory, therefore, advocates public investments in human capital not provided by the market, and focuses on government intervention to help coordinate economic factors to increase human capital (Siu 2005). In this sense, IP rights become more important due to its spirit.

Technology transfer is essential to all developing countries. Developing countries do not own large amount of protected technology upon which they can build new technology and research. Therefore, inward technology transfer is the primary source of new information for creating technical change and structural transformation in most developing countries. Innovation and technological progress can raise productivity through the introduction of new goods and/or the improvement of existing goods by reducing the costs of production. Technology transfer can be broken down into several needs. These are needs to create technology available for transfer, needs to encourage follow-on inventors, and needs to provide rapid technology transfer (Langford 1997:1580). However, developing countries lack sufficient resources to perform R&D in new technologies. Consequently, they need technology from developed nations to assist their growth (Smith 1999).

In the global economy, countries acquire improved technologies through a variety of channels, both directly and indirectly via spillovers. These channels include innovation, licensing, trade, foreign direct investment, imitation, and piracy. Innovation requires important costs for R&D activities. Any useful innovation, if not protected by a legally given right, can usually be reproduced or copied by others at low cost. So if it is not protected, the innovation means no potential profits for the innovator and therefore the innovator cannot be compensated for the costs entailed in R&D. A role for IP rights protection arises because IP displays many of the characteristics of a public good

(Falvey et al. 2006). As IP rights are typically nonrival and can be nonexcludable, these characteristics could remove the incentive to invest in R&D. Therefore, IP rights protection can restore that incentive (Maskus 2000a).

The IP protection governing pioneering and follow-on inventors is vital to the proper functioning of innovation markets and is the key determinant of the rate and nature of innovation. The design of IP rights structure influences technology transfer, as the IP rights can affect the nature of industrial development. Effective IP protection leads to the creation of more technology and the conditions required for the sale or licensing of this new technology (Maskus 2000a).

The relationship between IP rights and economic development is a complex issue. Many studies have explored the relationship between economic growth, competitiveness, and innovation (Maskus 1998, 2000a, b; Falvey et al. 2006; Chen and Puttitanun 2005; Schneider 2005). The evidence is sometimes difficult to interpret because many of the concepts involved are not well measured. Within these studies, there are several well-known arguments for protecting IP rights effectively (Langford 1997; Maskus 2000a, b). There is a growing consensus that stronger IP rights increase economic growth and improve development processes if they are properly structured. In general, it is recognized that innovation leads to significant social welfare benefits and is underinvested compared to socially optimal levels, and IP rights provide national incentives to create innovation. These rights also support the innovation process by disseminating information on innovations, which leads to subsequent adaptations, improvements, and research by others.

According to Maskus (2000a), there are two central economic objectives of any IP protection system. The first is to promote investments in knowledge creation and innovation by establishing exclusive rights for using or trading these newly developed technologies, goods, and services. In the absence of such rights, economically valuable information could be appropriated without compensation by competitive rivals. Firms would be less willing to incur the costs of investing in research and commercialization activities. In economic terms, weak IP rights create a negative dynamic externality. They fail to overcome the problems of uncertainty in R&D and risks in competitive appropriation that are inherent in private markets for information (Maskus 2000a).

The second objective is promoting widespread dissemination of new knowledge by encouraging rights holders to place their inventions and ideas on the market (Maskus 2000a). Unlike standard economic commodities, knowledge has a number of special characteristics. Most importantly, knowledge is nonrival, meaning that once an idea has been developed, others can use the idea at no additional cost. In addition, knowledge is characterized to varying degrees by an inability to exclude others from using a particular idea (Blakeley et al. 2005). As knowledge is a form of public good that is inherently nonrival and nonexcludable, the developers may find it difficult to exclude others from using it (Atun et al. 2006). In economic terms, it is socially efficient to provide wide access to new technologies and products at marginal production costs.

In Chen and Puttitanun's (2005:489) empirical analysis of IP rights and innovations in developing countries, they have found that while lower IP rights facilitate imitations of foreign technologies, which reduces the market power of foreign firms and benefits domestic consumers, a developing country may also need to increase IP rights in order to encourage innovations by domestic firms.

For developing countries, trade and foreign direct investment (FDI) are key sources of new technology, particularly in regions where the domestic R&D sectors are underdeveloped or nonexistent. Indeed FDI is essential for technology transfer and thereof economic growth. IP protection is important for nations competing to attract FDI, and for encouraging domestic investments in innovation (Langford 1997). FDI, the establishment or acquisition of production subsidiaries abroad by multinational enterprises, is particularly important because it is a source of capital and knowledge about production techniques (Maskus 1998). According to Falvey and Foster (2006), inward FDI is expected to deploy advanced technology to subsidiaries that may be diffused to the firms in the host country. FDI may occur when sufficient cost or technological advantage over firms in the host country to offset the higher costs of operating internationally (Maskus 2000b). Effective IP protection may encourage technology transfer through increased trade, FDI, and technology licensing (Falvey and Foster 2006). Therefore, IP rights are key determinant of the conditions and circumstances of entry of business partners or competitors into national and global markets for goods and services (Shapiro 2002).

In order to draw a conclusion, we can benefit several points from Maskus' study. According to him, countries with weak IP rights could be isolated from modern technologies and would be forced to develop technological knowledge from their own resources, which is a difficult and costly task. Second, those countries would obtain fewer spillover benefits and demonstration effects of new technologies in their economies. Third, technologies available to such nations would tend to be outdated. Finally, nations with weak IP rights would experience both limited incentives for domestic innovation and relatively few inward technology transfers (Maskus 2000a).

4.5 Summary and Conclusion

Nowadays technological progress is viewed as the prime determinant of long-run economic growth. Countries invest in R&D with the expectation of benefiting from the results of innovations. Therefore, IP rights have the incentive role for innovation. Additionally, in creating new products, innovative activities also make contribution to the society's stock of knowledge upon which subsequent innovations are based. This process is assisted by IP rights where the information is made available to other potential inventors. The global rate of growth then depends upon the rate of innovation, and the stock of knowledge and IP protection can increase growth by encouraging both (Falvey and Foster 2006).

Although overly protective system of IP rights could limit the social gains from invention by reducing incentives to disseminate its fruits, an excessively weak system could reduce innovation by failing to provide an adequate return on investment (Maskus 2000a). Inadequate protection of IP rights has significant harmful consequences with economical and social effects. It harms creativity by causing a drain of creators to foreign countries where protection is available and impedes local culture and identity. It harms production by causing lower volumes of sales, losses in sale revenues, profits, market share, image, and jobs. Such a high-risk environment negatively impacts upon both local and foreign direct investment, and it negatively affects international image by causing harm to international trade (Keplinger 2007).

In summary, studies show that innovation has a positive association with economic productivity. Benefits are best realized when IP rights system provides incentives for innovation and does not hinder diffusion of knowledge (Atun et al. 2006). Hence, IP protection is important to sustain competitive advantage. Undeniably, without enforceable IP rights, the fear of deprivation would discourage the productive activity without considering the development level of the country. The overall implication of IP rights can play an important role for enabling firms in developing nations to access and exploit technologies and know-how through licensing agreements with parties in the developed countries. Therefore, effective management of innovation and providing a protection via IP rights should be the fundamental strategic objective for developing countries.

References

Blakeley, N., Lewis, G. and Mills, D. (2005). The economics of knowledge: what makes ideas special for economic growth? *Policy Perspectives Paper 05/05*, New Zealand Treasury.

Chen, Y., and Puttitanun, T. (2005). Intellectual property rights and innovation in developing countries. *Journal of Development Economics*, 78, 474–493.

Falvey, R., and Foster, N. (2006). The role of intellectual property rights in technology transfer and economic growth: theory and evidence. *UNIDO Working Paper*, UNIDO, Vienna.

Falvey, R., Foster, N., and Greenaway, D. (2006). Intellectual property rights and economic growth. *Review of Development Economics*, 10(4), 170–179.

Gans, J. S., Williams, P. L., and Briggs, D. (2002). Intellectual property rights: a grant of monopoly or an aid to competition. *Working Paper No.07/02*, Intellectual Property Research Institute of Australia.

Gould, D. M., and Gruben, W. C. (1996). The role of intellectual property rights in economic growth. *Journal of Development Economics*, 48, 323–350.

Keplinger, M. S. (2007). The protection of rights in the information society, Paper presented "The policymaking role of Parliaments in the development of the Information Society", Rome.

Langford, J. (1997). Intellectual property rights: technology transfer and resource implications. *American Journal of Agricultural Economics*, 5, 1576–1583.

Maskus, K. E. (1998). The role of intellectual property rights in encouraging foreign direct investment and technology transfer. *Duke Journal of Comparative and International Law*, 9, 109–161.

Maskus, K. E. (2000a). IP rights and economic development. *Case Western Reserve Journal of International Law*, 32, 471–506.

Maskus, K. E. (2000b). *Intellectual Property Rights in the Global Economy*. Washington DC: Institute for International Economics.

Maskus, K. E., and McDaniel, C. (1999). Impacts of the Japanese patent system on productivity growth. *Japan and the World Economy*, 11, 557–574.

Maskus, K. E., and Penubarti, M. (1995). How trade-related are intellectual property rights? *Journal of International Economics*, 39, 227–248.

Schneider, P. (2005). International trade, economic growth and intellectual property rights: a panel data study of developed and developing countries. *Journal of Development Economics*, 78, 529–547.

Shapiro, C. (2002). Competition policy and innovation, *OECD STI Working Papers 2002/11*, Paris.

Smith, M. W. (1999). Bringing developing countries' intellectual property laws to TRIPs standards: Hurdles and pitfalls facing Vietnam's efforts to normalize an intellectual property regime. *Case Western Reserve Journal of International Law*, 31(1), 211–251.

Siu, Y. (2005). What role for intellectual property rights in economic development? Substantial Research Paper for the Master's Degree in International Development.

Su, E. (2000). The winners and the losers: TRIPS and its effects on developing countries. *Houston Journal of International Law*, 23, 169–181.

Todaro, M. P., and Smith, C. S. (2003). *Economic Development*. Eight Edition, New York: Addison Wesley.

Wattanapruttipaisan, T. (2004). Intellectual property rights and enterprise development: some policy issues and options in ASEAN. *Asia-Pacific Development Journal*, 11(1), 73–79.

5 Variables Affecting Innovation-Related Competitiveness in Turkey

A. Orçun Sakarya

Abstract

Innovation's relation with competitiveness can be considered as a part of its emerging importance for the global economy. Accordingly, the main goal of this quantitative study is to foresee the main "macro" variables affecting Turkey's innovation-related competitive performance in the long run by considering innovation concept, both in the global and European Union basis. Following the introductory part and literature review, the relationship between innovation and competitiveness has been emphasized in Section 5.3. In Section 5.4, European Union Innovation Scoreboard has been mentioned. In Section 5.5 and the final section of the chapter, innovation concept has been discussed as an extension to Summary of Innovation Index and factors affecting innovation-related competitiveness in Turkey have been examined. First, a brief exploratory factor analysis has been conducted to identify the relevance of selected variables. Then, for investigating factors affecting medium and long-run innovation-related competitiveness in the country, a VAR model has been utilized. Granger's causality test has also been used to detect the cause-effect relationships between variables. As a result, it has been deduced that basic variables affecting innovation-related competitiveness are the number of patent applications and per capita R&D expenses. Moreover, it is also concluded that the Gross Domestic Product may also be relatively important in the long run.

5.1 Introduction

Different definitions of innovation exist in the literature. For example, according to Oslo Manual, innovation is the implementation of a new

N. Aydogan (ed.), *Innovation Policies, Business Creation and Economic Development*,
International Studies in Entrepreneurship 21, DOI 10.1007/978-0-387-79976-6_5,
© Springer Science+Business Media, LLC 2009

or significantly improved product (goods or services) or process, a
new marketing method, or a new organizational method in business
practices, workplace organization, or external relations (OECD 2005).
Whereas, according to European Innovation Scoreboard 2004 paper,
innovation is defined as the renewal and enlargement of the range,
products and services, and the associated markets; the establishment
of new methods of production, supply and distribution, the introduction of changes in management, work organization, and working conditions; and the skills of the workforce (EC 2004). One of the implicit
goals of the innovation is solving a problem. In this framework, it
can also be deduced that innovation can also be managed. Moreover,
innovation has been assumed as one of the leading economic factors
that affect competitiveness; that is probably why innovation is defined
as "critical" by the policy designers. Therefore, innovation is a broad
concept that can be affected from different variables and that can be
considered in different perspectives. Accordingly, the aim of the study
is to evaluate Turkey's innovation performance, examine variables that
may potentially affect innovation, and to comment on them in the
framework of competitiveness through the horizon of harmonization
with the European Union (EU).

5.2 Literature Review

When the dimensions of innovation are envisaged, it can be seen that
the term itself contains many aspects. In a general point of view, it is
possible to place the innovation both in microeconomic and macroeconomic layers in a country's economy. For example, innovation at
corporate level means application of knowledge in order to acquire
productivity as well as creation of new products and services to be able
to survive in a competitive market. At this stage, a company's liaison
with applied policies in the country may begin with the legal framework concerning the innovative activities on firm basis. Then the company may also be indirectly affected by the national innovation policy
implications when it becomes a member of a cluster in the country. By
considering these two examples it can be said that, when evaluating
innovation activities in a country, variables that are related both with
the "firm" and "national" policy levels can be taken into account.

Regarding innovation's "micro" level, Tether and Hipp's (2002)
study yielded interesting results. They examined patterns of innovation

and sources of competitiveness amongst German service firms. The purpose of their study was to investigate how these patterns differ across services, and, in particular, how knowledge intensive and technical service firms differ from services. They reached the conclusion that a high degree of customization in the output of service firms the innovation activities are relatively more oriented to product innovation.

When the link between "micro" and "macro" dimensions of the innovation has been considered, the study by Hoskisson et al. (2004) can be focused. The authors have investigated how institutional congruence between capital and labor markets influence corporate governance systems, which in turn create differences in national corporate innovation and entrepreneurship systems, and subsequently global competitiveness in their study. They claimed that both market- and relationship-based systems have their own strengths and weaknesses. Dynamism, flexibility, and diversity of the market-based systems are supportive of explorative and revolutionary innovations while continuity, stability, and commitment of relationship-based systems are supportive of exploitative and incremental innovations. They also concluded that such linkages between national governance systems and innovation systems indicate that a country is more likely to gain global competitiveness in markets whose innovation requirements are well supported by its national governance system.

In some studies, the innovation has also been investigated mostly in "macro" level. For example, Kaplinsky and Paulino (2005) have examined the innovation-competitiveness relation with a different point of view. In their study, they have considered the links between price performance of globally traded goods and innovation intensity, and reached three conclusions. The first one is that taxonomies that focus on R&D inputs are a poor reflection of innovation intensity. Second, by using Lall's sectoral taxonomy, there appears to be a strong correlation between price behavior and innovation intensity, with the exception of resource-based manufactures. They claimed that the higher the innovation content, the less likely prices are to fall. Third conclusion is that the lower the income group of the exporting economy, the more likely exports will be to cluster in the low-innovation niches in these sectors.

With the same point of view, Parker (2004) has studied foundations of technology development, innovation, and competitiveness in the globalized knowledge economy. By examining of cross-national data, her study developed the proposition that particular elements of the domestic science, technology, and industry infrastructure—such as the stock of knowledge and competence in the economy, the capacity for learning and generation of new ideas, and the capacity to commercialize new ideas—vary cross-nationally and are related to the level of participation of a nation in knowledge-intensive activities.

Lastly, Solleiro and Castañón (2005) have studied the challenges for Mexico's insertion in the global context in a framework of competitiveness and innovation systems. They have proposed some basic elements for a science, technology, and innovation policy, such as expansion and modernization of the human resources training system for science, technology, and innovation; popularization of the concept of a society of knowledge; promotion alliances between governments and entrepreneurial organizations to generate technologies; and identification of specific development mechanisms aimed at decreasing the regional disparities in the country.

5.3 The Relationship Between Innovation and Competitiveness in the World

The relationship between innovation and competitiveness involves various stages. The first stage is the identification of the relationship between technologic validity and innovation. With a general definition, technologic validity is the ability of the current technologic infrastructure in providing technology transfer whereas innovation is the production of the new technologies by a country. Accordingly, when innovation and innovation's quick adoption to technology is applied with "technologic compatibility" support, it can also be observed that the competitive power of the country may be subject to increase. In this case, it can be better to internalize technology adoption in order to improve the competitiveness.

At the second stage, factors leading to competitiveness and innovation can be directly related to each other. In countries where innovation is made in the area of production, it has been observed that the productivity may be subject to increase. In this stage, which is generally called "innovation-related competitiveness," simultaneous improvements in the R&D activities and education infrastructure are also required. Moreover, increase in the number of projects held may also ease the focalization of the innovation in the area of policy implementation. Additionally, due to development in the human resources supported by supplementary investments, the entrepreneurship and so the competitiveness may also grow in the country.

At the third stage, the country will become an "innovation leaded" one. In such countries, high living standards accompanied by higher salaries may dominate the economy. As country oriented products will also become highly competitive ones, a gradual increase in national income may also occur via foreign trade.

The relationship between innovation and competitiveness has also been evaluated in a global point of view; Global Competitiveness Index (GCI) is one of them. One of the pillars that affect GCI is "innovation factors" that is a joint indicative result of business sophistication and innovation itself. This pillar, in a way, evaluates the adoption of new technologies and the position of innovation policies in a country's economy. Moreover, it also takes the effects of the implemented innovation policies into account. As a snapshot, according to GCI 2006 results, business sophistication and innovation yields positive results in Turkey, which achieved the 39th rank with a score of 4.58 in "business sophistication." The achievement had occurred particularly in the quality and quantity of the networks, and supporting industries that is above the average "new" (new members of EU and candidate countries) countries' average of 4.46. However, the "innovation" score of 3.35 is the one that still needs to be improved when compared to the average score of 3.54 obtained by the new member countries (Adopted from WEF 2006).

5.4 European Union Innovation Scoreboard

EU has an established innovation index founded within the Lisbon Decisions, which can also be seen as an extension of the intense work on innovation in the last decade. The "Lisbon Strategy" can be usefully broken down into eight distinct dimensions, considered to be critical for national competitiveness where one of them is developing a "European area for innovation, research and development" (adopted from WEF 2004). Accordingly, importance of the innovation concept has been underlined in many documents, such as the "Innovation Message document in 2003, "Innovation Action Plan," 2000 Lisbon, and 2002 Barcelona Summit Declarations in addition to the "Green Paper" that was launched in 1995. Innovation has also been considered as an important strategy within the Seventh Framework Programme (Framework Programme on Innovation and Competitiveness).

Undertaking of innovation activities in the market place, improvement of innovative abilities, and production for innovation are some of the notions mentioned in the EU's "New Action Plan on Innovation." Innovation has also been remarked as a critical point to reach the 2010 targets within policies mentioned in the R&D part of the plan.

European TrendChart on Innovation, which was launched in 2000, gives a general idea in the framework of performance evaluation for the countries. One the of the main indicators that has been used in the TrendChart is The European Innovation Scoreboard (EIS), which collects and analyzes trends in key indicators across the EU25, associated, and candidate countries as well as the United States and Japan. The EIS has become over time the standard for benchmarking of policy indicators (EC 2006b). TrendChart has been published in a yearly basis. The report also includes additional comparative results with the United States and Japan. EIS has been constructed by using 26 indicators' empowered methodology in conjunction with the Summary Innovation Index (SII), which gives an "at a glance" overview of aggregate national innovation performance. SII scale highest value is 1, whereas the lowest value is 0.

To have a better understanding of different aspects of the innovation process, 25 EIS indicators has been classified under 5 groups (MERIT 2006) in SII:

(a) Innovation Drivers: Indicators on structural conditions required for innovation potential. Some of the drivers are S&E graduates, population with tertiary education, and broadband penetration rate.
(b) Knowledge creation: These are the measures of the investments in R&D activities, considered as key elements for a successful knowledge-based economy. Some of the indicators are public and business R&D expenditures and share of enterprises receiving public funding for innovation.
(c) Innovation and entrepreneurship: These are the measures of the efforts toward innovation at the level of the firms. Some of the indicators are Information Communication Technology (ICT)

expenditures, and Small and Medium Enterprises (SMEs) innovating at house.

(d) Application: These are the measures of the performance expressed in terms of labor and business activities, and their value added in innovative sectors. Some of the application indicators are exports of high technology products as a share of total exports and new to market product sales.

(e) Intellectual property: These are the measures of the achieved results in terms of successful know-how. Some of the indicators are triadic patent families per million population, new community trademarks per million population, and new community designs per million population.

The policy response to each of the identified challenges was appraised based on a set of criteria ranging from a systematic and integrated approach responding to the challenge through a comprehensive set of measures to no specific measures addressing the challenge (EC 2006b). In this way, it can be said that the set of indicators give a broad idea for examining the innovation process in a country.

5.5 Identification of Factors that Affect Innovation-Related Competitiveness in Turkey

For Turkey, the process of EU harmonization brings constraints in many areas in addition to some that have to be improved. At this stage, innovation is one of the subjects that have been considered during the process of integration. Turkey is also one of the countries that have been included and quoted in the SII on the basis of its innovation performance. In this section of the study, the concept of innovation in the framework of EIS and SII for Turkey is discussed.

5.6 Turkey's Innovation Performance According to EIS and SII

In order to figure out the innovation performance of Turkey, some EIS performance indicators can be focused in relation with the indicators that has been mentioned in Section 5.4. Accordingly, main facilitators of the innovation in the country can be stated as public R&D expenditures, and university R&D activities financed by businesses. However, areas such as ICT, intellectual property, broadband penetration, and high technology exports are the ones that still need to be improved (adopted from EC 2006a).

Additionally, innovating businesses represent another potential in Turkey especially in the area of "application." According to a research conducted in 2004, the percentage of the innovating companies in the production sector is nearly 35 percent, whereas the EU average is 47 percent (adopted from Crowley 2005). When the high percentage of SMEs (which is nearly 99.6 percent as of 2001 [OECD 2004]) in the country is considered, this "scale-based" elastic infrastructure can be seen as an opportunity for faster dissemination of innovation within them. However, funding facilities (such as venture and risk capital, and others) should also be improved in order to support such dissemination. In the same framework, development and diversification of the current financial instruments may also yield positive results.

In relation with such a "scale-based" elastic infrastructure, it can also be added that entrepreneurship also plays a crucial role in promoting economic growth by serving as a mechanism facilitating the spillover of knowledge, according to Audretch (2004).

The strong and vulnerable points stated above provide a basis to comment on an innovation policy that may be implemented by Turkey in the future. Main goals of such a policy may be stated as

- Investment in human resources that will be able to innovate
- Increase in university and industry cooperation
- Increase in private sector's innovation activities
- Development of a national innovation system
- Development of regional innovation systems.

Accordingly, some of the national innovation policy objectives that have to be achieved until year 2010 have been summarized in Table 5.1.

5.6.1 Examination of the Variables Affecting Innovation-Related Competitiveness in Turkey

There are two main assumptions that lies behind the model developed for examining the innovation-related competitiveness in Turkey. The first assumption is the identification of the variables that may affect the country's innovation potential and the degree of their affection.

Table 5.1 Selected national innovation policy objectives (EC 2006a)

Goals	Target year
Increasing the gross domestic expenditure of R&D (GERD) as a percentage of GDP (%)	2010
Increasing the number of researchers per thousand employed	2010
Increase in the number of triadic patents	2010
Increase in the number of scientific publications and science citation per million	2010
Increasing the SMEs innovating in-house (% of all SMEs)	2010
Increasing the sales of "new to market" products (% of total turnover)	2010
Increasing the tertiary-type A education graduates participating in workforce (men) (%)	2010
Increase the global competitiveness ranking	2010
Improving the global competitiveness index ranking infrastructure	2010

In this framework, the inclusion of the country in the SII provides a basis for the model.

The second assumption is the usage of the variables obtained at the end of analysis for evaluating innovation-related competitiveness in the long run. As some of the GCI and SII index variables look similar, evaluation of the variables that may affect innovation in the long run may also give an indirect idea for commenting on the relationship between innovation and competitiveness with a general point of view.

5.6.2 Data Source and Selected Variables

In the study, basically World Bank Data has been used. Additionally, World Intellectual Property Organization (WIPO), EUROSTAT, Scientific and Technological Research Council of Turkey (TUBITAK), and Turkish Statistical Institute (TUIK) data have also been considered. Selected variables for the study between 1990 and 2006 are stated below:

- SII value (Yearly trend has been assumed as −4.3. Data on yearly basis has been produced via backward calculation).
- Number of patent applications (residents) (abbreviated as PATENT in result tables).

- High technology exports (% of manufactured exports; abbreviated as HTE in result tables).
- Per capita research and development expenses (US Dollars) (abbreviated as RDHEAD in result tables).
- World rank based on scientific publications with Turkish origin (RANK in result tables).
- Per capita GDP in US Dollars. All of the selected variables are endogenous.

During the analysis, SII has also been assumed as "an independent variable" on which the other's effect has been investigated. This assumption is based on the idea that SII appears as a holistic indicator that contains different innovation measures, including some that may be related to competitiveness. As a result, it is also possible to comment on Turkey's innovation-related competitiveness potential regarding its SII value.

5.6.3 Methodology

First, exploratory factor analysis has been conducted to understand the relevance of selected variables. Exploratory factor analysis (EFA) is generally used to discover the factor structure of a measure and to examine its internal reliability. In general, in an exploratory analysis, the rule is to put in as many variables as possible and see what loads on the relevant factor (Kline 1994). As we do not have any prior theory or hypothesis about the innovation variables affecting competitiveness, we use factor loadings to intuit the factor structure of the data. During the factor analysis, principal components analysis with varimax rotation has been used.

Second, to be able to notify the effect of selected variables in time, Vector Autoregression System (VAR) is applied. The goal of VAR analysis is to determine the interrelationships among the variables, not the parameter estimates (Burbidge et al. 1985) In the VAR systems, every equation has the same variables on the right-hand side that include lagged values of all the endogenous variables. In a way, it can also be stated that it is a system that contains n equations. Reduced form of the equations in the system can be shown as follows:

$$y_t = v + A_1 Y_{t-1} + \ldots + A_t Y_{p-t} + u_t \qquad (5.1)$$

In the VAR system, impulse response functions, variance decomposition, and Granger causality can be used in order to test the relationship between variables. In addition to that, an impulse response function describes the response of an endogenous variable to one of the innovations. Specifically, it traces the effect on current and future values of the endogenous variable of a one standard deviation shock to one of the innovations. At this stage, Granger causality indicates the power of explanation of variable to each other in the system Engel and Grangar (1987). The variance decomposition of the VAR gives information about the relative importance of the random innovations.

5.6.4 Results

5.6.4.1 Factor Analysis

Results indicate that the variables may be summarized under two factors. The first factor may be called as the "economic power" that accounts for about 67 percent of the total loadings where the second one may be called "technology." Technology factor accounts for about 23 percent of the total loadings. In this stage, it is also possible to claim that the "economic power" may be more important than "technology" on the competitiveness. Results after rotation give a detailed idea about the variables that affect the two factors.

When the first factor called "economic power" is considered, it can also be deduced that the number of patent applications has an important influence on the economic power other than per capita GDP. Besides, it can be seen that high technology exports in conjunction with the per capita R&D expenses is highly effective when the second factor "technology" is taken into account. Table 5.2 gives a general idea about the variables that may be significant for the VAR analysis that has been discussed in the next section.

5.6.4.2 VAR Decomposition

Unit Root Test Results

To make a VAR analysis, the stationary of the series must be assured. In this framework, Augmented Dickey Fuller (ADF) test has been executed to provide the stationarity the series in consideration. In this

Table 5.2 Rotated component matrix results

	Component	
	Economic power	Technology
PATENT	0.853	0.388
RDEXPHEAD	0.648	0.722
GDP	0.925	−0.103
RANK	−0.630	−0.720
HTE	−0.072	0.952

Extraction Method: Principal Component Analysis.
Rotation Method: Varimax with Kaiser Normalization.
Rotation converged in 3 iterations.

step, identification of the appropriate lag length in VAR systems plays an important role because if the lag length is too small, the assumed model may be misspecified, and if it is too large, degrees of freedom may be wasted. In this study, the optimum lag length is determined by the Akaike information criterion (AIC), for which the lag length for the annual data is deduced as one. Nonstationary variables become stationary after having been differenced. To be able to decide on the stationarity of the variables the existence of a unit root has been checked, and to comment on such an existence an ADF test is applied (Dickey and Fuller 1979). Test results are given in Table 5.3.

The optimum lag length determined to the AIC is obtained from the estimation of the unrestricted VAR model constructed to search for a Granger causality. The following model is an example of the unrestricted VAR model using GDP* and HTE* variables:

$$\text{GDP}_t^* = \mu + \sum \alpha \text{GDP}_{t-i}^* + \sum \beta_i \text{HTE}_{t-i}^* + u_t, \quad i = 1, 2, \ldots p.$$

$$\text{HTE}_t^* = \mu + \sum \gamma_i \text{GDP}_{t-i}^* + \sum \theta_i \text{HTE}_{t-i}^* + v_t, \quad i = 1, 2, \ldots p.$$

Granger Causality Test

According to the table, optimal lag length has been identified as 1 and the series became stationary to be able conduct the Granger Causality Test. The main reason for conducting the test is the expectance of finding a causal relationship between selected variables. In this test,

Table 5.3 Unit root test results

Variables observation; sample	T-statistics for ADF	Test results	Constant, trend
SII*	−3.42956	Unit root does not exist	
14; 1991–2004	p = 0.0021	Stationary	None
RDEXPHEAD*	−2.95228	Unit root does not exist	
14; 1992–2005	p = 0.0063	Stationary	None
PATENT*	−2.44130	Unit root does not exist	
15; 1992–2006	p = 0.0186	Stationary	None
GDP*	−4.24241	Unit root does not exist	
15; 1992–2006	p = 0.0059	Stationary	Intercept
HTE*	−3.20713	Unit root does not exist	
13; 1992–2004	p = 0.0038	Stationary	None
RANK*	−3.40985	Unit root does not exist	
15; 1992–2006	p = 0.0022	Stationary	None

*Denotes the first difference
If *p*-value is greater than 0.05 as a result of the ADF test, it can be decided that the variable has a unit root and vice versa. The results are obtained from MacKinnon's table by using Eviews5 software.

in order to declare a causal relationship between selected variables, their F values should be greater than those stated on the F values table. Accordingly, Table F values for the time series considered are as follows:

$F(1,14):4,60$
$F(1,15):4,54$
$F(1,16):4,99$

In conjunction with the F test for Granger Causality, detected relationships between variables are given in Table 5.4.

Table 5.4 Granger causality test results

Pairwise Granger Causality Tests			
Sample: 1990–2006			
Lags: 1			
Null Hypothesis:	Obs	F-Statistic	Probability
PATENT does not Granger Cause RDEXPHEAD	15	6.53171	0.02520
GDP does not Granger Cause RDEXPHEAD	15	4.74070	0.05013
PATENT does not Granger Cause GDP	16	10.3599	0.00672
GDP does not Granger Cause THE	14	7.71572	0.01798

Fig. 5.1 Granger
causality test results

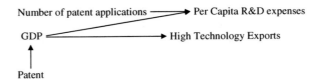

According to Table 5.4, at a 5 percent significance level, a number of patent applications appear as a one-way cause of the per capita expenses, where the GDP is the one-way cause of the per capita R&D expenses that might also be imagined as an expected result. Besides, when the causality between high technology exports and country economy is considered, it can also be deduced that high technology exports are indirectly affected from countries' economic power. Lastly, it can also be said that the number of patent applications is also a one-way cause of the GDP that might show the indirect contribution of the intellectual capital on the country's economy. Directions of the Granger Causality Test are shown in Fig. 5.1.

Impulse Response Functions

A shock to the i-th variable not only directly affects the i-th variable, but is also transmitted to all of the other endogenous variables through the dynamic (lag) structure of the VAR. The goal of using impulse response functions is to trace the deviations of a one-time shock to one of the innovations (impulses) on the current and future values of selected variables.

In accordance with the impulse response function, a standard deviation shock is given to patent application, per capita R&D expenses, high technology exports, per capita GDP, and scientific publications' rank. In Fig. 5.2, impulse response functions show that the response of SII expenses to patent production and to per capita R&D expenses is longer than the one to per capita GDP, high technology exports, and to the rank of scientific publications. This stipulates that the patent production and the per capita R&D expenses mostly affect SII in the long run.

Variance Decomposition

To analyze endogenous variables' medium and long-term effects (maximum 10 years) on the model, variance decomposition method have been applied.

Response to Cholesky One S.D. Innovations ± 2 S.E.

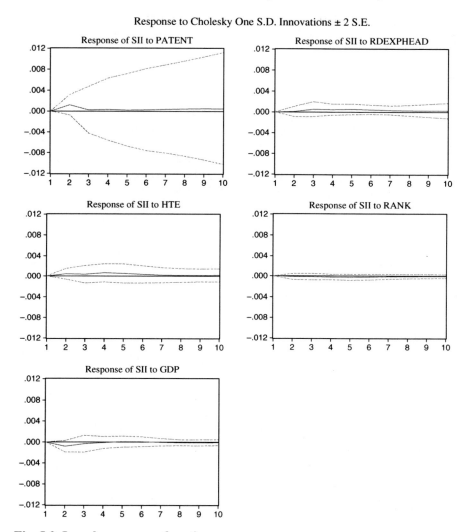

Fig. 5.2 Impulse response functions

The impulse response functions trace the effects of a shock to one endogenous variable on the other variables in the VAR, whereas variance decomposition separates the variation of an endogenous variable into the component shocks of the VAR. The variance decomposition is the percentage of the variance of the error made in forecasting a variable due to a specific shock at a specific time horizon.

The results are shown in Table 5.5. The second column, labeled "S.E.," gives the forecast error of the variable at the given forecast horizon. The source of this forecast error is the variation in the current

Table 5.5 Variance decomposition results

Variance decomp. of SII:

Period	S.E.	SII	PATENT	RDEXP HEAD	HTE	RANK	GDP
1	0.002116	100.0000	0.000000	0.000000	0.000000	0.000000	0.000000
2	0.003742	83.33112	10.59820	0.068375	1.326050	0.100683	4.575573
3	0.004007	81.68905	9.646035	1.839378	1.936158	0.213057	4.676323
4	0.004194	78.65687	9.529707	2.921414	4.138847	0.433447	4.319713
5	0.004293	75.90632	9.387360	4.302174	5.500120	0.750757	4.153272
6	0.004364	74.33504	9.504596	5.217811	5.936982	0.966279	4.039293
7	0.004441	73.48700	9.987994	5.640821	5.924926	1.049727	3.909531
8	0.004531	72.81169	10.72291	5.796934	5.787212	1.060803	3.820451
9	0.004616	72.06095	11.55742	5.892027	5.683162	1.055759	3.750678
10	0.004685	71.21076	12.38889	6.020137	5.648015	1.057879	3.674317

and future values of the innovations to each endogenous variable in the VAR. The remaining columns include the percentage of the forecast variance caused by innovation. The percentages in each row add up to 100.

According to Table 5.5, the SII is basically affected by two variables: number of patent applications and per capita R&D expenses in the long run. It can also be deduced that high technology exports may also play an important role on the country's competitive power within the same time frame. When the theoretical relationship between those variables is reconsidered, it can also be contemplated that increase in per capita R&D expenses may also yield positive results on patent applications, and indirectly contribute on high technology products' manufacturing and exports.

As a result, it can be stated that the most important potential for a higher SII value is the transformation of intellectual capital investments and knowledge creation into the trade power. Moreover, it can also be added that a higher GDP may also be theoretically needed for a potential increase in the GDP portion afforded for R&D activities when its loadings in Table 5.5 are taken into account. Lastly, it can also be added that all these factors may also contribute indirectly to the expansion of innovation to the country. At that stage, these factors may also facilitate the enhancement of "sustainable innovation systems" as proposed by Bonilla (2003) where innovation contributes to sustainable development of a country.

5.7 Conclusion

In a country, innovation-related competitiveness is an issue that is affected by many factors. When a country's performance is to be evaluated, EIS as well as GCI can be affirmed as two main compiling indexes. It can also be said that both indexes contain innovation criteria that can also be assumed as aggregate indicators during evaluation processes of the country. In this framework, Turkey has some potential strength and more goals to achieve in the future. For this reason, when the process of harmonization with the EU is considered, obtaining a higher SII value can also be important in developing innovation-related competitiveness as both processes can be seen as interrelated ones.

Regarding the analysis conducted, when the SII is taken as an indicator of innovation-related competitiveness, it can be concluded that Turkey's SII value is mostly affected by patent applications and per capita R&D expenditures. In this stage, two main conclusions can be reached. The first one is related with Turkey's innovation policy objectives, as shown in Section 5.1, where the increase in the number of patents is one of the goals to be reached. When this goal is evaluated in conjunction with the analysis results, it can be said that patent applications become one of the high priority goals. Moreover, investments made on human capital may also have a significant effect on improving the competitive power with the support of high technology products' exports. Second conclusion is that the economic power may also have a significant effect on SII value that may also bring the presence of an innovation cycle (when the causality between number of patent applications-GDP and GDP-high technology exports are considered altogether), where more innovative companies may also be more competitive, and consequently will contribute positively to the national income. Finally, it should not be forgotten that evaluating such a "cycle" with different index criteria may also yield different results and hence be the subject of further research.

Appendix: Variance Decomposition Results

Variance decomp. of PATENT:

Period	S.E.	SII	PATENT	RDEXP HEAD	HTE	RANK	GDP
1	95.99420	10.88380	89.11620	0.000000	0.000000	0.000000	0.000000
2	128.4679	10.00339	87.39762	0.875602	1.439898	0.000886	0.282607
3	158.5482	12.27016	84.64727	0.932846	1.482912	0.022680	0.644134
4	183.7847	13.15320	83.78002	1.107113	1.172475	0.020190	0.767002
5	203.7443	12.85965	83.97320	1.479575	0.956655	0.018527	0.712398
6	221.4732	12.42651	84.23616	1.867238	0.809662	0.025950	0.634481
7	238.5385	12.24557	84.26718	2.175516	0.700385	0.034221	0.577127
8	255.6600	12.39782	84.01296	2.383961	0.616548	0.038588	0.550125
9	272.7775	12.73955	83.59468	2.532242	0.547056	0.040617	0.545856
10	289.5197	13.08605	83.17315	2.664118	0.487179	0.042777	0.546727

Variance decomp. of RDEXP HEAD:

Period	S.E.	SII	PATENT	RDEXP HEAD	HTE	RANK	GDP
1	4.504428	7.804443	59.72043	32.47513	0.000000	0.000000	0.000000
2	7.472892	2.871409	74.90310	15.61928	4.967101	0.380176	1.258936
3	9.285218	2.077851	78.32008	13.96604	3.312316	0.661001	1.662712
4	11.14708	3.603107	81.02331	11.02710	2.681738	0.510987	1.153753
5	13.37786	8.524268	79.53041	8.161591	2.273643	0.354866	1.155220
6	15.41676	11.78600	78.29384	6.573588	1.814665	0.268412	1.263488
7	17.07206	12.86991	78.32708	5.893990	1.480213	0.220513	1.208296
8	18.45732	12.91922	78.84201	5.675243	1.276002	0.201749	1.085776
9	19.73412	12.80642	79.31132	5.590822	1.121281	0.196504	0.973650
10	21.00393	12.89992	79.54625	5.482782	0.989817	0.190249	0.890986

Variance decomp. of HTE:

Period	S.E.	SII	PATENT	RDEXP HEAD	HTE	RANK	GDP
1	0.649471	20.12781	1.042263	0.851638	77.97829	0.000000	0.000000
2	1.057224	21.74838	2.956474	7.412501	58.61607	3.205457	6.061119
3	1.284694	27.91985	7.349389	9.484367	42.12561	3.886987	9.233789
4	1.294127	27.60079	7.526699	9.824586	41.53114	4.154513	9.362275
5	1.341603	31.55079	7.150991	9.142453	39.03969	3.866029	9.250049
6	1.392539	35.31118	6.936274	8.488155	36.24598	3.601519	9.416892
7	1.408620	36.21671	6.832169	8.338679	35.69200	3.520755	9.399685
8	1.414436	35.96316	6.790280	8.455338	35.93090	3.533123	9.327198
9	1.419539	35.73512	6.792637	8.596665	35.97382	3.572786	9.328968
10	1.421287	35.64847	6.789856	8.680200	35.94804	3.601675	9.331755

Variance decomp. of RANK:

Period	S.E.	SII	PATENT	RDEXP HEAD	HTE	RANK	GDP
1	1.770784	0.159966	5.501873	73.88886	9.986050	10.46325	0.000000
2	2.267943	11.29324	11.14259	58.53330	10.34677	8.360319	0.323789
3	2.960265	25.28213	22.18922	38.39975	8.027259	5.683651	0.417992
4	3.452379	30.48456	26.85871	31.14739	6.390978	4.506668	0.611690
5	3.905570	33.24838	30.72826	26.10655	5.453085	3.692636	0.771088
6	4.271949	33.76121	33.92576	23.30388	4.985263	3.225481	0.798410
7	4.578551	33.32243	36.74464	21.56594	4.674149	2.929853	0.762993
8	4.856922	32.64780	39.33993	20.22595	4.362727	2.701892	0.721700
9	5.125219	32.01151	41.74394	19.02154	4.031427	2.497545	0.694038
10	5.390197	31.44609	43.95790	17.89648	3.709757	2.307675	0.682099

Variance decomp. of GDP:

Period	S.E.	SII	PATENT	RDEXP HEAD	HTE	RANK	GDP
1	374.2461	34.12791	20.60803	0.104623	5.041485	0.886825	39.23112
2	492.9631	20.11897	47.30485	0.149828	9.163850	0.612754	22.64975
3	646.3966	22.38717	48.43255	0.146472	13.26123	0.732819	15.03975
4	798.5153	26.70984	50.66597	0.204932	9.686679	0.789809	11.94277
5	865.0220	25.46020	54.71362	0.264013	8.254645	0.714619	10.59289
6	904.6187	23.45392	57.86447	0.676955	7.658985	0.659560	9.686111
7	939.9736	21.75690	60.31208	1.160222	7.118861	0.641306	9.010632
8	978.7185	20.45044	62.59531	1.451673	6.583725	0.606738	8.312110
9	1025.722	19.83948	64.37126	1.565886	6.059918	0.554248	7.609213
10	1076.844	19.66565	65.66887	1.627435	5.537653	0.502968	6.997431

References

Audretch, D.B. (2004). Sustaining Innovation and Growth: Public Policy Support for Entrepreneurship. *Industry and Innovation,* 11(3), 167–191.

Bonilla, O.S. (2003). Competitiveness, Systems of Innovation and the Learning Economy: The Forest Sector in Costa Rica. *Forest Policy and Economics, 5,* 373–384.

Burbidge, I.B., Megee, L., Veall, M.R. (1985). On the Seasonality of Vector Autoregression Residuals. *Economic Letters,* 18, 137–141.

Crowley, P. (2005). *Innovation Activity in the New Member States and Candidate Countries.* Brussels: Statistics in Focus: Science and Technology.

Dickey, D.A., Fuller, W.A. (1979). Distribution of the Estimators for Autoregressive Time Series with Unit Root. *Journal of the American Statistical Association*, 74, 427–431.

Engle, R.F., Granger, C.W.J. (1987). Cointegration and Error Correction: Representation, Estimation and Testing. *Econometrica*, 55, 251–276.

European Commission (2004) European Innovation Scoreboard 2004, Comparative Analysis of Innovation Performance. In: Pro Inno Europe http://www.trendchart.cordis.lu/scoreboards/scoreboard2004/pdf/eis_2004.pdf/ European Innovation Scoreboard 2004, Comparative Analysis of Innovation Performance. Cited 21 Sep 2007.

European Commission (2006a) *Annual Innovation Policy Trends and Appraisal Report: Turkey 2005–2006*. Brussels: Enterprise Directorate General.

European Commission (2006b) European Innovation Progress Report, 2006: Trendchart. In: Pro Inno Europe http://www.proinno-europe.eu/docs/Reports/Documents/EIPR2006-final.pdf/ European Innovation Progress Report, 2006: Trendchart. Cited 14 Oct 2007.

Hoskisson, R.E., Yiu, D., Kim, H. (2004). Corporate Governance Systems: Effects of Capital and Labor Market Congruency on Corporate Innovation and Global Competitiveness. *Journal of High Technology Management Research*, 15, 293–315.

Kaplinsky, R., Paulino, A.S. (2005). Innovation and Competitiveness: Trends in Unit Prices in Global Trade. *Oxford Development Studies*, 33(3–4), 333–355.

Kline, P. (1994). *An Easy Guide to Factor Analysis*. New Jersey: Routledge.

MERIT (2006) European Innovation Scoreboard 2006: Comparative Analysis of Innovation Performance. In: Report Prepared by Maastricht Economic Research Institute on Innovation and Technology and Joint Research Centre of the European Commission http://www.proinno-europe.eu/doc/EIS2006_final.pdf/ European Innovation Scoreboard 2006: Comparative Analysis of Innovation Performance. Cited 09 Oct 2007.

OECD (2004) Small and Medium Sized Enterprises in Turkey. In: Organization for Economic Cooperation and Development http://www.oecd.org/dataoecd/5/11/31932173.pdf/ Small and Medium Sized Enterprises in Turkey

OECD (2005). *Oslo Manual: Guidelines for Collecting and Interpreting Innovation Data*. Paris: A Joint Publication of OECD and Eurostat.

Parker, R. (2004). Foundations of Technology Development, Innovation and Competitiveness in the Globalised Knowledge Economy. *Prometheus*, 22(3), 293–309.

Solleiro, J.L., Castañón, R. (2005). Competitiveness and Innovation Systems: The Challenges for Mexico's Insertion in the Global Context. *Technovation*, 25, 1059–1070.

Tether, B.S., Hipp, C. (2002). Knowledge Intensive, Technical and Other Services: Patterns of Competitiveness and Innovation Compared. *Technology Analysis and Strategic Management*, 14(2), 163–182.

WEF (2004) The Lisbon Review, 2004: An Assessment of Policies and Reforms in Europe. In: World Economic Forum.
http://www.weforum.org/pdf/Gcr/LisbonReview/Lisbon_Review_2004.pdf/ The Lisbon Review, 2004: An Assessment of Policies and Reforms in Europe. Cited 20 Nov 2007.
WEF (2006) Global Competitiveness Index: 2006. In: World Economic Forum. http://www.weforum.org/pdf/Global_Competetiveness_Reports/Reports/gcr_2006/ Global Competitiveness Index: 2006. Cited 08 Dec 2007.

6 The Meaning of Innovation and Entrepreneurship in Developing Countries

Gökhan Çapoğlu

Abstract

The meaning of innovation and entrepreneurship and policies to promote innovation differ across groups of developing countries. On the one hand, there is a small group of countries such as China, South Korea, Brazil, and Mexico which has achieved a certain stage of capitalistic development that provides an institutional environment for encouraging innovation and entrepreneurship. On the other hand, there is a large group of countries in Africa and Asia as well as in Latin America which lacks the critical level of capital accumulation even for sustainable development let alone for the growth of innovation and entrepreneurship. There is also a group of countries such as India with a world-class high-technology clusters developing in the midst of increasing poverty. That is, a generalization of policy proposals will fail to address the specific needs of country groups with different institutional characteristics. Appropriate government policies need to be designed to address specific needs of different country groups.

There are two features of the capitalist development process that have exerted themselves continuously over the last 200 years: rapid technological change and the uneven development of nations leading to shifts in centers of power and growth over time. Unfortunately these are the features that the economic theory has been unable to account for. For example, the main body of economic theory simply assumes that technology is an exogenous parameter, or treats it as an unexplained residual as in Solow's famous article (Solow 1957). However, ever accelerating pace of technological change needs to be the focus of any

N. Aydogan (ed.), *Innovation Policies, Business Creation and Economic Development*,
International Studies in Entrepreneurship 21, DOI 10.1007/978-0-387-79976-6_6,
© Springer Science+Business Media, LLC 2009

theoretical approach that aims at analyzing the capitalist development process.

In a similar fashion, the uneven development of nations and shifts in the centers of power and growth over time has been the constant feature of the capitalist development process. Even the developments in the last 50 years have been very fascinating. From the absolute dominance of the United States in the early post-war period to the rise of Japan and Germany in the 1970s, East Asian countries in the 1980s to be followed by the European Union, China, and India in the 1990s, the dynamics of the world economy has changed dramatically asking for a holistic approach to account for these developments. Rapid technological changes and the uneven development of nations have been very closely interrelated to each other in this process.

The basic reason that the mainstream economic theory has been unable to account for rapid technological change lies in the peculiar conception of competition as a market structure. Even though competition has been the organizing principle for systematizing the fundamental forces at work in the capitalist economy and has provided the basis for the theories of value since Adam Smith, it has been stripped of its behavioral content by conceptualizing it as a market structure. Dennis (1977), in his thesis on "Competition in the History of Economic Thought," summarizes the development in conception of competition since then in the following words: "As classical 'free competition' was being transformed into neoclassical 'perfect competition,' the scientific account of economic behavior rendered by theorists grew more and more distorted, the almost absurd features of this 'perfect' type of behavior being designed not to explain reality but to accommodate the special requirements of the new mathematical methods of analysis." These methods of analysis have essentially led to the static equilibrium framework negating the role of profits and technological change in capitalist development process.

The deficiency of a conception of competition that concentrates exclusively on market structure is that price behavior alone does not encompass the means by which firms try to survive in a competitive environment nor their relation to the institutional structure of the economy. Both rapid technological change and the uneven development of nations are primarily results of the survival process taking place in certain institutional structures existing at a specific time in history. The basic characteristics of the survival process in capitalist economies are that firms are under continuous pressure to innovate to stay competitive. This raises the survival struggle beyond simple reproduction to reproduction at a continuously expanding level. The resulting technological dynamism is unique to the capitalist system. Since a particular form of the survival struggle develops in a particular institutional structure, the dynamics of capitalist economies show uneven development in the international context due to the historical specificity of the institutional structures in each country (Capoglu 1991).

The development of new technologies is embodied in firms' investment efforts. The continuous nature of the investment efforts by firms also reveals their attitude toward the uncertain future facing them. Uncertainty leads firms to take account of various possibilities—a matter of survival for firms. Firms do not know in advance which aspects of the technological dynamics, in the Schumpeterian sense, are being explored by other firms. By undertaking investments, firms explore those aspects of the technological dynamics that they think are the most profitable and possible ones to be searched by other firms. However, the conditions for the availability of funds for investment are determined by the institutional characteristics of the financial system.

The close relationship between the banks and incumbent firms, indeed the coownership of the banks and firms by the same family groups as it is mostly the case in the credit-based financial systems of developing countries, effectively prevents the entry of potentially successful firms into the industry. This eliminates the pressure on the existing firms to innovate, which to a large extent explains technological stagnancy in the developing countries. For example, in 2006, R&D expenditures in the world totaled US$ 478 billion. Of that total 43.7 percent was undertaken by the North American region, 28.9 percent by Europe, 21.5 percent by Japan, 4.8 percent by the rest of Asia, 0.6 percent by China and India, and 0.5 percent by the rest of the world. A global innovation study by Booz Allen Hamilton points out that R&D productivity and not R&D investment as the real challenge for global innovation.

If the survival pressure is induced by the institutional environment and institutions are product of historical development process, how can innovation and entrepreneurship be encouraged in developing countries especially taking into account big institutional differences existing even among developed countries in the presence of rapid globalization? In 2006, venture capitalists invested US$ 9 billion in the EU compared to US$ 45 billion invested in the United States. According to Kortum and Lerner (2003), there is a strong relation between venture capital and innovation, a dollar of venture capital being up to 10 times more effective in stimulating patenting than a dollar of traditional R&D. That is, the securities-based financial system of the United States is more responsive to innovation relative to the credit-based financial system of the EU. Of course, one also needs to consider the superiority of the entrepreneurial culture of the United States that encourages risk taking and absorbs failure.

As regards developing countries, one set of answers is provided by the most successful innovating developing countries namely by Israel, South Korea, and China. What is common to these countries is the existence of a very strong sense of national survival that dominated policy implementation philosophy. In these countries, all actors from policy makers deciding resource allocation to resource receiving firms or individuals shared the mutual understanding and pressure that they had to be successful in innovating to survive in the global arena. That is, the deficiencies of the domestic institutional structure for inducing competitive environment were overcome by policies subjecting domestic economic actors to international competition. Trade, exchange rate, tax, and industrial policies were rigorously implemented and followed up to this end.

The importance of mobilization of resources in developing innovative capacity through such policies and institutional building can be shown by comparing the experiences of Turkey and South Korea in the last 50 years. Almost 50 years ago, in 1955, Turkey and South Korea had similar populations—22.5 million and 21.4 million respectively. The Turkish GDP per capita was triple that of the South Korean GDP per capita—US$ 210 versus US$ 70. Institutional structures were not that different. In Turkey, family holdings dominated the economy, resembling the chaebols in South Korea. The Turkish exports were US$ 347 million in 1961, more than eight times that of the Korean exports that were only US$ 41 million. That is, the future of Turkey had looked much brighter than SouthKorea back in 1961. By 2006, the South Korean population increased to 48.4 million whereas the Turkish population more than tripled to 73 million. The GDP per capita in South Korea stood at US$ 17,690, more than triple that of the GDP per capita in Turkey at US$ 5,400. The South Korean exports were US$ 326 billion last year surpassing the Turkish exports of US$

85 billion. But most importantly, today the South Koreans own global brands such as Samsung, LG, Hyundai, Kia, in telecommunications, electronics, and automotive industries respectively, whereas Turkish companies are proud of producing few brands in blue jeans and refrigerators. Indeed, both Turkey and South Korea provided similar subsidy and tax incentives to their companies in the past. The difference was in the fact that the Turkish companies were protected from international competition leading to rent-seeking behavior, whereas the South Korean companies were forced to compete internationally subjecting them to survival pressure. The South Korean government had clear national priorities and targets, and all policy instruments were used to achieve those national priorities and targets. South Koreans shared the urgency of national sense of survival and realized the importance of technological development as a means to survive in the global arena. Educational policies and technological infrastructure were developed accordingly. In Turkey, rent-seeking behavior had become a national pursuit whether it be in industry, agriculture, unionized labor, or land development with no pressure for survival.

Another set of answers is provided by countries such as India and Brazil with thriving geographic clusters of innovation in the midst of poverty. Although Indian companies, such as Infosys, Wipro, and Tata Consultancy Services, excel in software service, raising Bangalore to global status, Tata Motors is developing a "people's car," which will sell for around US$ 2,500, and may revolutionize the process of design, manufacturing, and distribution. Brazilians are specializing in ethanol production, while Embraer is strengthening its position in commercial airplane production. Even though infrastructure problems have been solved only regionally in these countries, market friendly policies have been established well enough to encourage entrepreneurs to take advantage of new opportunities and bring about a match between innovation and market needs. Facing intensified competition, these entrepreneurs realize that innovation has to be integrally woven into their firm's strategy, and they have to derive and sustain competitiveness through innovation.

A third and large group consists of countries in Africa and Asia as well as in Latin America which lacks the critical level of capital accumulation even for sustainable development let alone for growth of innovation and entrepreneurship. This group of countries may aptly be described as left-out countries. Innovation and entrepreneurship in this case corresponds to creative ways of mobilizing human resources, transforming institutional structures, and adapting technological developments to local needs. Dr Muhammed Yunus's microfinance institutions in Bangladesh have been an excellent example of institution-building initiatives. There are specific organizations such as the National Innovation Foundation (NIF) and the Rural Innovation Network engaged in promoting innovations at the grassroots level in India. Various novel applications of solar photovoltaics and thermals have been developed to enhance the quality of life of the people in rural areas in India. Some of the areas include rural lighting, telecommunications, energy solutions for home, solar pumps for irrigation, solar-aided computer literacy, and solar power packs.

These examples emphasize the importance of survival pressure in innovation and entrepreneurship. Survival struggle between firms or entrepreneurs determines the dynamics of capitalist development process in advanced countries. Some developing countries, realizing the lack of the critical level of capital accumulation for the emergence of survival struggle, have implemented conscious policies in the last 40 years to overcome these deficiencies. Today they are no longer counted as developing countries, their companies are busy in determining their place in the global economy through appropriate applications in the frontier areas of nanotechnology, healthcare and biotechnology, material sciences, telecommunications, and alternative sources of energy. Some other developing countries are just realizing the urgent need to develop environment to support entrepreneurial skills so that technological developments can be translated into jobs and economic growth in these countries. Unfortunately, most of the developing countries are still failing in their struggle to meet basic survival needs of their population. Maybe what we most need is global social entrepreneurship to integrate these people into the global economy to meet their basic survival needs.

References

Capoglu G (1991) Prices, Profits, and Financial Structures: A Post-Keynesian Approach to Competition. Edward Elgar, Aldershot.

Dennis KG (1977) Competition in the History of Economic Thought. Arno Press, New York.

Kortum S, Lerner J (2003) Venture Capital and Innovation: Clues to a Puzzle. In: McCahery J., Renneboog L. (eds.) Venture Capital Contracting and the Valuation of High-Technology Firms. Oxford University Press, Oxford and New York.

Solow R (1957) Technical Change and the Aggregate Production Function. Review of Economics and Statistics V. 39.

Part II
Company Innovativeness and Growth

7 The Phenomenology of Creativity, Innovation, and Entrepreneurship

Lance B. Kurke

Abstract

In our social world, we find extreme variations in the patterns of creativity, innovation, and success at the entrepreneurial activities derived from those patterns. It is the author's assertion that greater rates of creativity can be achieved by joining the sociological study of phenomenology to that of the entrepreneurial and economic disciplines. In particular, this paper considers the culmination of 100 years of sociological theorizing that has not penetrated various other social disciplines and practical applications, like entrepreneurship, leadership, and strategic planning. Phenomenology is discussed using six assumptions: People have a *stock knowledge* that is their reality; this stock knowledge bestows a *taken-for-granted* sense of reality; we *learn* this stock knowledge from each other; we *assume that others share* our stock knowledge; there is *nothing intrinsic* about what we believe to be real in our social world; and there is a *presumption that the world is the same* for all other people that we inhabit a common social world. Three kinds of examples are provided—political, organizational/economic, and historical/military. In all three examples, the author applies phenomenology to show how creativity is unbounded by applying the concepts of phenomenology and thereby breaking the presumed constraints of our social beliefs.

This chapter is based upon a talk given at the Innovation and Entrepreneurship in Developing Countries Workshop, hosted by the Department of Economics at Cankaya University, Chaired by Dr. Nesli Aydogan and Dr. Mete Doganay in Ankara, Turkey on November 1–2, 2007. My appreciation to Dean Ahmet Yalmiz for his financial support.

N. Aydogan (ed.), *Innovation Policies, Business Creation and Economic Development*, International Studies in Entrepreneurship 21, DOI 10.1007/978-0-387-79976-6_7,
© Springer Science+Business Media, LLC 2009

7.1 Introduction

In this chapter, we will attempt to model the very behavior of the model proposed by the chapter itself. Our job here is to change the reader's beliefs in 30 min, or the time it will take you to read this chapter—an impossible task you may think. If your job is to change the world, you need an infusion of words that will have the effect of making you think differently for having read this manuscript. That is a huge burden on the author, so one may best take refuge in humor, entertainment, or intellectual legerdemain. Then, you would report that you felt good, your time was well spent, the author would be appreciated, and everyone would go home happy. Unfortunately the purpose of this chapter is not entertainment or "feeling good." The author is in the change, innovation, and creativity business. That is bad for you, unless you too want to change your world.

Look at our burden. The best predictor of your behavior tomorrow is to observe your behavior today and assume that your behavior tomorrow will mimic it. In other words, you are not going to change your behavior. Our burden, then, is to write something that will change your behavior tomorrow. We intend to share a few words whose purpose is to get you to see that the world is not at all like you believe it to be right now. When you finish this paper, you will believe differently because of our words. That is a substantial challenge, is it not?

7.2 Epistemology and the Acquisition of Social Knowledge

Why do you believe what you believe? First, let us accept that the reader is a brilliant scientist, who answers: "I know what I know because I employ the scientific method." That is a great answer, though horribly misleading, because you use the scientific method in so few situations. The simplest answer is that you know whatever you know to be true. You just *know* it.[1] You accept many things you have been

---

[1] There are entire literatures that explore these questions, but some of the most enduring in their influence or accessibility include among numerous others: Garfinkel (1967), Handel (1982), Husserl (1913, 1936), Mead (1934), Schutz (1932), Shaver (1975), Simmel (1922), Stryker (1980), and Weber (1947).

taught, and you do not question them. Sociologists say you have a *stock knowledge at hand*, which we will explain below. Our task now is to ask some basic questions, the purpose of which are to get you to think differently enough about what you think you believe to actually change what you believe.

An entry point to challenge your beliefs is to discuss epistemology. Epistemology is the philosophical study of the acquisition of knowledge. How do you know what you know? Philosophers say there are four ways of knowing things: tenacity, authority, intuition, and science (see, for example, Lave and March 1975). Since the first three are easily shown to be wrong except under very specific circumstances for "intuition" (Gladwell 2005); that is, they are not reproducible in many circumstances, we need to delve into science—in particular, scientific method.

Rather than lecture you on the methods that scientists use to come to agreement on "truth," whether that is how to make a laser so you can watch DVD movies or how to make a cell phone transfer your call from antenna to antenna while you move, we are going to delve into the social sciences to get a lever on epistemology.

Why do you believe what you believe?

This question is fundamental, whether you are a physician, a chemist, an economist, a home maker, a colonel, an engineer, a manager, a parent, a spouse or a sibling, an entrepreneur, or a leader. If you do not question what you believe, then one can predict your behavior tomorrow by assuming you will repeat today's behavior. You will be less creative and less successful. Since we have implicitly promised you that you will change what you believe based on this chapter, we will directly answer our question: Why do you believe what you believe?

The simple answer is that you just do and this paper explores why. You do *not* question what you believe. But there are sociologists who for more than 100 years have been systematically trying to answer this question in the most scientifically responsible fashion, and their answer is either the most disconcerting thing you will read, or else the most exhilarating thing you will read because this truth will set you free. (We apologize for the cliché.) Sociologist would yawn at the roots of this material; lay people may be shocked when they think through the implications.

So, why *do* you just accept what you believe? The answer lies in the sociological studies of symbolic interactionism, ethnomethodology, and phenomenology. Trust us, you probably do not want the details, but if you would like a fuller introduction, see Turner (1978). Sociologists have spent decades delving ever deeper into the details of how to characterize social reality (in this paper we accept the physical reality of say chemistry and physics, thought those sciences are also amenable to deeper examination) and in our written work we provide references for further exploration. For this audience, primarily economists, we have chosen to provide you with a synopsis of phenomenology—because it is a field of study we suspect few if any economists have broached and because as an adjacent field of knowledge, it may be very useful to you in your professional work.

7.3 A Brief Overview of Phenomenology

Let us start this exploration with that which is very easy for every reader to understand: your job. Most of us have a job, a career, a profession. For example, consider the author's situation in academe. Here, there are rules, expectations, demands, and processes that together make up the lifeworld of an academic. The problem is that *not one of them is real* in the sense that they cannot be changed in a blink. Recently, the author resigned his tenured faculty position. What did that act do to the lifeworld of academe? Not a thing for those who stayed behind, but everything for the author. Since the best predictor of tomorrow's behavior is today's behavior, actors know that they would continue the exact same rules, expectations, demands, and processes tomorrow as yesterday. But one cannot aspire to a very different future without making a very huge change, which the author did by fundamentally altering his lifeworld (a core concept in phenomenology that will be explained in a moment). The author now has a new "job," a new profession, and a new career. Most of our former colleagues think that the author is borderline insane for leaving such a cushy lifestyle—few hours, few constraints, moderate pay, very few demands, pension, benefits—but some recognize that this change of lifeworld changes everything. And your power to change your lifeworld, like the author's, is completely under your control. Bureaucrat to entrepreneur. Salaried wage earner to fee-based compensation. Income based on past performance to income based on current performance. Sales based on parent organization's reputation to sales based on own reputation. Tom Peters (2003) has talked for more than a decade about how professionals can offer their services on a fee-based plan (outsourcing) rather than as a member of a bureaucracy, and have greater income, greater freedom, and much greater control. The author's data point of one, while no "proof," supports Peter's assertion.

We started with this real life, and very personal example, to show how radically the lifeworld can be changed and how easy it is to change it. But you may not want to engage in such radical personal change. Like the author, you may face college tuition for your children, have a home mortgage, and enjoy the illusion of financial security and therefore you decide to stay put with your existing lifeworld. This staying put does not mean you cannot change your lifeworld in other respects, nor does it mean you cannot radically change the lifeworld of your organization: how the Board perceives its role, the expectations of senior leadership, the definition of the industry in which you compete, whether you compete with *anyone*, who is the customer, how you distribute your products or services, what are your products and services, why you use the vendors that you use, and the myriad of other questions and beliefs that you simply do not ask because you take all of these for granted. As a leader, it is one of your most important responsibilities to *not* take such questions for granted.

When leaders cease to take their own and their organization's lifeworld for granted, remarkable things can and do happen, but they rarely do because they are so predisposed to continue accepting their existing lifeworld.

7.4 A More Detailed Investigation of Phenomenology

Next, we will discuss phenomenology in more depth, which will prepare the reader for three examples—political, organizational, and military.

Phenomenology is "a generic term to include all the positions that stress the primacy of consciousness and subjective meaning in the interpretation of social action."[2] For a nonsociological audience, Turner (1978) provides an especially accessible summary of the work of Husserl (1913, 1936) and Shultz (1932). Although this section draws on Turner's organization of Shultz's work, the summary, explanation, and examples are the author's.

First, *a person's reality is their stock knowledge.* (Stock knowledge is amalgamation of the rules, processes, conceptions, and information that makes up the known world of the social actor.) This implies that we can "attack" the stock knowledge that people have about their world (or our own, of course). For example, consider a manufacturing organization that has for more than 100 years made industrial heaters. Many of the men and women on the shop floor are third generation family members who have worked for this company. They all have a lifeworld whose stock knowledge at hand is based upon what their parents and even grandparents have told them, what the union tells them, and what they observe. Not to be simplistic nor insulting, but to simplify this discussion for economy of exposition, consider that these factory workers view the tons of steel on the floor all around them, which we call work in process (WIP), as job security. It took weeks to stamp, press, weld, bend, cut, punch, and drill all that steel, and it will takes weeks more to finish all that is in process. But WIP *could* be seen to be job *insecurity.* Imagine a parallel company who does not share the stock knowledge at hand of our hypothetical company. This alternative company views any WIP as bad and wasteful. That means that at most this alternative company has one piece of steel at each work station, not tons of it. What, we ask rhetorically, is the inventory carrying cost of hundreds of tons of steel—in perpetuity?! The alternative company immediately has a cost advantage. Also, consider a quality problem. In our company, we now have to rework many thousands of pieces, at great expense. The alternative company need only modify that which is in the system currently. This one paragraph gives the essence of lean manufacturing with just these two examples. The lean (alternative) factory has higher quality, at lower cost, with much better response times. Accordingly, our company does not have job security in its work in process in this type of a competitive arena,

---

[2] Natonson, Maurice, "Philosophy and Social Science," in *Literature, Philosophy and Social Science* (The Hague: Nijhoff, 1968), p. 157.

but rather job *insecurity*. Our firm will simply not be able to compete in the long term.

So, as a leader in this case, your job would be to acquire the "appropriate" stock knowledge at hand, and convince the organizational members of the importance of this alternative world view—for everyone's best interest.

Second, this *stock knowledge* that gives a sense of reality *is taken for granted*. We essentially never reflect on it, but use its assumed existence to guide all of our behavior. The implication for leaders and strategic planners is that strategic planning is not strategic because we take strategic issues for granted. We enter a room with a facilitator and all sorts of assumptions that we never even identify, and we all take them for granted during the entire "planning" (read: continuing the past) process. What this phenomenological insight suggests is that the first steps in planning facilitation are to expose all of the assumptions. Do not kid yourself—this is a very difficult task. There will be essentially no person with an interest in overturning the status quo, and any who would lead the charge to undertake radical change would probably be viewed as an arsonist or an anarchist. Nevertheless, to be true to phenomenology, one would have to dig enough to expose the stock knowledge that is taken for granted. Keep in mind that if your organization does this and the competition does not, you will have an unparalleled opportunity to extinguish all competitors.

A short case will help the reader to see how taking the wrong things for granted can paralyze a firm. The author had a long-term planning client, who for 17 years opportunistically chased whatever product development would make some money. After our first strategic plan, the firm began to focus, doubling its sales in three years in an industry that was contracting. This firm has continued to thrive, because, put simply, senior leaders did not accept what everyone else in the industry took to be gospel. Namely, rather than remaining a replacement supplier of burner parts to the coal-fired electrical generation industry, they would become the provider of low nitrous oxide systems to help utilities meet Congressionally mandated low NOx targets. This simple change of stock knowledge made all the difference.

Third, *stock knowledge is learned*. It is acquired through socialization within a common social and cultural world, but it becomes *the* reality for actors in this world. The implications are profound, because

once we understand that our social beliefs are not real, but just our
learned opinions, our parents' prejudices, our organization's culture,
and our country's legacy, then we can begin to substitute alternative
knowledge that will lead to alternative beliefs. Let me take a simple
but distressing example. In the United States, there is a veritable explosion of obesity (as there is in many countries). The question of its
cause is not completely clear. We know well that there is a surplus
of food, but the culprit seems to be a surplus of the wrong kinds of
food. The United States Department of Agriculture (USDA) publishes
a "pyramid" that recommends what combination of foods to eat. Is the
stock knowledge at hand promulgated by the US government "right?"

There is growing evidence that the agricultural revolution has
caused a worldwide *decline* in health in the last 10,000 years. Our
bodies evolved as hunter–gatherers, and are not acclimated to eating
such high proportions of noncomplex grains. Doing so has caused all
sorts of health problems. The spate of diets lately centering around
reducing the amount of simple carbohydrates to be more in accord
with the diet our bodies evolved to eat are spectacularly successful
in helping dieters loose weight and become healthier when coupled
with exercise and a focus on *complex* carbohydrates. The problem is
of course that diet is learned. It is difficult to completely change the
way we see food, given our cultural heritage. In America, there is an
epidemic of adult onset diabetes, which is almost completely driven
by the consumption of the wrong mix of foods. Americans simply do
not know any other reality, so they eat what they think is right, which
is of course, completely wrong.

Fourth, humans *assume that others share their stock knowledge at
hand* and that *unique components of the other person's stock knowledge can be safely ignored.* Using the prior example of the USDA, let
us see how there can be unique components that can not be ignored.
The "recommendation" of the USDA is racist, prejudiced by big business (who essentially control the USDA), and is certainly wrong in
its advice. Let me give a single data point. The official policy of the
US government is that its citizens should eat two to three portions
of dairy products a day. It turns out, though, that people of African
decent (after the age of about five) are incapable of digesting lactose, an important component of dairy products, and so would suffer
greatly if they were to take their government's advice. Furthermore,

it is completely possible to have a perfectly healthy diet without *any* dairy products, as witnessed by more that three-quarters of the people on earth (who are lactose intolerant and eat no dairy products) who get by without any. Obviously the stock knowledge at hand of the USDA bureaucrats is very different from the citizens being advised. Why is dairy consumption part of the recommendation then? In part, the government subsidizes the production of milk and farmers respond by producing too much. Thus, the dairy industry responds by insisting that the products need to be sold. . .

It should be obvious to educated and traveled people that these assumptions are untrue. We do *not* have the same stock knowledge, and ignoring differences is a chronic source of conflict and lost opportunities for creative and innovative changes in our societies. It seems to follow that all readers, entrepreneurs, or those who study them would find a ripe field for research opportunities and for new product and service ideas by picking apart these two assumptions—shared stock knowledge and the ability to ignore differences.

Fifth, because we assume we share common stock knowledge, and because it is acquired through socialization, actors may believe falsely that there is reciprocity of perspectives; that is, we have a *presumption* that the world is the same for all actors. This presumption is part of the glue that holds society together. In everyday intercourse, this presumption is helpful, even essential. But for someone who is creating a new organization, product, or process, this presumption is an impediment. It can be a freeing empowerment of the human creative spirit to recognize that the presumptions we carry around all day, every day are not barriers, but can be removed at any time. (Conversely, for others, this is a very frightening realization and that fear warrants its own investigation about personal change in a different publication.) For example, the expedient, however devilish, of turning an airplane into a weapon worked precisely because everyone presumed that airplanes were not weapons. The recognition that medical personnel can use the mosquito to deliver a vaccine against mosquito-borne illnesses comes from *not* accepting the presumption that the insect needs to be eradicated.

Sixth, and finally, *because people presume that we share a common world*, we can *engage in a process of typification*. Here, people simplify their social worlds by finding actions that, in most situations, can be typified, scripted, or codified to such an extent that human interaction is socially lubricated. However, these typical actions are again not sacrosanct. Marketers and advertisers constantly take advantage of the routinization of human interaction. In stores, slow music is played to make you shop at a more leisurely pace and spend more. In grocery stores, the common items we need are placed at the back of the store so we must traverse all the other things we do not need to increase the chance of making an impulse buy. On a more macro scale, the phone has made a huge transition from verbal communication devise to camera, text messenger, calendar, et cetera. It was the insight of an entrepreneur who saw that we need not take typification as a constraint. Even now, some technology users live in a world that is very different than others'.

Here then is a succinct summary of the field of phenomenology as articulated in the prior several pages.

This characterization of the social world makes social interactions easier, but it can be destructive to those trying to forge new realities—entrepreneurs, innovators, planners, researchers, and leaders, for example. It is possible to violate every single assumption and become more creative, innovative, and successful as an entrepreneur, planner, or leader.

7.5 Three Examples of the Power of Phenomenology

This section provides three examples of the power of using phenomenology to change our stock knowledge at hand and thereby change our world. We consider a political example, two business examples, and a military example that is historically based.

7.5.1 A Political Example of Phenomenology

Let us consider a very specific example of how this stock knowledge at hand can so deeply influence our thinking, that it renders us typically unable to see alternative worlds. Consider a fringe statement. So fringe that normally you would simply ignore it. So fringe that you would dismiss it completely out of hand. So fringe that you would turn to other matters at hand and give it no more of your valuable attention.

The statement that you are about to read is not consistent with your world view, so it is therefore wrong. However, in the context of this chapter, maybe you will open your mind briefly and consider a belief so radically different from what you believe that you will ponder it. Please take seriously for a few moments the next sentence, which you right now do not believe.

Turkey is the most important country in the world.

OK, the author is out of his mind. How stupid, et cetera, et cetera. This statement is incompatible with your beliefs and most of the members of the audience where this paper was originally delivered were Turkish, so they were inclined to dismiss it as well. But bear with us for a few moments. Wrap your mind around how someone could make such an assertion. When you are done with this example, we can go back to phenomenology and why we believe what we believe.

Turkey? It is poor, backward, has few resources, caught between east and west, has an Islamic legacy, must deal with the intractable problem of the Kurds, was on the wrong side of World War I ... and all the other standard things that political commentators blather on about. How could it be the most important country in the world?

But, the same data can be configured quite differently. The statement is not that Turkey was the most powerful, the richest, or the strongest. It said "important." Why would someone assert that? Well, look at the centrality of the country, both geographically and politically. It is not *that* poor and its economy is rapidly expanding. It is not *that* backward, and in numerous ways is first world, world class. For example, Turkey spends more money relative to GDP per capital on teachers' salary than any other society on earth. Relative to the region, it can be seen to have many important resources. And rather than seeing Turkey as being "caught" between east and west, it can be seen to be the crucial "go between." It does have an Islamic legacy, but it has done a better job of secularizing Islam—the legacy of Ataturk—based probably upon the success of the Ottoman Empire's handling of its multicultural empire for 600 years. Yes, the Kurds must be dealt with, but Turkey can be broadly seen as the most important country in the world if it handles this matter well. We could go on, but you get the idea. A different stock knowledge (based on the same raw data) gives a different reality.

People would assert that the United States is the most important country in the world. But look at her failings, which we will not catalog here. Just take the Middle East. The United States has been systematically unable to effect change. But look at Turkey. It is a secular, Islamic country that has excellent relations (or at least some relations) with all the major players in the Middle East, especially including Israel, Syria, Jordan, Iraq, and Iran. It is a member of NATO, it has a powerful and professional army, and it is in talks to join the EU. It spans Europe and Asia literally and figuratively. This set of facts coupled with its centrality make it the most important country in the world. If the "world powers" want to get anything done in the Middle East, Turkey is central to getting anything done. Since Europe, Japan, China, and the United States all are dependent upon the raw materials of the Middle East, Turkey is the lynchpin that controls the world's outcomes.

So you now are able to see a different Turkey than you did before you started this chapter. Your beliefs have changed (or at least some readers). If you understand how this occurred in so short a time, you may use that process and change any social belief you hold. You can reconceive of industries, products, processes, plans, cultures, or even whole societies. Look back at Table 7.1 and see assumptions two, five, and six.

7.5.2 Two Organizational Examples of Phenomenology

For more than a 100 years in the United States, organizations that mine coal underground have had a huge problem: that of eliminating the naturally occurring gases (methane, propane, and butane) that seep out of the seams of coal. When these gases fill the mines, they become bombs that are easily ignited and can not just kill miners, but destroy the mine. The solution has been to vent these gases or, since they are harmful to people on the surface, to burn them off at the surface. Any one who has seen a coal mine is familiar with this problem and its solution.

A young man, working for Consol, the largest owner and operator of coal mines in North America, recognized that the gases could be captured and sold. His insight was the basis for a new industry. He wrote a strategic plan that created a subsidiary unit, which

Table 7.1 Assumptions and implications of phenomenology

	Assumption	Implication
1	People have a *stock knowledge* that is their reality	This paramount reality shapes and guides all social events
2	This stock knowledge bestows a *taken-for-granted* sense of reality	Assumptions, processes, rules, agreements, and procedures help us navigate our social world
3	We *learn* this stock knowledge from each other	It becomes our reality
4	We *assume that others share* our stock knowledge	Differences between our unique components can be safely ignored
5	There is *nothing intrinsic* about what we believe to be real in our social world	Unique components of the other person's stock knowledge can be safely ignored
6	There is a *presumption that the world is the same* for all other people; that we inhabit a common social world	Allows us to typify our actions and this typification greatly simplifies our world

subsequently had a public offering. He is now the CEO of CNX Gas, which has sales of more than US$ 4 billion dollars and is a fortune 500 firm after just a few years in existence. His entrepreneurial insight was to violate all phenomenological assumptions.

The second example is that of PPG, a Fortune 500 company headquartered in the United States. Originally, PPG was known as Pittsburgh Plate Glass, and soon after the invention of the automobile, it specialized also in glass for cars, and was the first to figure out how to curve automobile glass. Thus, most of their history is inextricably mixed up with glass and automobiles. Glass is a commodity business, and Wall Street has not only treated PPG as a commodity company, but used other types of commodity businesses for comparison to its balance sheet. Accordingly, the former CEO assiduously followed the impeccable logic of all strategic planners, that to make money in a commodity business you must be the low-cost provider (cut costs) and operate at high volume (economies of scale). This is the stock knowledge at hand: it is taken for granted, it is learned, shared, no companies are unique, and stock knowledge is the same for all in the industry.

Contrast this reality with that of the new CEO, who violated several phenomenological assumptions. First, he said that PPG is no longer a glass business, and therefore not a commodity business. His attempt to teach Wall Street, based on hard data about the ratio of earnings derived from coatings versus glass, for example, was ignored by Wall Street analysts, precisely because of the shared stock knowledge. To more clearly make his point, the CEO set out to sell off the highly symbolic older automobile glass business units, so that the firm could not be seen as a glass company. Indeed, PPG's web site makes this transition clear. Finally, Wall Street understood the transformation in the company.

The essence is to recognize that stock knowledge at hand is *not* the real world. That stock knowledge is *not* universally shared; that it is learned; that it is taken for granted. By systematically undoing these prejudices, one can change another's stock knowledge. Entrepreneurs and leaders, more than anyone else, need to be on guard about their taken-for-granted assumptions about the social world.

7.5.3 An Historical Example of Phenomenology[3]

Alexander the Great, in the third century BCE was invading the Persian Empire. His water-borne food supply was being interdicted by the 200 ship Persian fleet with impunity. To secure his food supply, Alexander had to find a way to eliminate the enemy fleet. (As an example of how standard this stock knowledge at hand is, consider that hundreds of years later, the expedient of building a fleet was used by Julius Caesar to defeat the Veneti in what is modern day Belgium, but Alexander did not have the bottomless resources of the Roman Empire to call upon, nor did he have the two years or so that would have been required to build this enormous fleet. Finally, the Persians would have been unlikely to confront his untested fleet and lose to it in a pitched battle.)

What Alexander did was to reason that if he could control all of the sources of fresh water within the operating range of the fleet (the fleet could not distill salt water and so had to put into port every couple of

---

[3] This section draws on the author's book, *The Wisdom of Alexander the Great*, NY: AMACOM, 2004.

days), it would cease to be able to operate and interdict his food. His plan to defeat a navy on land—the first time ever done so in history—was working well by garrisoning wells and fresh water outlets, selectively poisoning other sources, and in general gaining control over all fresh water that the enemy could use. But the independent city-state of Tyre systematically sold water to the Persian fleet from their impregnable fortified island, where there was a huge upwelling aquifer.

Alexander with an entourage rowed out to the island (it was about a kilometer off the coast of modern-day Northern Israel). He asked to conduct a religious ceremony, but the implication of this ceremony would implicitly make Alexander the ruler of Tyre, so the Tyrians declined. Indeed, they unceremoniously threw him back in his boat and told him to leave, as the Tyrians withstood a siege of 13 years by the very 200 ship fleet now harassing Alexander, and thus they considered their island citadel to be impregnable.

One can imagine Alexander the "soon to be great" standing on the coast looking covetously at the island of Tyre, and picturing himself going down in history as a footnote to his already great father, Philip II, who invented the professional army. How could he conquer an island without benefit of a fleet, which had failed at the task for the Persians? Well, this chapter would propose to you that the use of Tables 7.1 and 7.2 could be helpful if we were to confront any such unsolvable problem.

There were three things that characterized Alexander's army: the cavalry, his engineers, and his logistical supply. Presumably his supply could keep his army fed, even though the cavalry would be useless for a while. What could he do with his engineering strength? The answer derives from denying the stock knowledge of hand, learning a new reality, accepting his unique components of his stock knowledge, and

Table 7.2 Applying the assumptions of phenomenology to violate them

	Assumption	Application by violating assumption
1	*Stock knowledge*	Deny stock knowledge
2	*Taken-for-granted*	Do not take anything for granted
3	*Learned*	Learn a new reality
4	*Others share*	Unique components should not be nurtured
5	*Nothing intrinsic*	We all have unique components
6	*World is the same for all*	Do not typify—complicate your world

recreating a new reality. He reasoned that if he could just besiege the city as a land city, it would fall quickly. How to bring land to island? Why, fill in the ocean of course. And that is what he commanded his engineers to do. The army took seven months of heavy labor, but when they were done, they simply rolled their siege equipment out to the island, and it fell in two weeks.

7.6 Conclusions

This chapter has tried to cross over disciplines and show that there is real power of moving knowledge across parallel disciplines. Economics and the studies of entrepreneurial behavior, innovation, and creativity can all benefit from even a shallow appreciation of phenomenology.

We have tried to show the power of eliminating social constraints on our beliefs. Economists, leaders, and entrepreneurs can benefit from understanding the presumed constraints articulated by phenomenology, and enhancing their creativity accordingly. We have tried to show the power of tools of phenomenology to change our beliefs and thereby make us more creative, innovative, and entrepreneurial.

The following Table 7.2 is meant to convey the approach an entrepreneur, planner, or leader might take to escaping the taken-for-granted nature of our social world. Entrepreneurs can benefit by understanding and escaping from the presumptions that constrain us all. We leave the application of violating these assumptions to each of you, for a lifetime homework assignment.

References

Garfinkel, Harold. (1967). *Studies in Ethnomethodology*. Englewood Cliffs, NJ: Prentice-Hall.

Gladwell, Malcolm. (2005). *Blink*. New York, NY: Little Brown and Company.

Handel, Warren. (1982). *Ethnomethodology*. Englewood Cliffs, NJ: Prentice-Hall.

Husserl, Edmund. (1965, originally published 1936). *Phenomenology and the Crisis of Western Philosophy*. New York, NY: Harper and Row.

Husserl, Edmund. (1969, originally published in 1913). *Ideas: General Introduction to Pure Phenomenology*. London: Collier-Macmillan.

Kurke, Lance B. (2004). *The Wisdom of Alexander the Great*. NY: AMACOM.

Lave, Charles A. and March, James G. (1975). *An Introduction to Models in the Social Sciences*. New York, NY: Harper and Row.

Mead, George Herbert (1934). *Mind, Self, and Society*. Edited by Charles W. Morris. Chicago: University of Chicago Press.

Natonson, Maurice. (1968). Philosophy and Social Science. In *Literature, Philosophy and Social Science*. The Hague: Nijhoff.

Peters, Tom. (2003). *Re-imagine!*. London: Doring Kindserley.

Schutz, Alfred. (1967, originally published in 1932). *The Phenomenology of the Social World*. Evanston, IL: Northwestern University Press.

Shaver, Kelly G. (1975). *An Introduction to Attribution Processes*. Cambridge, MA: Winthrop.

Simmel, Georg. (1955, originally published in 1922). *Conflict and the Web of Group Affiliations*. Glencoe, IL: Free Press

Stryker, Sheldon. (1980). *Symbolic Interactionism*. Menlo Park, CA: Benjamin/ Cummings.

Turner, Jonathan. (1978). *The Structure of Sociological Theory*, revised edition. Homewood, IL: Dorsey.

Weber, Max. (1947). *The Theory of Social and Economic Organization*. New York, NY: Free Press.

8 Innovativeness: Is It a Function of the Leadership Style and the Value System of the Entrepreneur?

Alev Katrinli, Gulem Atabay, Gonca Gunay, Burcu Guneri, and Ahenk Aktan

Abstract

Innovativeness as an organizational cultural phenomena affects innovation and, in turn, performance. Hence, antecedents to innovativeness, namely the value system and leadership style of the entrepreneur, were investigated in this study. Results indicate that innovativeness is significantly related to different leadership dimensions such as demand reconciliation, integration, initiation of structure, production emphasis, role assumption, predictive accuracy, and external stakeholder orientation. Likewise, the intensity of values of power and security of the entrepreneur are significantly related with innovativeness. According to the regression results, innovativeness is a function of demand reconciliation, integration, and power.

8.1 Introduction

Increasing competition and globalization of market force organizations to find new ways for surviving and sustaining their performance. This makes the concept of innovation as one of the important subjects for practitioners, scholars, and policy makers. In order to understand the concept of innovation, scholars attempted to identify the antecedents of innovation. One of the antecedents of innovation is labeled as innovativeness, which is defined as "the notion of openness to new ideas as an aspect of a firm's culture" (Hurley

N. Aydogan (ed.), *Innovation Policies, Business Creation and Economic Development,*
International Studies in Entrepreneurship 21, DOI 10.1007/978-0-387-79976-6_8,
© Springer Science+Business Media, LLC 2009

and Hult 1998). Thus, innovativeness constitutes the cultural base
for innovation. Literature suggests that creative capacity and personal
mastery (Garcia-Morales et al. 2006), market orientation (Jaworski
and Kohli 1993), learning orientation (Slater and Narver 1995), entrepreneurial orientation (Lumpkin and Dess 1996), and leadership
styles (Dackert et al. 2004) affect innovativeness. Amongst the points
mentioned above, this chapter focuses on the effect of values and
leadership styles of entrepreneurs on innovativeness with the belief that they are the vital factors for explaining innovativeness in
organizations.

In order to identify how value system and leadership styles influence innovativeness, this paper examines innovativeness as a dependent variable and value system, and leadership styles of entrepreneurs
as independent variables. Since our aim is to examine the effect of the
value system and leadership styles of entrepreneurs, not the managers,
study is conducted in SMEs.

8.2 Theoretical Background

8.2.1 Innovation and Innovativeness

As competition becomes tough, markets turn global, product life cycles get shorter, the dynamics of success become more complex, and
innovation gains growing importance in the field of business administration. Innovation is defined as "the renewal and enlargement of
the range of products and services and the associated markets; the
establishment of new methods of production, supply, and distribution;
the introduction of changes in management, work organization, and
the working conditions and skills of the workforce" (European Commission 1995).

Innovation is regarded as an input for growth of nations, industries,
or firms (Dess and Pickens 2000; Mansfield et al. 1971; Schumpeter
1934). Analyses show that countries, which are capable in innovation
creation, have relatively high income. The country whose innovative effect remains constant, with more innovative sectors and firms,
has higher productivity levels (European Innovation Progress Report
2006; Oslo Manual 2005; Slow 2001). Besides productivity, innovation is found to be strongly related to overall business performance
(Lin and Chen 2007). Karagozoglu and Brown (1988) argue that firms,

which demonstrated below-average performance, involve little innovation. The argument that innovation contributes to firm performance is supported by different studies conducted in different sectors (Zahra et al. 1999). Mone et al. (1998) explain the reason of the existence of the relationship between innovation and firm performance as innovation strengthening the competitive advantage, which is the key for the firms' performance. Deshpande and Farley (2003) conducted a research in large companies, and investigated the effect of innovation and market orientation on the overall firm performance. They showed that in the industrial world, innovation has more impact than the market orientation on firm performance.

Innovation is also crucial for small and medium sized enterprises (SMEs) due to the fact that they compete with limited financial and human resources. As stated by Lee et al. (2001), head-to-head competition generally results with failures for SMEs because of resource shortcomings, scale diseconomies, and questionable reputation. Vermeulen et al. (2005) support this argument through their research and showed that SMEs, which develop new products, grow faster than the others. Thus, SMEs can differentiate themselves from their rivals and show superior performance through innovation. Rivals cannot easily imitate innovation since it depends on complex social relationships.

Since innovation is accepted as one of the major determinants of growth and performance, scholars pay considerable attention to identifying the antecedents of innovation. This requires a holistic and multidisciplinary approach due to the fact that innovation is the outcome of complex social processes (Hurley and Hult 1998; Menguc and Seigyoung 2006). Many external and internal factors including venture capital (e.g. Kortum and Lerner 2000; Timmons and Bygrave 1986), interfirm cooperation (e.g. Cooke 1996; Tsai 2001), legal system (e.g. Aoki and Hu 1999; Teece 1986), R&D capabilities (e.g. Becker and Dietz 2004; Fritsch and Franke 2004), and business strategies (e.g. Olson et al. 2005) affect innovation. Additionally, innovation is influenced by human-related factors.

Understanding human-related factors and how they affect innovation has substantial importance, since all the other factors mentioned above are tools that are created and utilized by human beings. Hence, their effect on innovation depends on people. Thus, studies, which ignore human-related factors in the antecedents of innovation, reported inconsistent findings (O'Regan et al. 2004). Addressing this issue, some decades ago Minnesota Innovation Research Program called upon researchers to take into consideration the knowledge of psychology (Van de Ven 1986). Responding to this call, scholars have attempted to identify the effect of psychological factors on innovation. Values of members and entrepreneurs (Thomson and Strickland 1986; Verbees and Meulenberg 2004), creativity (Amabile et al. 1996; Miron et al. 2003), leadership styles (Krause 2004; O'Regan et al. 2006; Somech 2006), and organizational culture (Anderson and West 1998; Deshpande and Farley 2004; O'Regan et al. 2006) are the factors that are identified as human-related antecedents to innovation. Those factors influence innovation through affecting people's and organizations' tendency or willingness to innovation. Zaltman et al. (1973) suggest that willingness to innovation is critical especially at the initiation stage of innovation. Van de Ven (1986) defines this as a part of organizational culture. Hurley and Hult (1998) name it as innovativeness and define it as "the notion of openness to new ideas as an aspect of a firm's culture." They also show that innovativeness has a significant and positive impact on innovation. Thus, innovativeness constitutes the cultural base for innovation. Hult et al. (2003) show that it is an important factor for company performance. Menguc and Seigyoung (2006) support this argument and they show that when market orientation is complemented with innovativeness, innovation capabilities and firm performance will significantly increase. Hence, innovativeness appeared as an important factor for identifying the concept of innovation.

Although innovativeness emerges as an important factor for stimulating innovation in the literature, the antecedents of innovativeness are still not well documented and require attention from the scholars. In the literature, creative capacity and personal mastery (Garcia-Morales et al. 2006), market orientation (Jaworski and Kohli 1993), learning orientation (Slater and Narver 1995), entrepreneurial orientation (Lumpkin and Dess 1996), and leadership styles (Dackert et al. 2004) are identified as the antecedents of innovativeness. Amongst the points mentioned above, this chapter focuses on the effect of values and leadership styles of entrepreneurs on innovativeness with the belief that they are the vital factors for explaining it in organizations. Values of entrepreneurs are important since they are influential in the initiation, development, and ongoing maintenance of an organization's culture (Kelly et al. 2000). Similarly, leadership styles of entrepreneurs may affect innovativeness in idea generation, evaluation, and implementation processes (Elenkov and Manev 2005; Mumford et al. 2003).

In order to identify how value system and leadership styles influence innovativeness, this chapter examines innovativeness as a dependent variable and value system, and leadership styles of entrepreneurs as independent variables. Since our aim is to examine the effect of the value system and leadership styles of entrepreneurs, not the managers, study is conducted in SMEs where the owner and the entrepreneur are the same people.

8.2.2 Value System and Innovativeness

Values represent concepts or beliefs about desirable end-states or behaviors that transcend specific situations, guide selection, or evaluation of behavior and events, and are ordered by relative importance (Schwartz 1992). Values are terminal if they describe end-states of existence, or instrumental if they refer to preferable modes of behavior or means of achieving terminal values (Rokeach 1973).

Values are evaluative statements, and they are important determinants of how people perceive and react to their social environment. Thus, values affect people's professional life as well as their social life. The review of values literature by Meglino and Ravlin (1998) suggest that values directly affect behavior in an organizational setting because they encourage individuals to act in accordance with their values. Hence, values have been in extensive research for many years.

Specifically, values of entrepreneurs, managers, and leaders attracted the attention of scholars (Kotey and Meredith 1997) due to their effects on organizational culture. Kelly et al. (2000) reported that founders' values have a significant influence on initiation, development, and ongoing maintenance of organizational culture. Supporting this proposition, Morris and Schindehutte (2005) found linkages between the entrepreneur's values and specific operational practices. For example, when honesty is an important value for the entrepreneur, it is one of the key traits sought during an employee selection process. Similarly, Kane-Urrabazo (2006) suggested that managers have an important function in establishing and maintaining an organization's culture.

The impact of entrepreneurs and managers on organizational culture has important implications for innovation capabilities and business performance since it is well known that organizational culture has a substantial impact on innovation capabilities of the firms, firm strategy, and performance (Deshpande and Farley 2004; O'Regan et al. 2006). Thomson and Strickland (1986) and Kotey and Meredith (1997) show that values of the owners or managers affect the business strategy and eventually the performance of the businesses. Especially in SMEs, innovativeness, which is a dimension of organizational culture, entailed a willingness of the owner to learn about and adopt innovations (Verbees and Meulenberg 2004).

Three universal requirements were thought to be at the root of values: needs of individuals as biological organisms, requisites of coordinating social interaction, requirements for the functioning of society, and the survival of groups. As summarized by Spini (2003), 10 individual level values were derived based on these three basic goals: (a) Achievement: personal success through the demonstration of competence according to social standards; (b) Benevolence: concern for the welfare of others in everyday interaction; (c) Conformity: restraint of actions, inclination, and impulses likely to upset or harm others and violate social expectations and norms; (d) Hedonism: pleasure and sensuous gratification for oneself; (e) Power: attainment of social status and prestige, and control or dominance over people and resources; (f) Security: safety, harmony, and stability of society, relationships, and self; (g) Self-direction: independent thought and action; (h) Stimulation: excitement, novelty, and challenge in life; (i) Tradition: respect, commitment, and acceptance of the customs and ideas that one's culture or religion impose on the individual; (j) Universalism: understanding, appreciation, tolerance, and protection for the welfare of all human beings and nature.

Previous research supports the view that values of entrepreneurs have effects on their perceptions and behaviors, and, in turn, on organizational performance and innovativeness (Kane-Urrabazo 2006; O'Regan et al. 2006; Morris and Schindehutte 2005; Deshpande 2004; Verbees and Meulenberg 2004; Kelly et al. 2000; Meglino and Ravlin 1998; Kotey and Meredith 1997; Thomson and Strickland 1986).

One of the 10 individual values that may motivate organizational innovativeness is tradition. Although the research results by Kwang et al. (2005) reveal that innovators are more likely to subscribe to conservative values such as tradition and security, the study conducted by Sosik (2005) rely on a totally different point of view. In this study, he confirmed that while promoting change, leaders must appeal to employees' cherished values because followers seek continuity between the past, present, and future. Therefore, tradition as a value does not necessarily mean insistence on traditional practices for the sake of tradition. Rather, it represents recognition that time-honored values embody important aspects of collective identity and culture, and provide a meaningful link between the past, present and future. Thus:

Hypothesis 1. *Entrepreneurs' tradition value intensity will be positively related to organizational innovativeness.*

Similarly, although security may be seen as a conservative value opposing innovation (Kwang et al. 2005), value of security may assume a substantial role in promoting innovativeness. Today, organizations are facing a very dynamic environment where rapid changes require innovation for survival and stability. No organization can be secure without innovating. Hence, when the security is an important value for owners, they know that they have to innovate to assure security. Hence:

Hypothesis 2. *Entrepreneurs' security value intensity will be positively related to organizational innovativeness.*

Another value, which may be related to organizational innovativeness, is stimulation. According to Dionne et al. (2004), stimulation can create an environment, where questioning assumptions and inventing new uses for old processes are considered a healthy form of conflict that results in innovation. Thus:

Hypothesis 3. *Entrepreneurs' stimulation value intensity will be positively related to organizational innovativeness.*

One of the important issues in literature is the distinction between creativity and innovation. In the review by McLean (2005), creativity was defined as the production of novel and useful ideas while innovation was defined as the successful implementation of creative ideas within an organization. Hence, no innovation is possible without creativity. The study by Rice (2006) posits that value of achievement is positively related to creative behavior while conformity is negatively related. Accordingly, creative people demonstrate a strong achievement motive, and they tend to be independent and follow their own ideas without being overly concerned about socially imposed expectations for certain kinds of behavior or how others will view them. Since it is accepted that innovation is an engine without fuel, without creativity to feed the innovation pipeline, achievement, and conformity may also be related to organizational innovativeness. Thus:

Hypothesis 4. *Entrepreneurs' achievement value intensity will be positively related to organizational innovativeness.*

Hypothesis 5. *Entrepreneurs' conformity value intensity will be negatively related to organizational innovativeness.*

As suggested in the same study by Rice (2006), the defining goals of the value type and power are social status and prestige, typical of an outward orientation, and they hinder the creation of novel and useful ideas. Therefore, hindrance of creativity may affect organizational innovativeness. Hence:

Hypothesis 6. *Entrepreneurs' power value intensity will be negatively related to organizational innovativeness.*

8.2.3 Leadership Styles

Leadership is defined as "the process of transforming organizations from what they are to what the leader would have them become" (Dess and Lumpkin 2003). Therefore, by definition, the concept of leadership includes some type of innovation (O'Regan et al. 2006).

Literature suggests that leadership styles and behaviors of entrepreneurs affect innovation in business organizations in many ways (Elenkov and Manev 2005; Mumford et al. 2003). Entrepreneurs, like the leaders, may produce creative ideas, stimulate innovation in evaluating creative ideas of employees, or promote innovation through creating an innovative culture. Therefore, they play active roles both in idea generation and implementation, which are essential processes of innovation creation. This argument is supported by different scholars. Yadav et al. (2007) show that the CEOs' attention is the major driver of innovation even when the intention of the CEO is not always creating innovation. West et al. (2003) examine that leadership has an impact on innovation and reveal that when the teams lack identifiable leader, their innovation capabilities significantly decrease.

As the above-mentioned studies prove, leadership styles have an important impact on innovativeness. Hence this concept attracts attention from scholars for identifying its complex nature. Therefore, different characteristics of leaders and entrepreneurs are investigated in order to identify how they affect innovation process and what common characteristics these innovative leaders have (Krause 2004; O'Regan et al. 2006; Somech 2006; Yadav et al. 2007). Yadav et al. (2007) study revealed that the future and external focus of CEOs increased innovation outcomes. Among the scholars who investigated the relationship between leadership styles and innovation, O'Regan et al. (2006) show that transformational and human resource leadership styles have greater success in achieving innovation. They explain this finding of these two leadership styles having a long-term outlook, which is important for innovation. Garcia-Morales et al. (2006) also report similar findings about the impact of transformational leadership on innovation. Krause (2004) investigates the relationship between innovation related behaviors of middle managers and leadership behaviors of their superiors in the context of influence-based leadership. She examines influence-based leadership behaviors with five dimensions, namely: identification, expert knowledge and information, the granting of degrees of freedom and autonomy, support for innovation, and openness in the decision-making process. She reports positive significant correlations between innovation-related behaviors in all dimensions except openness for decision-making process. Somech (2006) examines how participatory and directive leadership styles affect team innovation and performance. She also found that participative leadership fostered team innovation but decreased team in role performance.

To examine the effect of leadership styles on innovativeness, we employ Ohio State University leadership description questionnaire (LBDQ) (Stogdill 1974). Instead of examining consideration and initiating structures as leadership styles, we prefer to investigate the effect of leadership dimensions that constitute the leadership styles on innovativeness. This way, we aim to identify the relationship between each leadership dimensions and innovativeness. Stogdill (1974) defines 12 leadership dimensions, namely: representation, demand reconciliation, tolerance of uncertainty, persuasiveness, initiation of structure, tolerance of freedom, role assumption, consideration, production emphasis, predictive accuracy, integration, and superior orientation. It may not be meaningful to involve superior orientation for explaining behaviors of entrepreneurs since they do not work under superiors. On the other hand, it can be considered that they need to build positive relationships with their external stakeholders instead of the superiors to be successful. Thus, in this study, superior orientation was transformed to external stakeholders' orientation.

We developed the following hypotheses about the relationship between leadership dimensions and innovativeness based on literature. Two leadership dimensions, representation and persuasiveness, were not formulated as hypothesis due to the fact that there was no information suggesting any association between them and innovativeness in the literature.

Demand reconciliation is defined as to what extent and how well the leader reconciles conflicting demands and reduces disorder in the system (Stogdill 1974). Thus, it can be concluded that by these types of behaviors, leaders keep conflicts among the members at optimum levels. Literature suggests that innovation could be a product of conflict but if it stays at a healthy level (Gobeli et al. 1998). Hence, the hypothesis is formulated as:

Hypothesis 7. *Entrepreneurs' demand reconciliation leadership behaviors will be positively related to innovativeness.*

Tolerance of uncertainty refers to what extent the leader is able to tolerate uncertainty and postponement without anxiety or getting upset. Since entrepreneurs' ability of coping with uncertainties is found positively associated with innovativeness (Blanchflower and Oswald 1998), hypothesis is formulated as:

Hypothesis 8. *Entrepreneurs' tolerance of uncertainty will be positively related to innovativeness.*

Initiation of structure measures to what degree the leader clearly defines own role and lets followers know what is expected. Findings of previous studies showed that innovation was positively associated with transformational and participative leadership that are the opposite forms of leadership behaviors (Krause 2004; O'Regan et al. 2006). Thus, in this study, we expected a negative association between initiation of structure and innovativeness.

Hypothesis 9. *Entrepreneurs' initiation of structure leadership behaviors will be negatively related to innovativeness.*

Tolerance of freedom reflects to what extent the leader allows followers scope for initiative, decision, and action. When the leader shows high tolerance of freedom to the employees, they have opportunities to express their ideas and test them. In this respect, it is positively correlated with participatory and delegative leadership (Krause 2004). Thus, tolerance of freedom is required for innovation (Anderson and King 1993; Mumford et al. 2002).

Hypothesis 10. *Entrepreneurs' tolerance of freedom leadership behaviors will be positively related to innovativeness.*

Role assumption measures to what degree the leader exercises actively the leadership role rather than surrendering leadership to others. Since it is known that teams, which do not have identifiable leaders, are not successful in innovation creation (West et al. 2003), it is expected that this dimension is positively associated with innovativeness.

Hypothesis 11. *Entrepreneurs' role assumption leadership behaviors will be positively related to innovativeness.*

Consideration depicts to what extent the leader regards the comfort, well-being, status, and contributions of followers. Northouse (2004) stated that consideration and human orientation could be used interchangeably. Since previous studies suggested that human orientation was positively associated with innovation (O'Regan et al. 2006), it is expected that there is a positive association between consideration and innovativeness.

Hypothesis 12. *Entrepreneurs' consideration leadership behaviors will be positively related to innovativeness.*

Production emphasis measures to what degree the leader applies pressure for productive output. Since this type of leadership behaviors pursue the quantity at lower cost, they are considered as a part of cost leadership. Miller (1986) reported that cost leadership was negatively associated with innovation due to the fact that innovation might increase the cost of products. Also, this type of leadership behaviors are directed to the use of subordinates for the purpose of work and do not take into consideration the need of skill development (Dackert et al. 2004).

Hypothesis 13. *Entrepreneurs' production emphasis leadership behaviors will be negatively related to innovativeness.*

Predictive accuracy measures to what extent the leader exhibits foresight and ability to predict outcomes accurately. It is very similar to future focus of leadership and having a long-term outlook, which were found positively associated with innovation (O'Regan et al. 2006; Yadav et al. 2007). Thus, it is expected that predictive accuracy is positively correlated with innovativeness.

Hypothesis 14. *Entrepreneurs' predictive accuracy leadership behaviors will be positively related to innovativeness.*

Integration reflects to what degree the leader maintains a close-knit organization and resolves intermember conflicts. Integration, similar to demand reconciliation, keeps the conflict among the followers at optimum level. Besides, integration is required to share knowledge, which plays a vital role for innovation (Hansen and Morten 1999; Liebowitz 2002) among the followers. Therefore, we expect that there is a positive association between integration and innovativeness.

Hypothesis 15. *Entrepreneurs' integration leadership behaviors will be positively related to innovativeness.*

External stakeholder orientation measures to what extent the leader maintains cordial relations with external stakeholders such as suppliers and customers, and efforts to influence them. Hence, it can be concluded that it is very similar to the market or external orientation, which were found positively associated with innovation (Yadav et al. 2007).

Hypothesis 16. *Entrepreneurs' external stakeholder orientation leadership behaviors will be positively related to innovativeness.*

8.3 Method

8.3.1 Participants and Procedures

Data was collected from the small businesses' owners, who were actively managing their enterprises, in Izmir, which is the third largest city in Turkey. For data collection, a questionnaire that consisted of two parts was designed. The first part involved the measures for leadership style of the entrepreneur and the innovativeness level in the business enterprise. Hence, the first part was filled out by the employee that worked closest to the owner. The second part consisted of a measure for the value system of the owner, demographic properties of the entrepreneur, and properties of the business. This part was filled out by the owner.

Five hundred questionnaires were distributed in different parts of the city. Of the 500, 307 businesses responded to the questionnaire. Thus, response rate was approximately 62 percent. However, for the values scale to give reliable results, it has been suggested to the researcher to clean data when a scale anchor is repeated more than 15 times for the scale with 57 items (www.crossculturalcentre. homestead. com). Hence, after data cleaning, only 251 usable questionnaires were left. Among 251 business enterprises, 48 percent were micro businesses with less than 10 employees, and 37 percent were small businesses with more than 10 employees but less than 50 employees. The rest were medium sized businesses with more than 50 but less than 250 employees. Based on their year of establishment, 41 percent were established after year 2000, 40 percent in the 1990s, 12 percent during the 1980s, 3 percent in the 1970s, and the rest before 1970. Seventy-nine percent of the owners were male while the rest were female; 19 percent of the entrepreneurs were 30 years old or younger; 39 percent were 40 or younger, 28 percent were 50 or younger; and 14 percent were older than 50. Regarding education, 49 percent were high school graduates, 40 percent were university graduates, 3 percent had primary education, and 8 percent had graduate degrees.

8.3.2 Measures

8.3.2.1 Organizational Innovativeness

Innovativeness of the business was measured through a scale adapted from Hurley and Hult (1998). This scale was chosen due to the fact that there are numerous studies that employed the same scale and tested its reliability (for example Keskin 2006; Tanriverdi and Zehir 2006; Hult et al. 2004). The original scale contained five items, but the last item was stated as "innovation is perceived as too risky and is resisted." Since the item referred to two different cases at the same time, it was divided into two components. The fifth item became "innovation is perceived as too risky" and the sixth became "innovation is resisted." The measure used a five-point Likert scale ranging from "never" to "all the time." The Cronbach alpha for this scale was 0.63.

8.3.2.2 Value System

The value system of the entrepreneur was measured through Schwartz Value Survey for the individual values (Schwartz and Sagiv 1995; Schwartz 1994; Schwartz 1992). Individual level value scales of tradition (alpha = 0.66), stimulation (alpha = 0.58), achievement (alpha = 0.62), conformity (alpha = 0.71), power (alpha = 0.67), and security (alpha = 0.72) were utilized. Schwartz Value Survey is one of the more widely used tools for measuring values at the individual and cultural level, and as it had been translated to Turkish, it was employed in research by Turkish scholars (Sener and Hazer 2007; www.crosscultural centre.homestead.com). Stimulation was excluded from the analysis since its reliability was lower than 0.60.

8.3.2.3 Leadership Style

The leadership style of the entrepreneur was measured through the LBDQ (Stogdill 1974). It has been extensively used in a previous research (Lok et al. 2005; Hollander 1979; Schriesheim and Stogdill 1975). With the questionnaire, the following dimensions were measured: demand reconciliation (alpha = 0.60), tolerance of uncertainty (alpha = 0.31), initiation of structure (alpha = 0.67), tolerance of freedom (alpha = 0.70), role assumption (alpha = 0.77), consideration (alpha = 0.55), production emphasis (alpha = 0.67), predictive accuracy (alpha = 0.62), integration (alpha = 0.72), and superior orientation (alpha = 0.81). The dimensions with lower than 0.60 reliabilities, which are tolerance of uncertainty and consideration, were excluded from the analysis. All dimensions except superior orientation were used in their original forms. Questions measuring superior orientation were reformulated for this study due to the fact that the sample of the study was constituted by entrepreneurs who do not have superiors.

8.4 Results

The descriptive statistics regarding variables involved in the research are summarized in Table 8.1.

According to Table 8.2, there was not enough evidence to support Hypotheses 1, 4, and 5. However, as stated in Hypothesis 2, entrepreneurs' security value intensity was positively related to organizational innovativeness. On the other hand, as stated in Hypothesis 6, power value intensity was negatively related to organizational innovativeness.

Hypotheses 7, 11, 14, 15, and 16 were supported since demand reconciliation, role assumption, predictive accuracy, integration, and external stakeholder orientation among leadership dimensions were positively related to organizational innovativeness at a significant level. However, contrary to Hypotheses 9 and 13, initiations of structure and production emphasis behaviors of the entrepreneur were

Table 8.1 Descriptive statistics for research variables

Dimensions	Mean	Standard deviation
Innovativeness	3.5429	0.7019
Tradition	4.4640	1.3669
Achievement	5.4000	1.0169
Power	5.0200	1.2714
Conformity	5.1853	1.2422
Security	5.2153	0.9266
Demand reconciliation	3.5017	0.7695
Initiation of structure	3.7307	0.5378
Tolerance of freedom	3.2996	0.6236
Role assumption	3.5504	0.7245
Production emphasis	3.7258	0.5617
Predictive accuracy	3.7238	0.6767
Integration	3.8241	0.6940
External stakeholder orientation	3.9399	0.6179

Table 8.2 Correlations between study variables

	1	2	3	4	5	6	7	8	9	10	11	12	13	14
1. Innovativeness	1.000	-	-	-	-	-	-	-	-	-	-	-	-	-
2. Demand reconciliation	0.494**	1.000	-	-	-	-	-	-	-	-	-	-	-	-
3. Initiation of structure	0.326**	0.351**	1.000	-	-	-	-	-	-	-	-	-	-	-
4. Tolerence of freedom	0.118	-0.090	0.468**	1.000	-	-	-	-	-	-	-	-	-	-
5. Role assumption	0.461**	0.672**	0.157*	-0.390**	1.000	-	-	-	-	-	-	-	-	-
6. Production emphasis	0.299**	0.403**	0.696**	0.202**	0.302**	1.000	-	-	-	-	-	-	-	-
7. Predictive accuracy	0.269**	0.245**	0.589**	0.396**	0.092**	0.603**	1.000	-	-	-	-	-	-	-
8. Integration	0.390**	0.408**	0.622**	0.435**	0.248**	0.580**	0.576**	1.000	-	-	-	-	-	-
9. External stakeholder orientation	0.382**	0.420**	0.644**	0.294**	0.330**	0.626**	0.618**	0.703**	1.000	-	-	-	-	-
10. Tradition	-0.093	-0.136*	-0.109	0.010	-0.219	-0.070**	-0.051	-0.139*	-0.133*	1.000	-	-	-	-
11. Achievement	-0.021	0.011	-0.019	-0.013	0.057	-0.076	-0.002	0.001	-0.090	-0.308**	1.000	-	-	-
12. Power	-0.199**	-0.210**	-0.018	0.091	-0.140	0.017	0.145*	0.054	0.035	-0.162*	0.249**	1.000	-	-
13. Security	0.189**	0.275**	-0.020	-0.263**	0.389	0.066	0.018	0.050	0.060	-0.259**	0.008	-0.082	1.000	-
14. Conformity	-0.102	0.036	-0.043	-0.018	-0.037	-0.063	-0.034	0.045	-0.034	0.081	-0.107	-0.259**	-0.011	1.00

**Correlation is significant at the 0.01 level (2-tailed).
*Correlation is significant at the 0.05 level (2-tailed).

Table 8.3 Regression analysis results for predicting innovativeness

	b	SE	β
Demand reconciliation	0.374	0.062	0.429**
Integration	0.224	0.069	0.229**
Power	−8.625E-02	0.043	−0.129*

**p<0.01
*p<0.05

positively related to organizational innovativeness. There was not enough evidence to support Hypothesis 10.

Based on their correlations with innovativeness, shown in Table 8.2, only power and security were included from the value survey and demand reconciliation, initiation of structure, role assumption, production emphasis, predictive accuracy, integration, and superior orientation were included from the leader behavior descriptions in the regression analysis.

According to the stepwise regression analysis, only the value of power and leadership descriptions of demand reconciliation and integration predicted innovativeness significantly, and the model explained a significant portion of variance in innovativeness as shown in Table 8.3 (R^2=0.35, $F_{(3, 165)}$=30.526, $p<0.01$). The coefficient for power is negative while the coefficients for demand reconciliation and integration are positive.

8.5 Discussion

The relationship between organizational innovativeness, entrepreneurs' values, and leadership style was investigated in this study. Results reveal that power and security values of the entrepreneur were related to organizational innovativeness in the way postulated in the hypothesis. Also, findings show that most of the leadership dimensions, namely demand reconciliation, role assumption, predictive accuracy, integration, and external stakeholder orientation were related to organizational innovativeness, and all of these results were in line with the postulated hypothesis. However, in the case of initiation of structure and production emphasis, the results contradicted the expectation of a negative relation between variables.

Regarding production emphasis, although productivity is the main focus as stated in the postulation of the related hypothesis, productivity and low cost may not always be in contradiction with innovation as suggested by the findings. On the contrary, innovation may help the enterprise to decrease its costs and increase its productivity at the same time. Thus, production emphasis may require the organization culture to be more innovative in order to achieve goals of the production function through innovation. Especially for SMEs, to compete with large scale enterprises, low cost, and productivity through innovation is a requirement.

With respect to initiation of structure, as stated in the formation of the related hypothesis, when leader structures the expectations from employees, innovativeness may be inhibited. Though sometimes in some cultures people need to be clear about those expectations in order to be productive and innovative. Accordingly, Elenkov and Manev (2005) suggest that the sociocultural context directly influences leadership and moderates its relationship with organizational innovation. Hence, initiation of structure may be a requirement for innovation in the Turkish context.

Although the findings have interesting implications, there are several limitations to our research. First, the sample of the study consists of SMEs in a certain region in Turkey, which restricts the generalizability of the results. Moreover, the findings may represent the Turkish culture and may require further research in other cultures. As the desirable leadership behaviors change across cultures (Littrell 2002), the variables of leadership behavior and values related with innovativeness may change from culture to culture.

8.6 Implications

As the results of the study imply, entrepreneurs have to pay attention to the leadership style they adopt and increase their awareness about the intensity of their values. Attaching great intensity to the power value may inhibit innovativeness and produce severe results. If entrepreneurs are trying to increase the innovativeness in their organizations, they should be careful that power does not become an intensely shared value among employees. When power becomes a dominant value in the organizational culture, employees may start being motivated by extrinsic factors such as status and prestige, and this may hinder their innovativeness. Regarding security, although it seems that this value is positively related to innovativeness, entrepreneurs should be very careful in communicating to their employees that security can be achieved through innovation.

The results provide a direction to entrepreneurs in terms of leadership behaviors, too. First, demand reconciliation seems to be one of the most important dimensions for organizational innovativeness. The entrepreneur as the leader of the enterprise should provide guidance in reconciling conflicting demands and reduce disorder. Moreover, with respect to integration, the entrepreneur will try to maintain a close-knit organization. In both dimensions, it is implied that keeping conflict at an optimum level may help organizational innovativeness.

References

Amabile, T. M., Conti, R., Coon, H. Lazenby, J., Herron, M. (1996). Assessing the work environment for creativity. *Academy of Management Journal*, 39(5), 1154–1184.

Anderson, N. R. and King, N. (1993). Innovations in organizations. In Cooper, C. I., Robertson, I. T., *International Review of Industrial and Organizational Psychology*, 8, 1–33.

Aoki, R. and Hu, J. L. (1999). Licensing vs. litigation: the effect of the legal system on incentives to innovate. *Journal of Economics and Management Strategy*, 8(1), 133–160.

Becker, W. and Dietz, J. (2004). R&D cooperation and innovation activities of firms: evidence for the German manufacturing industry. *Research Policy*, 33(2), 209–223.

Blanchflower, D. and Oswald, A. (1998). What makes an entrepreneur? *Journal of Labor Economics*, 16, 26–60.

Cooke, P. (1996). The new wave of regional networks: analysis, characteristics and strategy. *Small Business Economics*, 8(2), 159–171.

Dackert, I., Loov, L. A., Martensson, M. (2004). Leadership and climate for innovation. *Economic and Industrial Democracy*, 25(2), 301–318.

Deshpande, R. and Farley, J. U. (2004). Organizational culture, market orientation, innovativeness and firm performance: an international research odyssey. *International Journal of Research in Marketing*, 21, 3–22.

Dess, G. G. and Pickens, J. C. (2000). Changing roles: leadership in the 21st century. *Organizational Dynamics*, 28, 18–34.

Dess, G. G. and Lumpkin, G. T. (2003). *Strategic Management: Creating Competitive Advantages*. New York, NY: McGraw-Hill

Dionne, S. D., Yammarino, F. J., Atwater, L. E., Spangler, W. D. (2004). Transfor-
    mational leadership and team performance. *Journal of Organizational Change
    Management*, 17(2), 177–193.
Elenkov, D. S. and Manev, I. M. (2005). Top management leadership and influence
    on innovation: the role of sociocultural context. *Journal of Management*, 31(3),
    381–402.
European Commission (1995). Small and medium-sized enterprises: a dynamic
    source of employment, growth and competitiveness in the European Union. Re-
    port presented by the European Commission for the Madrid European Coun-
    cil. Available via DIALOG. http://aei.pitt.edu/2839/01/069.pdf Cited 20 October
    2007.
European Innovation Progress Report (2006). Available via DIALOG. http://trend
    chart.cordis.lu. Cited 20 October 2007.
Fritsch, M. and Franke, M. (2004). Innovation, regional knowledge spillovers and
    R&D cooperation. *Research Policy,* 33(2), 245–255.
Garcia-Morales, V. J., Llorens-Montes, F. J., Verdu-Jover, A. J. (2006). An-
    tecedents and consequences of organizational innovation and organizational
    leaning in entrepreneurship. *Industrial Management and Data Systems*, 106(1),
    21–42.
Gobeli, D. H., Koenig, H. F., Bechinger, I. (1998). Managing conflict in software
    development teams: a multilevel analysis. *Journal of Product Innovation Man-
    agement*, 13(1), 52–62.
Hansen, M. T. and Morten, T. (1999). The search-transfer problem: the role of weak
    ties in sharing knowledge across organization subunits. *Administrative Science
    Quarterly*, 44(1), 82–111.
Hult, G. T. M., Hurley, R. F., Knight, G. A. (2004). Innovativeness: its antecedents
    and impact on business performance. *Industrial Marketing Management*, 33,
    429–438.
Hult, G. T. M, Snow, C. C., Kandemir, D. (2003). The role of entrepreneurship
    in building cultural competitiveness in different organizational types. *Journal of
    Management*, 29(3), 401–426.
Hurley, R. F. and Hult, G. T. (1998). Innovation, market orientation and organiza-
    tional learning: an integration and empirical examination. *Journal of Marketing*,
    62, 42–54.
Jaworski, B. and Kohli, A. (1990). Market orientation: antecedents and conse-
    quences. *Journal of Marketing,* 57, 53–70.
Kane-Urrabazo, C. (2006). Management's role in shaping organizational culture.
    Journal of Nursing Management, 14, 188–194.
Karagozoglu, N., Brown, W. B. (1988). Adaptive responses by conservative
    and entrepreneurial firms. *Journal of Product Innovation Management,* 5(4),
    269–281.
Kelly, L. M., Athanassiou, N., Crittenden, W. F. (2000). Founder centrality and
    strategic behavior in the family-owned firm. *Entrepreneurship Theory and Prac-
    tice*, 25(2), 27–42.

Keskin, H. (2006). Market orientation, learning orientation and innovation capabilities in SMEs: an extended model. *European Journal of Innovation Management*, 9(4), 396–417.

Kortum, S. and Lerner, J. (2000). Assessing the contribution of venture capital to innovation. *RAND Journal of Economics*, 31(4), 674–692.

Kotey, B. and Meredith G. G. (1997). Relationships among owner/manager personal values, business strategies, and enterprise performance. *Journal of Small Business Management*, 35(2), 37–64.

Kwang, N. A., Ang, R. P., Ooi, L. B., Shin, W. S., Oei, T. P. S., Leng, V. (2005). Do adaptors and innovators subscribe to opposing values? *Creativity Research Journal*. 17(2), 273–281.

Lee, C., Lee, K. and Pennings, J. M. (2001). Internal capabilities, external networks, and performance: a study on technology based ventures. *Strategic Management Journal*, 22, 615–640.

Liebowitz, J. (2002). Facilitating innovation through knowledge sharing: a look at the US naval surface warfare center-carderock division. *Journal of Computer Information System*, 42(5), 1–6.

Lin, C. Y. and Chen, M. Y. (2007). Does innovation lead to performance? An empirical study of SMEs in Taiwan. *Management Research News*, 30(2), 115–132.

Littrell, R. (2002). Desirable leadership behaviors of multi-cultural managers in China. *Journal of Management Development*, 21(1), 5–74.

Lok, P., Westwood, R., Crawford, J. (2005). Perceptions of organisational subculture and their significance for organizational commitment. *Applied Psychology: An International Review,* 54(4), 490–514.

Lumpkin, G. T. and Dess, G. (1996). Clarifying the entrepreneurial orientation construct and linking it to performance. *Academy of Management Review*, 21(1), 770–791.

Mansfield, E., Rapaport, J., Schnee, J., Wagner, S., and Hamburger, M. (1971). *The Production and Application of New Industrial Technology*. New York, NY: W.W. Norton and Co.

McLean, L. D. (2005). Organizational culture's influence on creativity and innovation: a review of the literature and implications for human resource development. *Advances in Developing Human Resources,* 7(2), 226–246.

Meglino, B. M. and Ravlin, E. C. (1998). Individual values in organizations: concepts, controversies, and research. *Journal of Management*, 24, 351–389.

Menguc, B. and Seigyoung, A. (2006). Creating a firm level dynamic capability through capitalizing on market orientation and innovativeness. *Academy of Marketing Science*, 34(1), 63–73.

Miller, D. (1986). Configurations of strategy and structure: towards a synthesis. *Strategic Management Journal,* 7, 233–249.

Miron, E., Erez, M. and Naveh, E. (2003). Do personal characteristics and cultural values that promote innovation, quality, and efficiency compete or complement each other? *Journal of Organizational Behavior*, 25(2), 175–199.

Mone, M. A., McKinley, W., Bargar, V. L. (1998). Organizational decline and innovation: a contingency framework. *Academy of Management Review*, 23, 115–132.

Morris, M. H. and Schindehutte, M. (2005). Entrepreneurial values and the ethnic enterprise: an examination of six sub-cultures. *Journal of Small Business Management*, 43(4), 453–480.

Mumford, M. D. and Licuanan, B. (2004). Leading for innovation: conclusions, issues, and directions. *The Leadership Quarterly*, 15, 163–171.

Mumford, M. D., Scott, G. M., Gaddis, B. and Strange, J. M. (2002). Leading creative people: orchestrating expertise and relationship. *The Leadership Quarterly*, 13, 705–750.

Northouse, P. G. (2004). *Leadership: Theory and Practice*. London: Sage Publications

Olson, E. M., Slater, F. S., Hult, G. T. M. (2005). The performance implications of fit among business strategy, marketing organization structure, and strategic behavior. *Journal of Marketing*, 69, 49–65.

O'Regan, N., Ghobadian, A., Sims, M. (2006). Fast tracking innovation in manufacturing SMEs. *Technovation*, 26(2), 251–261.

OECD & Eurostat (2005). Oslo Manual: guidelines for collecting and interpreting innovation data. Available via DIALOG. http://epp.eurostat.cec.eu.int/cache/ITY_PUBLIC/OSLO/EN/OSLO-EN.PDF Cited in 10 October 2007.

Rice, G. (2006). Individual values, organizational context, and employee creativity: evidence from Egyptian organizations. *Journal of Business Research*, 59, 233–241.

Rokeach, M. (1973). *The Nature of Human Values*. New York, NY: Free Press.

Santos-Vijande, M. L, Alvarez-Gonzales, L. I. (2007). Innovativeness and organizational innovation in total quality oriented firms: the moderating role of market turbulence. *Technovation*, 27(9), 514–532.

Schwartz, S. H. (1992). Universals in the content and structure of values: theory and empirical tests in 20 countries. *Advances in Experimental Social Psychology*, 25, 1–65.

Sener, A. and Hazer, O. (2007). Degerlerin kadinlarin Surdurulebilir tuketim davranisi uzerindeki etkilerine iliskin bir araştirma. *Hacettepe Universitesi Sosyolojik Araştirmalar E-dergisi*.

Slater, S. and Narver, J. (1995). Market orientation and the learning organization. *Journal of Marketing*, 59, 63–74.

Solow, R. (2001). Competitiveness and the CMI mission. Available via DIALOG. http://www.cambridge-mit.org/events/article/?objid=1176. Cited 20 October 2007

Somech, A. (2006). The effects of leadership style and team processes on performance and innovation in functionally heterogeneous teams. *Journal of Management*, 32, 132–157.

Sosik, J. J. (2005). The role of personal values in the charismatic leadership of corporate managers: a model and preliminary field study. *The Leadership Quarterly*, 16, 221–244.

Spini, D. (2003). Measurement equivalence of ten value types from the Schwartz Value Survey across 21 countries. *Journal of Cross-Cultural Psychology*, 34(1), 3–23.

Tanriverdi, H. and Zehir, C. (2006). Impact of learning organizations' applications and market dynamism on organizations' innovativeness and market performance. *The Business Review*, 6(2), 238–246.

Teece, D. J. (1986). Profiting from technological innovation: implications for integration, collaboration, licensing and public policy. *Research Policy*, 15, 285–305.

Thomson, A. A. and Strickland A. J. (1986). *Strategy Formulation and Implementation: Task of General Manager.* Plano, TX: Business Publications, Inc.

Timmons, J. A. and Bygrave, W. D. (1986). Venture capital's role in financing innovation for economic growth. *Journal of Business Venturing*, 1(2), 161–176.

Tsai, W. (2001). Knowledge transfer in intraorganizational networks: effects of network position and absorptive capacity on business unit innovation and performance. *The Academy of Management Journal*, 44(5), 996–1004.

Van de Ven, A. (1986). Central problems in the management of innovation. *Management Science*, 32, 590–607.

Verbees, F. J. H. and Meulenberg, M. T. G. (2004). Market orientation, innovativeness, product innovation, and performance in small firms. *Journal of Small Business Management*, 42(2), 134–154.

Vermeulen, P. A. M., Jong, J. P. J., O'Shaughnessy, K. C. (2005). Identifying key determinants for new product introductions and firm performance in small service firms. *The Services Industries Journal*, 25(5), 625–640.

West, M. A., Borrill, C. S., Dawson, J. F., Brodbeck, F. (2003). Leadership clarity and team innovation in health care. *The Leadership Quarterly*, 14, 545–568.

Yadav, M. S., Prabhu, J. C., Chandy, R. K. (2007). Managing the future: CEO attention and innovation outcomes. *Journal of Marketing*, 71, 84–101.

Zahra, S. A., Nielsen, A. P., Bognar, W. C. (1999). Corporate entrepreneurship, knowledge and competence development. *Entrepreneurship Theory and Practice*, 23(3), 169–189.

Zaltman, G., Duncan, R., Holbek, J. (1973). *Innovations and Organizations.* New York, NY: Wiley.

9 Ankara Technology Development Zones Within the Context of Innovation Strategies in Turkey

Cigdem Varol, N. Aydan Sat, Asli Gurel Ucer, and Gulsen Yilmaz

Abstract

Contemporary discussions on new economy have displayed that competitiveness of regions greatly depend on innovation regarded as a complex process involving many different functions, actors, and relationships. To improve the innovative performances of agents of production in the system and to promote interactions between them, national and regional innovation systems are developed. As a part of regional innovation systems, technology development zones (TDZs) appear as an environment that transforms innovative ideas to marketable products by utilizing collective learning processes among universities, innovative firms, and innovation support institutions. The aim of this study is to discuss the innovative strategies, thus the various instruments and institutional arrangements to encourage technology development in Turkey, and the efforts of building innovation capacity through the initiatives of TDZs in Ankara. Within this context, first of all, the innovation capability of Turkey in terms of R&D activities, policies, actors, and spatial repercussions under the name of TDZs are discussed. Second, the three TDZs in Ankara are analyzed

The authors gratefully acknowledge the funding provided for this research by Gazi University Scientific Research Project under grant no. BAP 06/2004-29. We would like to thank to the firms and management of the three TDZs in Ankara for realizing face-to-face interviews. We are also grateful to the editor for her great efforts.

N. Aydogan (ed.), *Innovation Policies, Business Creation and Economic Development,*
International Studies in Entrepreneurship 21, DOI 10.1007/978-0-387-79976-6_9,
© Springer Science+Business Media, LLC 2009

137

in details. At the end, with the comparison of the three TDZs, the innovative capacity of TDZs and the effects of government support in this process are evaluated briefly.

9.1 Introduction

Contemporary discussions on new economy have displayed that competitiveness of regions greatly depend on innovation that is basically defined as radical and incremental changes to products, processes, or services. Innovation is regarded as a complex process involving many different functions, actors, and relationships that interact in the production, diffusion, and use of new and economically useful knowledge. According to Lundvall (1992), this is defined as the system of innovation that includes "organizations and institutions involved in searching and exploring—such as research and development (R&D) departments, technological institutes and universities." In a broader definition, it includes "all parts and aspects of the economic structure and the institutional set-up affecting learning as well as searching and exploring" (Lundvall 1992:12).

To improve the innovative performances of agents of production in the system and to promote interactions between them, governments pursue science and technology policies, and create a network of institutions that form the national innovation systems (NISs) (Lundvall 1992; Nelson 1993). The accumulation of knowledge and provision of infrastructure for knowledge generation and the implementation of technology policy have been brought together in NISs approach, and in this system, innovations are viewed as part of a larger process of development of knowledge and as an important determinant of economic growth.

NISs contribute to the development of specific innovation policies, setting out the fields of public intervention. Alongside NISs, there has been an increasing interest in the role of regional innovation systems (RISs) in promoting the competitiveness of regional economies. RISs emphasize the existing interactions between actors, the capability of support mechanisms to create an innovative environment, and the potential sources for knowledge creation and learning processes. It is argued that innovation capabilities are the results of local agglomeration of industrial, technological, and scientific activities in RISs. In this point of view, innovation is connected to space and to the factors that ensure favorable conditions in shaping the innovation environment (Cooke et al. 2004).

As a part of RISs, in the spatial formation of innovation systems, technoparks appear as an environment that transforms innovative ideas to marketable products by utilizing collective learning processes among universities, innovative firms, and innovation support institutions. There are different definitions and terms for technoparks around the world, such as the science park, research park, technopolis, industry parks, and technology development zones, but the common approach lies in the "cluster effect," which would make it easier for agents of production to exchange ideas, attract labor, and share equipment. Bringing innovative actors and universities together can potentially benefit various sides: companies can easily recruit from the universities and interact with scientists; universities can keep students and faculty members engaged in local research; and thus the whole region gains by holding the "intellectual capital" (Galbraith 2002).

The idea of establishing technoparks arose in the 1980s as a national policy in Turkey, and the first project was started with the initiation of the State Planning Organization (DPT) in the early 1990s. The first regulation including the establishment, organization, and maintenance of technoparks was published in 1996, and in 2001 the Law of Technology Development Zones came into force. From here on, through the principals of creating RISs, TDZs have established supporting university–industry collaboration in Turkey.

In this scope, the aim of this study is to discuss the innovative strategies, thus the various instruments and institutional arrangements to encourage technology development in Turkey, and the efforts of building innovation capacity through the initiatives of TDZs in Ankara. Within this context, first, the innovation capability of Turkey in terms of R&D activities, policies, and actors, and spatial repercussions under the name of TDZs are discussed. Second, the three TDZs in Ankara are analyzed in details. Finally, with the comparison of the three TDZs, the innovative capacity of TDZs and the effects of government support in this process are evaluated briefly.

9.2 Innovation Capability of Turkey and Technology Development Zones (TDZs)

In this section, the innovation capability of Turkey is analyzed under three topics: R&D indicators; the science and technology policies, and actors of innovativeness; and spatial formations of innovation that appear as TDZs.

9.2.1 R&D Indicators in Turkey

Given the widely acknowledged importance of industrial R&D as the primary drivers of national capacity for development, several researches have suggested different ways to measure and rank R&D capacities of countries through calculating various composite indices (Soubbotina 2006). For example, UNCTAD has focused on education and R&D facilities, UNIDO has emphasized the industry technology relationship, and OECD has prepared three different manuals for measurement of science and technology activities (i.e. the Frascati, Oslo, and Canberra Manuals). Among these, according to the Frascati Manual, R&D data covers both "inputs" and "outputs." Although R&D inputs are defined as R&D expenditures and personnel, R&D outputs are defined as patents, trademark registration, utility model, SCI journal publications, projects, and so on (OECD 2002a). In this study, R&D indicators in Turkey are evaluated due to the classification of the Frascati Manual.

9.2.1.1 R&D Inputs

In Turkey, the share of R&D expenditures in GDP is quite low when compared to developed countries. Although the total gross domestic expenditure on R&D (GERD) as a percentage of GDP was 0.45 percent in 1996, it increased to 0.66 percent in 2004 and 0.79 percent in 2005. This percentage is above 1.0 percent in developed countries, such as 6.4 percent in Israel, 3.98 percent in Sweden, 3.15 percent in Japan, and 2.68 percent in the United States in 2004.

When the total number of R&D personnel (full time equivalent [FTE]) is analyzed, it appears that 21,983 R&D personnel in 1996 increased to 49,252 in 2005 in Turkey (TUIK 2007). FTE R&D personnel per thousand employees appeared as 1.1 percent in 2004 in

Turkey, although this ratio generally appears between 3 and 10 percent in developed countries; there are also extreme cases such as 17.7 percent in Finland and 10.4 percent in Japan in 2004 (OECD 2005).

Sectoral distribution of FTE R&D personnel occurred as 61.9 percent in higher education, 22.1 percent in the private sector, and 16.0 percent in the public sector in 2004. Statistics show that each year the share of private sector increases, which means the required emphasis be given to R&D activities in industry and service sectors (OECD 2005).

To sum up, although there is a gradual increase over the years in the GERD and R&D personnel in Turkey, this is not sufficient for catching up to the level of developed countries and for the effective use of R&D in competitiveness.

9.2.1.2 R&D Outputs

When the number of SCI journal publications is analyzed as R&D outputs, it is observed that Turkey has increased the number of publications from 206 in 1973 to 12,229 in 2004. However, when compared to other OECD countries, Turkey ranked 27 in 1997, whereas the United States, England, and Japan were ranked within the first three countries (TUBITAK 1997).

According to the distribution of patent numbers per thousand people, it was only 1 in Turkey, while it was 154.5 in USA and 166.7 in Japan in 2002 (OECD 2002b). For triadic patents, the number of patents per million people was 0.13 in Turkey while the OECD average was 54.04 in 2004. Another crucial point about patent numbers in Turkey is that most of the patents approved by the Turkish Patent Institute (TPE) were developed by international firms (97 percent in 2006).

As a result, the input and output indices of R&D analyzed here show that, although science and technology policies do not have a long history in Turkey, as will be mentioned in the next section, there are still too many steps that must be taken for increasing R&D capabilities and competitiveness of Turkey.

9.2.2 Policy and Actors for Innovativeness in Turkey

The important steps for creating national innovation policy of Turkey were taken after the 1960s. Turkey's Five Year Development Plans have formed the basis for innovation policy by providing the necessary financial allocation. Parallel to these plans, several institutions were established especially after 1990 for the development of NIS. DPT, Supreme Council of Science and Technology (BTYK), and Scientific and Research Council of Turkey (TUBITAK) are some of the most important institutions that prepare and coordinate Turkish science and technology policy.

For the creation of national innovation policy, the first step was taken by the First Five-Year Development Plan (1963–1968) with the establishment of TUBITAK. After this, topics on technological development and technology transfer were included in the Annual Programs of the Second (1968–1972) and Third (1973–1977) Five-Year Development Plans. The Fourth Five-Year Development Plan (1979–1983) referred to "technology policies" and emphasized the need for "integrating technology policies with industry, employment and investment policies, and enhancing certain industrial sectors in a way that they develop their own technologies" (Elci 2003).

In 1983, the Government issued the first policy document on creating NIS, the "Turkish Science Policy, 1983–2003" that mainly focused on increasing R&D activities in the country and defined priority technology areas (Goker and Akarsoy 1996). Although these technology areas were previously defined, this document could be regarded as the first attempt toward defining "critical technologies" in Turkey. With the Fifth Five-Year Development Plan (1984–1989), the first step for the foundation of technoparks was taken (DPT 1985) and details on the preparation of legal framework for these technoparks were given. During this period, DPT and United Nations Industrial Development Organization (UNIDO) derived a document on establishment of university–industry relations (Pakpese 1996).

In the Sixth Five-Year Development Plan (1990–1995), the requirement for constituting the legal framework for university–industry cooperation was mentioned and wide spreading of technoparks was intended (DPT 1990). Additionally, this plan aimed to increase the activities of BTYK and establish TPE. In the Seventh Five-Year Development Plan (1996–2000), the objectives about science and technology were determined as constituting the venture capital, purchasing technological goods by the state, increasing R&D performance of the private sector, establishing the national R&D network, revising the duties, authority and responsibilities of TUBITAK, supporting the participation of academicians in R&D activities, and establishing TDZs (DPT 1996).

In the 1990s, two other policy documents "Turkish Science and Technology Policy, 1993–2003" and "The Project for Impetus in Science and Technology" were prepared by TUBITAK and approved by BTYK with the objective of raising Turkey's science and technology capacity to the level of developed countries. Referring to these documents, the main objective of science and technology policy was defined as "establishment of the NIS that would enable systematic operation of the whole institutions and mechanisms required to carry out scientific and technological R&D activities and to transform the results of those activities into economic and social utility" (Elci 2003).

In the 2000s, constitution and development of Turkey's science and technology policies and implementations have been determined by the Eighth (2001–2005) and Ninth (2007–2013) Five-Year Development Plans in which objectives are mentioned as building encouraging system on technological development, maintaining the coordination, purchasing technological goods, establishing technology development zones, supporting the venture capital, and revising other institutional and legal arrangements.

Recent efforts on science and technology policies of Turkey for the near future started with the "Vision 2023: Strategies for Science and Technology" in 2002 under the coordination of TUBITAK (TUBITAK 2007). Vision 2023 is an ongoing project, which aims to build the science and technology vision of Turkey and involves the subprojects of technology foresight, technological capacity, and R&D labor and infrastructure. This project has been accordingly detailed in order to determine strategic technologies and priority areas of R&D, and to formulate science and technology policies of Turkey for the next 20 years. Within the context of this project, Turkish Research Area is defined so as to designate the relations between the foundations and institutes that realize, utilize, and fund R&D activities.

Turkey has attempted to build NIS by policy-making and empowering the institutional structure based on a top-down linear model until the 2000s. However, after the 2000s, in creating sustainable innovation system, the importance of bottom-up interactive model has been realized. Important steps have been taken for the establishment of RIS, which includes collective capacities and a local system of technical knowledge to strengthen the links between local firms and technology supply institutions. TDZs emerge as one of the most essential repercussion of RIS in Turkey.

9.2.3 Spatial Formations of Innovation: Technology Development Zones in Turkey

In Turkey, the thought for the establishment of technoparks was taken into agenda in the 1980s and became concrete by the Fifth Five-Year Development Plan. In 1990, DPT had started projects on the development of technoparks (Cilingir 2004), however the constitution of incubation centers had been determined more feasible in the first stage. The initial incubation centers—Istanbul Technical University Technology Development Center (ITU-TDC) and Middle East Technical University Technology Development Center (METU-TDC)—were established in 1991 with the cooperation of universities and Small and Medium Sized Industry Development Organization (KOS-GEB). During this period, without the support of KOSGEB, another technology development center Marmara Research Center (MRC) was built by TUBITAK.

In 1998, the first legal frame for technoparks; "KOSGEB Technopark Regulation" was approved, and TUBITAK-MRC and METU-TDC were accepted as the initial technoparks of Turkey. After this Regulation, the Law of TDZs (no. 4691), as the main current law, came into force in 2001. This Law is an important step to formalize the cooperation between university and industry. The objectives of the TDZs determined by the Law are to produce technological knowledge by providing cooperation between universities; research centers; manufacturing; to commercialize technological knowledge; to create investment opportunities in technology intense areas; to supply employment opportunities for researchers; to realize technology transfer; and to develop technological infrastructure attracting foreign direct investment. Related to this Law, Implementation Regulation of TDZs (no. 24790) came into force in 2002. According to this Regulation valid until the end of 2013, various financial supports and tax exemptions are provided to the management of TDZs, entrepreneurs, and members of the universities located at these zones.

Table 9.1 Technology development zones in Turkey, 2007

TDZs	Location	Year	Area (ha)	Firms	Employees
TUBITAK Marmara Research Centre Technopark	Gebze	1998	56.0	26	158
METU Technopolis TDZ	Ankara	1998	121.9	176	3200
Izmir TDZ	Izmir	2002	218.8	26	220
Ankara TDZ (Cyberpark-Bilkent University)	Ankara	2002	37.3	161	2305
Gebze Industrial Zone Technopark TDZ	Gebze	2002	12.4	15	269
ITU Ari Technocity TDZ	Istanbul	2003	198.9	25	566
Yildiz Technical University TDZ	Istanbul	2003	10.3	**	**
Hacettepe University TDZ	Ankara	2003	211.7	35	248
Eskisehir (Anadolu) TDZ	Eskisehir	2003	50.3	12	75
Istanbul University TDZ	Istanbul	2003	20.0	**	**
Kocaeli University TDZ	Kocaeli	2003	20.0	32	*
Selcuk University TDZ	Konya	2003	32.5	23	37
Bati Akdeniz Technocity (ATEK) TDZ	Antalya	2004	182.1	4	33
Trabzon (Karadeniz Technical University) TDZ	Trabzon	2004	1.8	**	**
Erciyes University TDZ	Kayseri	2004	27.7	*	*
Cukurova TDZ	Adana	2004	86.0	**	**
Erzurum Ata Technocity TDZ	Erzurum	2005	6.0	**	**
Goller Bolgesi TDZ	Isparta	2005	11.2	*	*
Mersin TDZ	Mersin	2005	9.6	4	*
Ulutek (Uludag University) TDZ	Bursa	2005	51.3	9	*
Ankara University TDZ	Ankara	2006	11.5	**	**
Gaziantep University TDZ	Gaziantep	2006	16.3	**	**
Pamukkale University TDZ	Denizli	2007	5.0	**	**
Firat (Firat University) TDZ	Elazig	2007	7.9	**	**
Cumhuriyet TDZ	Sivas	2007	9.1	**	**
Trakya University Edirne TDZ	Edirne	2007	5.4	**	**
Dicle University TDZ	Diyarbakir	2007	29.6	**	**
Gazi Technopark (Gazi University) TDZ	Ankara	2007	5.8	**	**

* no information, **not in operation.
Sources: Karabulut 2006, Sanayi Bakanligi 2007

With the help of these legal arrangements, the number of TDZs has increased rapidly. Until the end of 2007, 28 TDZs (Table 9.1) have been approved by the Council of Ministers; 15 of these TDZs are currently in operation (Sanayi Bakanligi, 2007). The first examples of TDZs were established in the metropolitan cities. Most of them are located in the campuses of universities, except the TDZs in Eskisehir and Gebze located in industrial zones.

Table 9.2 General information about TDZ's in Turkey

	2003	2004	2005	2006
Number of firms	169	318	500	533
Number of employees	2453	4196	5042	7757
Number of projects	250	700	1500	2470
Value of export (million US$)	0	28	43	34
Number of foreign firms	0	7	20	23

Source: Karabulut 2006

Among all of the TDZs in Turkey, Izmir (218.8 ha) and Hacettepe University (211.7 ha) TDZs are the largest in terms of their appropriated area. According to the number of firms and employment capacities, METU-Technopolis (176 firms—3200 employers) and Ankara TDZ-Cyberpark (161 firms—2305 employers) appear as the leaders.

In general, innovative firms working on software, informatics, electronic, nanotechnology, biotechnology, and renewable energy predominantly take place in the TDZs. The active TDZs have 533 firms out of which 23 are foreign firms and have 7,757 employees (Table 9.2). The number of R&D projects has reached 2,470 and the value of export has gone beyond US$ 34 million in 2006 (Karabulut 2006).

In the developing university–industry collaboration, Technology Development Centers (TEKMERs) built by KOSGEB, play an important role since the 1990s. These centers that act as incubators are

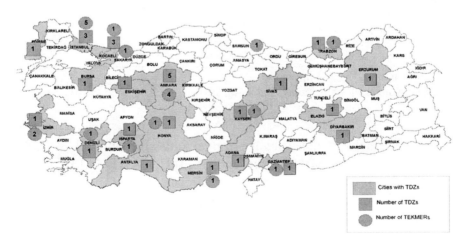

Fig. 9.1 TDZs and TEKMERs in Turkey, 2007

established for the purpose of supporting TDZs, so most of them are located in TDZs (Fig. 9.1). There are currently 20 TEKMERs where firms specialize in computer, software, and electronic sectors. KOS-GEB provides various tax exemptions and other supports to these start-up firms. Within these supports, there are provisions for initial capital, improvement of working conditions, and leasing aid.

9.3 Technology Development Zones and Incubation Centers in Ankara

Within the development process of TDZs, Ankara appears as the leading city. The first TDZ attempts in Turkey began with the initiation of METU in Ankara in 1987. Efforts to establish METU Technopolis went on till 1998 and with the Regulation of Technoparks accepted by KOSGEB, METU Technopolis and TUBITAK-MAM were regarded as the first TDZs in Turkey. After the Law of TDZs came into force in 2001, two more TDZs—Ankara TDZ-Cyberpark (Bilkent University) (2002) and Hacettepe University TDZ (2003)—went into action. In 2006, within Ankara University and in 2007 within Gazi University, two more TDZs were established. Besides the leading role of Ankara in the establishment of TDZs, it has a crucial place among other TDZs in Turkey in terms of number of firms, number of employment, and number of foreign investments (Table 9.3).

This study focuses on three active TDZs in Ankara: METU Technopolis, Ankara TDZ-Cyberpark (Bilkent University), and Hacettepe University TDZ. All these TDZs are located in the campuses of the universities and they have TEKMERs built in their campuses. They are located along a university corridor and close to each other (Fig. 9.2).

Table 9.3 General characteristics of TDZs in Ankara and Turkey (2006)

	Ankara (#)	Turkey (#)	% of Ankara in Turkey
Firms	372	533	69.7
Employees	5753	7757	74.2
Foreign firms	19	23	82.6

Source: Karabulut 2006

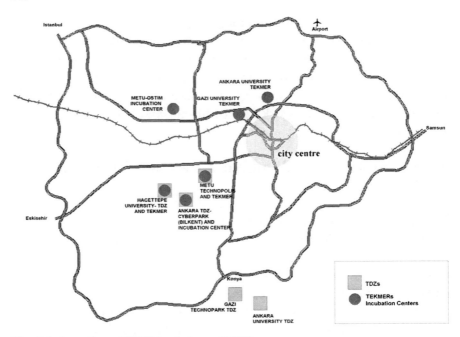

Fig. 9.2 Location of TDZ in Ankara (2007)

The methodology of this study is based on both qualitative and quantitative approaches to investigate the innovative structure of three active TDZs in Ankara. The quantitative analysis of innovation process may help to draw conclusions of statistical generalizations, and qualitative approach is used in order to understand complex structure of innovation process. To collect the data, a field survey was conducted. In the field survey, in-depth interviews with the management of TDZs, three incubation centers, and 10 percent of the selected firms were held (Varol et al. 2007). To analyze the efforts of building innovation capacity of TDZs and incubation centers in Ankara, input and output indicators of R&D and relations among actors taking place in these TDZs were evaluated. The R&D inputs are considered as R&D employees in total employment, the percentage of R&D expenditures, and R&D facilities. On the other hand, the R&D outputs are considered as the number of patents and the amount of technology export in TDZs. The number of university member researchers, the number of firms owned by university members, and the projects held by national and international institutions are the indicators denoting the level of relations among actors.

9.3.1 Middle East Technical University (METU) Technopolis

METU Technopolis project was started in 1987 with the aim of contributing university–industry relations and supporting high-tech development. With the support of KOSGEB, the first incubation centre was built in METU in 1991. Based on the Technopark Regulation of KOSGEB, the implementation projects of METU Technopolis were prepared, and in 1998 together with TUBITAK-MAM, they were accepted as the first technoparks in Turkey.

Since their establishment, the numbers of firms and employees have been growing steadily each year. The number of firms was 135 in 2002, which was increased to 170 in 2006. When the sectoral distribution of the firms is analyzed, it is seen that informatics sector with 69 firms (39 percent) appears as the dominant sector in Technopolis where the defense sector with 37 firms (21 percent) and the electronics sector with 23 firms (13 percent) follows. It is observed that micro firms with 1–9 employees formed the majority (66 percent) in METU Technopolis. Firms with 10–50 employees had a share of 26.8 percent and firms with more than 51 employees had a share of 7.3 percent in 2006.

When R&D inputs are analyzed in METU Technopolis, it is seen that, due to R&D facilities, the firms located in the Technopolis have the opportunity to access Internet connection and to use the library, laboratories, and research centers within METU. However, the firms limited their utilization of these facilities. Due to R&D employees in total employment, there were 3,200 employees in the total and 69 percent of them were R&D personnel (2,213) in 2006 (METU-Technopolis, 2006). Additionally, considering the education level of employees in 2006, 64 percent of them were graduates and 14 percent of them had M.S. or Ph.D. degrees. The firms allocated more than 75 percent of their budget for their R&D expenditures.

When R&D outputs are analyzed in METU Technopolis, it is observed that the amount of export realized by the firms in Technopolis was US$ 2.9 million in 2002 and increased to US$ 56.6 million in 2006. Parallel to the increase in the number of firms established and the projects performed, the amount of export has been increasing each year. In the METU Technopolis, 67 percent of the firms have not had any *patents* yet. Between 2004 and 2005, METU Technopolis firms had only 2 patents out of a total 27 patents in all TDZs in Turkey.

In METU Technopolis, the number of researchers from university and the number of firms owned by academicians, steadily increased each year. This emphasizes the increasing *relations between the firms and the university*. The rate of university member researchers was 5.6 percent in 2006 and the rate of firms owned by academicians was 17 percent in 2005. Parallel to this, the number of projects held together with the firms and the academicians also support these relations. In 2006, 963 (58.5 percent) of the total 1,647 projects were held by firms in cooperation with academicians. Within these projects, 88 were supported by national foundations such as KOSGEB, TUBITAK, and TTGV.

9.3.1.1 METU-TEKMER and OSTIM Incubation Centre

METU-TEKMER was established when the official record was signed between METU and KOSGEB in 1992, with the aim of transferring technological knowledge of the universities to the industry and supporting qualified young entrepreneurs. The firms functioning in METU-TEKMER are usually micro and small-sized (2–5 employees), and they utilize the financial supports of KOSGEB and technical supports of METU Technopolis.

Between 1992 and 2007, 117 firms had been supported where 80 of them had completed the incubation phase and graduated successfully. When the sectoral distribution of the firms was analyzed, it was seen that informatics, electronics, mechatronics, and biotechnology sectors were dominant. Firms that were able to grow enough preferred to work in their offices built after graduation. Twenty-one firms (18 percent) have been transferred to TDZs and built their own workplaces until 2007.

With the increasing demand for incubation centers and efforts to strengthen university–industry relations, another incubation center was established in OSTIM Organized Industry Zone with a protocol signed between the management of OSTIM and METU. The center was thought to be an implementation area of EU technology development projects related with small and medium sized enterprises (SMEs), and a place for developing R&D culture of manufacturing firms in OSTIM and their opening to international markets.

9.3.2 Ankara Technology Development Zone-Cyberpark (Bilkent University)

Ankara Technology Development Zone-Cyberpark was declared on November 12, 2002 in the Official Gazette. Ankara TDZ-Cyberpark that had only 9 firms in its first year has been developing rapidly at the rate of approximately 30 firms per year. According to the 2006 data, 161 firms, in which 6 of them were foreign investments, actively took place in Ankara TDZ-Cyberpark. When sectoral distribution of the firms is considered, it is seen that informatics sector, that has been given priority by the management of Ankara TDZ-Cyberpark, has the biggest share with 80.1 percent. Additionally, telecommunication (3.4 percent), electric/electronic (3.4 percent), nanotechnology (1.4 percent), and space and aeronautics sectors take part in the Ankara TDZ-Cyberpark. According to the 2006 data, it is seen that micro firms with 1–9 employees dominated (72 percent), firms with 10–50 employees had a share of 23 percent, and firms with more than 51 employees had a share of 5 percent.

Considering R&D inputs in Ankara TDZ-Cyberpark, it is seen that, due to R&D facilities, the firms utilize Internet infrastructure, libraries, laboratories, and research centers within Bilkent University. Due to R&D employees in total employment, there were 2,305 employees in total, out of which 1,307 (56.7 percent) were R&D personnel in 2006. When the education level of employees was analyzed in 2006, it was observed that 52.4 percent of them were graduates from a university and 10.9 percent had M.S. or Ph.D. degrees. Firms allocated more than 75 percent of their budget for their R&D expenditures.

According to the R&D outputs of Ankara TDZ-Cyberpark, the amount of export realized by the firms in TDZ was nearly US$ 7 million, which was 15 percent of total exports of all TDZs in 2006. Parallel to the increase in the number of firms and the projects performed, the amount of export has been increasing each year. In Ankara TDZ-Cyberpark, firms had 9 *patents* out of a total 27 patents in all TDZs in Turkey between 2004 and 2005.

When the *relations between firms and university* are analyzed, it is seen that the number of researchers from universities was 24 (19.5 percent) and the number of firms that are owned or shared by an academician was 70 (24 percent) in 2006. One of the objectives of Ankara

TDZ-Cyberpark is to provide an atmosphere that creates synergy among the academicians, students, and tenants. In order to create this synergy, the management established the "University Communication and Synergy Mechanisms" platform. The firms of Ankara TDZ-Cyberpark have an opportunity to form partnerships with universities via this platform. The firms in Ankara TDZ-Cyberpark realize R&D projects with the support of national and international institutions such as TTGV, TIDEB, TUBITAK, KOSGEB, World Bank, and EU.

9.3.2.1 Ankara Cyberpark Incubation Center

The incubation center was established through the partnership of Cyberpark with TTGV, KOSGEB, and Bilkent University in 2004. This center appears as the first incubation center in Turkey that was founded via the partnership of an NGO, the public sector, and the private sector. Its main aim is to create employment and business opportunities, and to ensure the growth of small firms. Start-ups and entrepreneurs are supported through office space and equipment allocation, consultancy, and training services.

The Incubation Center is established on over 2,000 m^2 office space, where 25 start-up firms are supported per year. The firms work on information technology, biotechnology and gene engineering, energy production and transformation technologies, chemical and new material technologies, and aerospace technologies. They utilize the resources and opportunities of the University.

9.3.3 Hacettepe University Technology Development Zone

Hacettepe University TDZ was declared on January 10, 2003 in the *Official Gazette*. Hacettepe University TDZ had 22 firms in its first year and, with an increase of 59 percent, the number of firms reached 35 in 2006. The percentage of foreign firms in Hacettepe University TDZ was 6 percent in 2006. The firms from almost all sectors such as informatics, electronics, machinery, automotive, chemistry, food, mine, geology, and physics take place in the Hacettepe University TDZ. According to the 2006 data, it is seen that firms with 1–9 employees had a share of 62.9 percent, firms with 10–50 had a share of 25.7 percent, and firms with more than 51 employees had a share of 11.4 percent.

When R&D inputs are analyzed in the Hacettepe University TDZ, it is seen that firms limit their use of the R&D facilities due to lack of sufficient infrastructure. The percentage of R&D employees in total employment was 73 percent, and among the total employees the percentage of postgraduates was 44 percent in 2006. R&D expenditure was more than 75 percent in the Hacettepe University TDZ.

Considering the R&D outputs in the Hacettepe University TDZ, it is observed that the amount of export was dramatically low compared to the other two TDZs in 2006. So far, no patents have been taken out by the firms.

The firms in TDZ generally perform their R&D projects with the national support. When the supporting foundations and the support amounts are examined, it is concluded that TUBITAK appeared as the leading supporter in 2006. So far, the *relations between the firms and the university* have been quite limited.

9.3.3.1 Hacettepe TEKMER Incubation Center

Hacettepe TEKMER was founded in the Hacettepe University TDZ in collaboration with KOSGEB on November 9, 2005 with the aim of providing appropriate physical conditions for young entrepreneurs. The firms in this center can benefit from the incentives and supports provided by KOSGEB. There were 20 SMEs in Hacettepe TEKMER where 65 percent were in the software sector, 30 percent in the machine and electronics sector, and the remaining 5 percent in the medicine sector in 2007.

9.3.4 Comparison and Evaluation of TDZs in Ankara

Within the debate of innovativeness, the input and output indicators of R&D activities, and the relations among the main actors in TDZs are evaluated for the three TDZs in Ankara, according to the field survey (Table 9.4).

As can be seen from Table 9.4, in general, related with the R&D inputs, the percentage of R&D employees and expenditures are crucial indicators for the innovativeness of the firms above 50 percent. R&D employees in METU and Ankara TDZ-Cyberpark are above 70 percent, (i.e. tax-incentives provided by the government for R&D employees are effective). However, similar situation does not exist in

Table 9.4 Main findings on innovativeness in TDZs in Ankara

Innovativeness	METU	Ankara	Hacettepe	Explanation
Inputs				
R&D employees in total employment	69 percent	57 percent	73 percent	The R&D employees in firms with 1–25 employees that built the general firm structure in TDZs are above 50 percent. This is directly related with the tax incentives provided in TDZs for R&D employees.
The percentage of R&D expenditures	More than 75 percent	More than 75 percent	More than 75 percent	When compared to other firms out of the TDZs, the percentage of R&D expenditures are extremely high.
R&D facilities	Facilities supplied by TDZs not utilized adequately	Facilities supplied by TDZs not utilized adequately	Facilities limitedly supplied by TDZs not utilized	Firms limitedly utilize the facilities like the library, laboratory, etc.
Outputs				
Patents	67 percent of the firms do not have any patent. Between 2004 and 2005, 2 patents of a total of 27 patents in all TDZs	53.3 percent of the firms do not have any patent. Between 2004 and 2005, 9 patents of a total of 27 patents in all TDZs	40 percent of the firms do not have any patent. Between 2004 and 2005, none of the firms had a patent	The number of patents are very limited when compared with a total of 5,100 patents taken between 2004 and 2005
Technology export rate (2005)	73 percent in total export of TDZs	15 percent in total export of TDZs	0.25 percent in total export of TDZs	Three TDZs in Ankara have the greatest share in total exports of all TDZs
Relations among actors				
Relations with other firms	60 percent of the firms have relations with other firms (project and subcontracting issues)	35.7 percent of the firms have relations with other firms (project development issue)	20 percent of the firms have relations with other firms (subcontracting relations)	The synergy for innovative capacity is limited since the firms are generally closed. Trust-based relations are more effective in METU as being the oldest TDZ
Relations with universities	40 percent of the firms have consultancy relations with academicians, 13.3 percent utilize technical facilities of the university	13.3 percent of the firms have consultancy relations with academicians, 6.7 percent utilize technical facilities of the university	40 percent of the firms have consultancy relations with academicians, 20 percent utilize technical facilities of the university	The firms have relatively strong relations with academicians rather than utilizing technical facilities of the universities

terms of R&D facilities supported by the TDZs, since none of the three TDZs utilize the facilities effectively. This can be explained by the TDZs being in the early phase of their development.

Compared to R&D inputs, R&D outputs are very limited in terms of patents and export rates in the TDZs. This limited number could be explained by TDZs being new initiations. Another interesting point here is that, although these three TDZs have limited export rates, they have the greatest share in total export of all TDZs in Turkey.

To sum up, in all of the TDZs in Ankara, it is seen that there are efforts for R&D activities that are essential for innovativeness. However, it is not sufficient enough for a competitive global system. For creating the synergy and increasing the innovation capacity, the share of knowledge, based on university–industry and interfirm relations are crucial. However, in all of the TDZs it has not been established sufficiently yet.

9.4 Conclusion

In the integration to the global system and catching-up competitiveness, it is required to build up innovative capacity in the regions and thus in the nations. Innovativeness as a system requires different organizations where various interactive actors take place. The affective role of government in terms of the provision of supportive institutional arrangements as well as funding for R&D and skill development for the support of science and technology and the interactions between firms and other organizations for the creation of knowledge help to build up national and regional innovation systems.

In building national and regional innovation systems, Turkey tries to integrate two models of innovation, the top-down linear model and the bottom-up interactive model simultaneously. From a top-down approach, based on thinking and policy-making, there have been substantial developments for the past two decades in Turkey. The input and output indices of the R&D in Turkey show that there has been an effort to increase the expenditures on R&D, with the expectation to increase the innovativeness of the society. On the other hand, by the new millennium, TDZs have possessed a fundamental role in order to create an interactive model from a bottom-up approach. In this approach for a regionally embedded innovation system, there is the need to establish collective capabilities, raise awareness of enterprises about new developments and their access to the system, and develop a local system of technical knowledge and services by strengthening the links between local firms and technology supply institutions in the long run.

For building up RIS in Ankara, five TDZs have been approved by the Council of Ministers since 2001 with the acceptance of the Law of TDZs. Among these five TDZs, three of them are active, which shows that it takes time to create an integrated system of local firms...

The three TDZs in Ankara, in supporting innovativeness, provide various facilities for high-tech firms both by incubation centers and TDZs. For start-up firms, incubation centers have crucial roles to play, but there are some difficulties in the transfer of start-up firms to TDZs after their graduation. For maintaining the innovativeness, it is important for the firms to pass from start-up to on-going business period. For this reason, successful start-up firms should be supported by different mechanisms to get over these difficulties.

The relations with the firms located in TDZs and universities appear to be limited, whereas it is crucial to integrate the scientific knowledge with production. It is seen that technology transfer from university to industry, creation of spin-off firms established by academicians, and commercialization of research findings are limited in all the TDZs. The advantages of spatial closeness between university and industry cannot be utilized effectively in Ankara as yet. Furthermore, university–industry linkages may become stronger after the experiences lived by the actors. By supporting sectoral specializations in each technopark, it might be more possible to increase this interaction and create an interactive learning-based system.

Within this context, it is early to evaluate the innovativeness of TDZs since they are still new initiations for Turkey. Time is needed for creating an innovative milieu where trust-based networks among firms and institutional thickness are maintained. It is believed that in the coming years with the support of its ever-growing young population, and their request for knowledge and learning, Turkish economy and innovativeness will take new strides with the boost it will get from the wider recourse to R&D.

References

Cooke, P., Heidenreich, M. and Braczyk H.J. (2004). Regional innovation systems: the role of governance in a globalized world. London, 2nd edition, New York, NY: Routledge.

Cilingir, C. (2004). Technology development zones: tools for enhancing university industry relations, Knowledge Economic Forum. Barcelona: Unpublished Presentation.

DPT (1985). Besinci bes yillik kalkinma plani 1985–1989. Ankara: Devlet Planlama Teskilati Mustesarligi, Yayin No: 1974. http://ekutup.dpt.gov.tr/plan/plan5.pdf. Cited 18 Nov 2006

DPT (1990). Altinci bes yillik kalkinma plani 1990–1994. Ankara: Devlet Planlama Teskilati Mustesarligi, Yayin No: 2174.

http://ekutup.dpt.gov.tr/plan/plan6.pdf. Cited 18 Nov 2006

DPT (1996). Yedinci bes yillik kalkinma plani 1995–2000. Ankara: Devlet Planlama Teskilati Mustesarligi.

http://ekutup.dpt.gov.tr/plan/vii/. Cited 18 Nov 2006

Elci, S. (2003). Innovation policy in seven candidate countries: the challenges, innovation policy profile: Turkey. Final Report, Volume 2, ADE—SSEES—LOGOTECH.

Galbraith, K. (2002). Technology parks become a force in Europe, Chronicle of Higher Education, 48(18), 120–35.

Goker, A., and Akarsoy, T. (1996). Turkiye'nin bilim ve teknoloji politikasi. I. Turkiye Endustri Muhendisligi Ogrencileri Bulusmasi, Teknoloji Politikalari ve Teknoloji Yonetimi Semineri. Denizli.

Karabulut, Z. (2006). Teknoloji gelistirme bolgeleri. 3. Teknoparklar Zirvesi. Istanbul: ITO Meclis Salonu Bogazici Universitesi.

http://teknozirve.org.tr/files/documents/ZiyaKarabulut.ppt. Cited 21 Feb 2007

Lundvall, B.A. (ed.) (1992). National systems of innovation: towards a theory of innovation and interactive learning. London: Pinter.

Nelson, R.R. (ed.) (1993). National systems of innovation: a comparative study. Oxford: Oxford University Press.

OECD (2002a) The measurement of scientific and technological activities. Frascati Manual 2002: Proposed standard practice for surveys on research and experimental development. Paris: OECD.

OECD (2002b). Benchmarking industry-science relationships. Paris: OECD.

OECD (2005) Science, technology and industry: Scoreboard 2005. http://oberon. sourceoecd.org. Cited 08 May 2006.

Pakpese, O. (1996). Dunyada teknopark uygulamalari ve Turkiye'de serbest bolge statusunde teknopark modeli. Ankara: Basbakanlik Dis Ticaret Mustesarligi: Unpublished Document.

Sanayi Bakanligi (2007). Kurulusu tamamlanan teknoloji gelistirme bolgeleri. http://www.sanayi. gov.tr. Cited 08 May 2007

Soubbotina, T. P. (2006). Generic models of technological learning by developing countries. World Bank: draft papers prepared for WB science and technology program.

TUBITAK (1997). Turkiye'nin bilim ve teknoloji politikasi, Bilim ve Teknoloji Strateji ve Politika Calismalari, Ankara: BTP 97/04.

TUBITAK (2007). Vizyon 2023. Bilim, teknoloji ve yenilik politikalari daire baskanligi.

http://www.tubitak.gov.tr/home.do?ot=1&sid=472&pid=468. Cited 19 May 2007

TUIK (2007). 2005 yili arastirma ve gelistirme faaliyetleri arastirmasi. Haber Bulteni, 129.

Varol, C., Sat, N.A., Gurel Ucer, Z.A. & Yilmaz, G. (2007). Kuresel sisteme entegrasyonda yenilikci uretim kapasitesinin rolu: Turkiye teknoparklari uzerinden bir degerlendirme (The Role of Innovative Production Capacity in the Integration to the Global System: An Evaluation over Technoparks in Turkey). Ankara: Unpublished Research Report.

10 Innovation Ability of Small Firms in Turkish Industrial Clusters: Ankara-Ivedik Industrial Region Case

Özlem Özkanli and Erdal Akdeve

Abstract

Research and development activities (R&D) of small firms forming innovation have to be improved because of the insufficiency of financial, technical, and human resources. Innovation ability, which would actually support firm activity, is uncommon by small firms. This fact evidently causes a disadvantage for the small firms to compete in comparison with middle and large-scale firms. However, the disadvantaged situation of small firms arising from their economies of scale can be converted to an advantageous situation by forming a network of organizations in clusters. According to the literature reviewed, small firms within clusters improve in the field of innovation by intensity of communication and interaction, relative ease of information flow, ability of creating collective learning effects, and mutual budget for R&D studies. This study examines the existence of this interaction among firms, as in the case of Ankara-Ivedik Organized Industrial District by a survey depending upon questionnaire information.

10.1 Introduction

Today, competition has become much more dynamic. Global procurement business activities can compensate the disadvantages brought by the costs of factors of production, whereby the age-old idea of competitive capacity loses its importance (Arndt and Sternberg 2000).

During the last decades, regional concentration and competitiveness of small firms became important topics of discussion on how to develop the competitive ability of small firms, whereby large firms

N. Aydogan (ed.), *Innovation Policies, Business Creation and Economic Development,*
International Studies in Entrepreneurship 21, DOI 10.1007/978-0-387-79976-6_10,
© Springer Science+Business Media, LLC 2009

enjoy economies of scale and scope. In order to overcome difficulties resulting from economies of scale, small firms require the benefit arising from the effects of network interaction. Hence, small firms operating under network interaction within industrial clusters would have greater competitive ability, which cannot be attained by the small firms individually. In a study conducted by Hoen (2001), it was found that industrial clusters were, in general, inclined to use more innovations, knowledge spillovers, and experience faster diffusion of technologies and knowledge, which result in an increase in their competitive advantages.

By developed countries or by countries where the economic policies rely upon industrialization as an indispensable factor to achieve growth, R&D, innovative activities, gaining ability generating diversity, and competitiveness, proximity and allied concepts became crucial issues of the economic research and debate. Consequently, innovation has increasingly been viewed as the deciding factor on whether a company, business sector, region, or country will be able to retain and improve its competitive position in the world economy (OECD 2000).

Comparing Turkey with the developed countries, it will be observed that the R&D activities are rather lower than usual (Taymaz 2001). R&D's share in GNP is about 2 percent in developed countries, whereas about 40 personnel among every 10,000 economically active populations are employed in the R&D activities. On the other hand, in Turkey, total R&D expenditures reaches 0.8 percent of the GNP, and only about 10 personnel are engaged in R&D activities among every 10,000 economically active populations (KOSGEB 2007). In this respect, it is noteworthy that the small-scale firms of Turkey are usually not capable of forming a program and an appropriate budget for an R&D unit for reasons related to market position, organizational peculiarities, and certain social effects, although there is no lack of intention to set up such a unit (Akgemici 2001).

This chapter will focus on an empirical study of industrial clusters and innovation capability of small firms in the Ankara-Ivedik industrial region. The methodology and findings of the case study will be explained after a short discussion on the subject and research problems within a theoretical framework on industrial clusters and innovative capability.

10.2 Theoretical Framework

10.2.1 Industrial Clusters and Small-Sized Firms

The literature cluster and industrial district are frequently used interchangeably. However, the term "cluster" will rather be used for a more extensive perspective with respect to the term "industrial districts." Isaksen (2001) explains that every industrial district is a cluster, whilst a cluster is not necessarily an industrial district. Actually, both clusters and industrial districts generate external economies. In this context, the cluster concept relates to the achievement of increased efficiency through extensive external division of labor within the networks of specialized firms (Isaksen 2001). Regional cluster and regional innovation systems have started to take a critical place in the world economy for both the traditional (e.g. in the industrial districts in Turkey) and high technology products (e.g. in the Silicon Valley).

The industrial–district environment places each district company within a web of relationships, which deeply influence its activities and performance. Within this context, the business idea embodies, ever since the company's start-up, certain specific interfirm relationships as an essential feature of its survival and performance potential. Access to the market, marketing, and R&D activities would then start to execute with the help of joint initiatives among many firms (Ritter and Gemünden 2003). That strategic cooperation will in turn increase interaction among firms.

According to conventional classification, industrial clusters in terms of important linkages, complementary and technological abilities, knowledge, marketing, and customer demands determine the spillovers in some broader sense. Such linkages for firms and industries are essential bases for competition and efficiency, and especially for direct new business areas and innovation (Porter 1998).

Industrial clusters are defined and referred as key structures for competitive ability of small and medium firms. Porter (1998) points out the rivalry as an explanation for the success of the clusters. Cooperation among firms in clusters has been viewed and deeply studied as a powerful determinant of the competitive advantage of clusters and of the individual firms in such clusters (Boari et al. 2003). Clustering of economic activity seems to enable firms, and especially the SMEs to grow and upgrade more easily (Altenburg and Meyer-Stamer 1999). Moreover, geographical agglomeration provides capital market, pool of labor, and interfirm relations for SMEs. Capello (1999) claims that if SMEs are located in a cluster, they would be initially influenced by greater capital and higher labor productivity.

Nadvi (1995) mentions that clusters offer unique opportunities for SMEs to engage in the wide array of domestic linkages between users and producers that stimulate learning and innovation (e.g. especially by the knowledge producing sectors). Reaching external knowledge is not quite easy for SMEs. However, cluster can help SMEs to provide external knowledge by its mechanism of information flows among different economic actors. Firms of cluster exchange and create knowledge through face-to-face interactions together with the creation of a common language among institutions and associations.

The emergence of clusters can be explained by several theoretical approaches. In the literature, studies by Krugman (1991) and Porter (1998) are well known as presenting fundamental sources about the emergence of clusters. While Krugman attempts to stress upon the role of interaction between factors that cause localization, Porter points out the positive effects of "agglomeration economies" as the reason for the existence of clusters Hoen (2001). A model designed by Krugman (1991) tries to explain the emergence of clusters on the transportation costs, mobile production factors, and economies of scope and scale.

10.2.2 Innovation and Small Firms in Industrial Cluster

Thompson (1965), who forwarded one of the essential studies about innovation, defines it as diffusion, acceptance, and execution of new ideas concerning process, product, or service. Similarly, Zaltman (1973), Roger (1995), Amabile et al. (1996), Johnson et al. (1997), Moorman and Miner (1998), and Verona (1999) reflect innovation process as acquisition, diffusion, and explosion of new knowledge.

Calantone et al. (2002) associate innovation factor studying the relationship among learning orientation, firm innovativeness, and firm performance with organizational learning, and also adopt learning orientation as a model approach that is a start point or basement for firm innovativeness effecting firm performance.

The importance of knowledge spillover and innovation inputs emphasize that R&D activities do not develop in isolation (Nelson 1993). Several studies in the literature reveal direct linkages between innovation level and the existence of R&D in industrial clusters (Braunerhjelm and Carlsson 1999).

Since the end of the 1960s, industrial economists, sociologists, and local economists have begun to take interest in the constellations of small companies being concentrated in specific areas that have been termed as industrial districts (Brusco and Pezzini 19990). Firms in industrial districts dispose of capabilities to store and develop knowledge through their established rules and routines as well as through specific documentation procedures, as Nelson & Winter (1982) have shown. In recent approaches to the theory of the firm, firms have been considered not only as repositories of knowledge, but also as processors of knowledge (Amin and Cohendet 2000).

Baptista and Swann (1998), in their study stating that firms in clusters have more innovative activities, explain the relationship between clusters and innovations from four different aspects, namely: nature of clustering process, nature of technology, nature of innovation process, and nature of economic growth. One of the main reasons for the existence and success of clusters' technological innovation seemed to be the wider spread of knowledge or spillovers (Baptista and Swann 1998).

10.2.3 Innovation Capability of Small Firms

The largest problem to determine the factors of innovation ability was a lack of appropriate and qualified technology or R&D personnel. The next most important problem was excessive economic risk, since most of an enterprise's main information sources come from customers. The third category arose within the enterprises (Hsien-Ta Wang et al. 2003).

In the early 1990s in particular, increasing criticism was leveled at the exclusive orientation of R&D support toward large enterprises, which were mostly enhancing their competitive advantage by downsizing operations and reducing employment EC (2003). In parallel with the development of the theoretical approach toward the national systems of innovation, practitioners (especially in the EU) were pointing out the existence of the SME problem. In practice, the innovation-systems approach stimulates policy actions in SMEs, in order to enhance technology diffusion between actors, and to increase the absorptive capacity of these companies.

Relatively smaller scale of firms might also prevent the achievement for specialized and effective internal division of labor that, according to classical economic theory, fosters cumulative improvements in productive capabilities and innovation (Ceglie and Dini 1999).

In particular, although dynamic SMEs have a strong potential to create new ideas, innovations, and employment, they will be, on the other hand, hindered by weak access to knowledge resources and finance due to relatively high fixed costs, and especially high information and administrative costs, if they intend to participate in research programs (Bessant 1999).

10.3 Research Methodology

10.3.1 Research Questions

The present research work depends upon a developed model to determine effects influencing research and development activities of SMEs. After specifying the effects on the availability R&D leading to the creation of a new product, the relationship between the innovation and the availability of R&D activity was investigated. Innovation capability is then evaluated by the degree of introducing the new product. R&D activities here are considered as a process to form a new product, which would locate the firm into a competitively advantageous position in the market. The R&D activity gives rise to knowledge, which is valuable both for directly commercializing a product, and for being the basis for a new and better version of the product (Fosfuri and Ronde 2002).

In this respect, it should be kept in mind that shortage of skilled personnel in small-scale firms prevents these firms from realizing effective technological R&D activities and bringing out technological innovation. Moreover, laboratory activities might be intended to provide testing and certification services, but will eventually be fully engaged in technology development (Cooke 2001). Also to be taken into consideration is that the trade fairs, which provide leading sources of information within the industrial clusters, will have a core function in improving flows of technical and marketing know-how, in providing quality and fashion feedback, and in enhancing the competitiveness of clustered and networked producers (Nadvi 1995). In that sense, participation in fairs would mean that new potential customers will be contacted, and that results in new interactions that bring in ideas and opportunities for innovation.

Accordingly, the first research question in the study defines the determinants of the R&D activities related to new product development as:

- Skilled personnel,
- Quality improvement initiatives,
- Availability of laboratories,
- Training and development activities,
- Use of computer for production, and
- Participation in fairs.

The question can be set as follows: *Is there a relationship between these determinants and the availability of research and development activities?*

Related to the preceding question, the second level of the investigation concerns the innovation ability of the firms. In order to determine the innovation ability of the firms in the industrial district, the relationship between the degree of new product development and the availability of R&D might be analyzed. R&D activities are defined as one of the main effects for making innovation. Firms with increased degree of R&D availability have strong intentions to realize innovations (Taymaz 2001). From this point of view, the research examines the relationship between the level of innovation ability and the R&D activities.

Hence the related question might be formulated as follows: *Does the level of innovation ability depend on the availability of research and development activities leading to new product innovation?*

As a result, firms being surveyed are (according to the determinants defined in the preceding sentence) classified as "potential innovators" and "noninnovators." Potential innovators are then defined as firms with R&D activities, while noninnovators are found being deprived of R&D activities.

10.3.2 Background Data

The study as such is a theory application. Hence it utilizes a research methodology based on a questionnaire survey. The questionnaire survey was applied on the small-sized manufacturing firms in the "Ankara-Ivedik Organized Industrial District" (Ivedik OID). Ivedik OID, established on an area of 477 hectares, is one of the most important small-sized industry complexes in Turkey. Machinery, chemicals, metal works, wood works, plastics, printing, and construction equipment are the main manufacturing sectors of the district. Ivedik OID is a center, which brings all support units required for quality manufacturing together with manufacturers.

Data were collected from 314 firms. In order to determine the present situation exactly and to reach at accurate results, "face-to-face interview" method was used for collecting data. For that reason, there was no problem of response rate. In accordance with the statistical criterion of the EU for small firms, the small firms were composed of 10–50 employees. The EU definition entails furthermore that SMEs should yearly have achieved less than € 25 million sales. (OECD 2004; TOBBKOSGEB 2002).

Data obtained by applying questionnaire forms were systematically analyzed. The interpreted results came out as shown in the coming section.

10.3.3 Analysis

Concerning the first research question, the analysis was based upon the data as shown in Table 10.1. The relationship between independent variables has been listed in the table, and the availability of R&D activities has been tested. There were 202 firms, for which it was stated that they had research and development activities (i.e. Yes group), and there were 112 firms for which the answer was negative (i.e. No group).

Binomial test has been used to find out whether the variables listed in Table 10.1 have an impact on the availability of R&D activities and, therefore, in terms of the statistical hypotheses.

$H_0 : p = 0.5$

$H_1 : p \neq 0.5$

Table 10.1 Availability of R&D activities

Independent variables	Availability of R&D activities	
	Yes	No
Skilled personnel	1582	366
Quality improvement initiatives	136	70
The availability of laboratories	66	15
R&D activities	120	29
Use of computer for production	140	40
Participation in fairs	104	41

If a variable has an impact on the availability of research and development, it is expected that the proportion of that variable to the total is higher in the "yes" group—of course at its computed level of significance. On the other hand, if the same proportion is higher in the "no" group, it would result in the opposite (e.g. in case of quality improvement initiatives, it would mean that the majority of firms do not have adequate quality improvement initiatives)—again the result to be accepted at its level of significance. If "yes" and "no" are distributed evenly, this fact would rather imply that, for example the quality improvement initiatives will not be considered as a significant factor.

We started by considering the results of the binomial test for the number of skilled and nonskilled personnel. Note that only in this group the number of persons is taken as a unit of measurement, and by all of the others the data presented are given in number of firms. The criterion for success (denoted by 1) in the "yes" group (X1) is the number of skilled persons, and criterion of success (denoted by 1) for the "no" group (X2) is the number of nonskilled personnel. Skilled persons were composed of university, vocational school, or technical high school graduates. The others were classified as nonskilled personnel.

The results of the significance test are presented in Table 10.2. As can be seen from Table 10.2, the hypothesis $p = 0.5$ is rejected for both possibilities. So the proportion of nonskilled personnel is higher in each group. But this proportion is 0.64 in the "yes" group and 0.22 in the "no" group. In the light of the data, it can be said that the proportion of nonskilled personnel is higher in the "no group".

For the binomial test being used for quality improvement initiatives, the results are presented in Table 10.3 where $p = 0.5$ is again rejected.

Table 10.2 Test results for the existence of skilled persons

		Category	N	Observed prop.	Test prop.	Asymp. sig. (2-tailed)
X1	Group 1	1	1581	0.36	0.50	0.000
	Group 2	0	2789	0.64		
	Total		4370	1.00		
X2	Group 1	1	1304	0.78	0.50	0.000
	Group 2	0	366	0.22		
	Total		1670	1.00		

Table 10.3 Test results for quality improvement initiatives

		Category	N	Observed prop.	Test prop.	Asymp. sig. (2-tailed)
X1	Group 1	1	136	0.67	0.50	0.000
	Group 2	0	66	0.33		
	Total		202	1.00		
X2	Group 1	1	42	0.38	0.50	0.011
	Group 2	0	70	0.63		
	Total		112	1.00		

Table 10.4 Test results for the availability of laboratories

		Category	N	Observed prop.	Test prop.	Asymp. sig. (2-tailed)
X1	Group 1	1	66	0.33	0.50	0.000
	Group 2	0	136	0.67		
	Total		202	1.00		
X2	Group 1	1	97	0.87	0.50	0.000
	Group 2	0	15	0.13		
	Total		112	1.00		

Interestingly enough, the proportion of firm managers saying that they have quality improvement initiatives is approximately the same for both groups.

The results of the test concerning the impact of availability of laboratories on the availability of R&D activities are presented in Table 10.4 where $p = 0.5$ will again be rejected. But the impact of the laboratory possession reveals clearly different proportions between two groups. Although most of the firms do not possess any laboratory

Table 10.5 Test results on the existence of training and development activities

		Category	N	Observed prop.	Test prop.	Asymp. sig. (2-tailed)
X1	Group 1	1	120	0.59	0.50	0.009
	Group 2	0	82	0.41		
	Total		202	1.00		
X2	Group 1	1	83	0.74	0.50	0.000
	Group 2	0	29	0.26		
	Total		112	1.00		

in two groups, the proportion of the laboratory availability is higher in the "yes" group.

In the variable of "training and development activities," $p = 0.5$ hypothesis at 5 percent significance is rejected for both groups. Most of the firms have training and development activities in the "yes" group (59 percent of them have training and development activities). On the other hand, most of the firms in the "no" group do not have training and development activities (74 percent of the firms do not have training and development activities). The results are presented in Table 10.5. Firms in the "yes" group seem to be more willing to train employees and develop their processes than the firms in the "no" group.

Use of computer in production was also subjected to the binomial test. As can be seen from Table 10.6, $p = 0.5$ is again rejected for both groups. However, the proportion of computer use in production for the "yes" group is substantially higher than that of the "no" group. Whilst 69 percent of firms in the "yes" group use the computer in production process, just 36 percent of the firms in the "no" group make use of computers in production.

Table 10.6 Test results on the Computer use in production

		Category	N	Observed prop.	Test prop.	Asymp. sig. (2-tailed)
X1	Group 1	1	140	0.69	0.50	0.000
	Group 2	0	62	0.31		
	Total		202	1.00		
X2	Group 1	1	72	0.64	0.50	0.003
	Group 2	0	40	0.36		
	Total		112	1.00		

Table 10.7 Test results on the participation in the fairs

		Category	N	Observed prop.	Test prop.	Asymp. sig. (2-tailed)
X1	Group 1	1	104	0.51	0.50	0.725
	Group 2	0	98	0.49		
	Total		202	1.00		
X2	Group 1	1	71	0.63	0.50	0.006
	Group 2	0	41	0.37		
	Total		112	1.00		

As a last variable defined for impact on R&D activities, the test results for participation in fairs indicates that the $p = 0.5$ hypothesis is accepted for the "yes" group, meaning that half of the firms in the "yes" group are participating in the fairs. On the other hand, the hypothesis for the "no" group is rejected and, as can be seen from Table 10.7, 63 percent of the firms in the "no" group are not participating in the fairs.

As an overall evaluation, it can be asserted that the proportions of skilled persons, of firms stating that they have quality improvement initiatives, possess laboratory, training and development activities, use computer in their activities, and participate in the fairs are higher for the firms stating that they have R&D activities.

It should be taken into account that all of these firms are SMEs. As can be seen from Table 10.2, although the proportion of skilled personnel is higher in the "yes" group, most of their employees are nonskilled. Table 10.3 shows that the proportion of firms that have quality improvement initiatives is approximately the same for both the "yes" and "no" group of firms. These results indicate that both groups of firms do emphasize quality improvement. The managers attribute greater importance in production than R&D. However, if Table 10.4 is examined, it will be seen that most of the firms in the "yes" and "no" groups do not possess laboratories, which is enough evidence that their main concern is not R&D. These findings confirm that most SMEs are production oriented rather than being interested in creating designs and trademarks.

As for the second research question of the paper, the relationship between the new product development and the availability of R&D was tested. The fundamental data for this test is presented in Table 10.8.

Table 10.8 Availability of R&D activities and new product development

Independent variable		New product development	
		Yes	No
Availability of R&D	Yes	118	84
	No	62	50

Table 10.9 Results of the Chi-squared analysis upon the fourfold data in Table 10.8

	Value	Df	Asymp. sig. (2-sided)	Exact sig. (2-sided)	Exact sig. (1-sided)
Pearson Chi-square	0.276	1	0.600		
Continuity correction	0.165	1	0.685		
Likelihood ratio	0.275	1	0.600		
Fisher's Exact test				0.635	0.342
Linear-by-linear association	0.275	1	0.600		
N of valid cases	314				

The analysis was done by means of applying chi-squared test. Here, one of the variables is "availability of R&D" and another variable is "new product development." Chi-squared analysis was performed on the bases of the following hypothesis:

H_0 = There is no relationship between availability of R&D and new product development.

Test results are presented in Table 10.9.

As can be seen from Table 10.9, the hypothesis is not accepted at appropriately high levels of significance. The finding thus reveals that there is no sensible relationship between "availability of R&D" and "new product development."

10.4 Conclusion

The determinants of the R&D activities related to new product development were taken as the number of skilled personnel, quality improvement initiatives, availability of laboratories, training and development activities, use of computer on production, and participation in the fairs. The relationship between these determinants and the availability of R&D activities were investigated. According to the binomial test results, for most of the SMEs the hypotheses for the determinants (except the hypotheses of "training and development activities" and "participation in fairs") of the R&D activities are rejected. On the other hand, the proportion of independent variables with impact on availability of the R&D activities are found higher in the "yes" group, which indicates the availability of R&D activities in the firms under investigation.

In case the hypotheses are accepted, there is a positive impact of "training and development activities" on the availability of R&D activities. In industrial complexes (such as a cluster, a district, or a network of small-scale firms), training and development activities that were organized by district administration seem to be very important for the R&D performance. The firms attending these training and development activities are considered to increase their competitive advantage, since the output of R&D activities is usually new product development.

"Participation in fairs" is another hypothesis being accepted by means of statistical analysis. It is determined that there is a direct impact of participation in fairs on the availability of R&D activity in firms. Participation in fairs enables the firm managers to meet R&D experts and reach the know-how of new products in the sector.

Furthermore, the relationship between innovation and the availability of the R&D activity was investigated by the chi-square test. Innovation capability was represented by the new product development. In the light of the statistical analysis, it is found that there is no relationship between availability of R&D and new product development in the Ankara-Ivedik Industrial Region case. It is interesting to note that the managers from the firms without R&D activities have stated the availability of new product development. This paradox can be explained with the high participation rate in the fairs. The managers of these firms participating in the fairs may adopt or integrate the new product forms easily into their production processes without intensive R&D activities.

It is evident that the nature of the compiled data restricts the outcomes. Future research providing longitudinal studies might contribute to theory. This research may then be comprehended as a basis for a further macro study.

References

Bapista, R., Swann, P. (1998). Do firms in clusters innovate more? *Research Policy*, 27, 525–540.

Bessant, J. (1999). The rise and fall of 'Supernet': a case study of technology transfer policy for smaller firms. *Research Policy*, 28, 6, 601–614.

Boari, C., Odorici, V., Zamarian, M. (2003). Clusters and rivalry: does localization really matter? *Scandinavian Journal of Management*, 19, 467–489.

Brusco, S., Pezzini, M. (1990). Small-scale enterprise in the ideology of the Italian Left. In: F. Pyke, G. Becattini, W. Sengenberger (1992), *Industrial Districts and Inter-firm Co-operation in Italy*, International Institute for Labour Studies. Geneva (142–159).

Ceglie, G., Dini, M. (1999). SME cluster and network development in developing countries: the experience of UNIDO. UNIDO Private Sector Development Branch: Vienna.

Cooke, P. (2001). Strategies for Regional Innovation Systems: Learning Transfer and Applications. Prepared for UNIDO World Industrial Development Report (WIDR). Centre for Advanced Studies, Cardiff University: Cardiff CF10 3BB.

EC (2003). European Commission, Third European Report on Science & Technology Indicators, Toward A Knowledge Based Economy. European Commission Directorate-General for Research Information and Communication Unit: Brussels

Fosfuri, A., Ronde, T. (2002). High-tech clusters, technology spillovers, and trade secret laws. Scandinavian Working Papers in Economics, No: 07-2002, Copenhagen Business School: Copenhagen.

Hsien-Ta Wang et al. (2003). A survey for technological innovation in Taiwan. *Journal of Data Science*, 1, 337–360.

Hoen, A. (2001). Clusters: determinants and effects. CPB Memorandum 17, CPB Netherlands Bureau for Economic Policy Analysis. Available via http://www.cpb.nl/eng/pub/memorandum

KOSGEB (2007). Tekmer'ler ve Ar-Ge Destekleri, Available via www.teknokent.org.tr

Krugman, P. (1991). *Geography and Trade*. Cambridge: MIT Press.

Nadvi, K. (1995). Industrial Clusters and Networks: Case Studies of SME Growth and Innovation, Paper commissioned by the Small and Medium Industries Branch, UNIDO.

OECD (2004). Small and Medium-Sized Enterprises in Turkey: Issues and Politics. OECD Publications. Available via www.oecd.org.

Porter, M. (1998). Clusters and new economics of competition. *Harvard Business Review*, 76 (6), 77–90.

TOBB-KOSGEB (1997). KOBI Rehberi. Ankara: TOBB Genel Yayını.

Part III
Small and Medium-Sized Enterprises and Growth

11 Innovation Strategies and Innovation Problems in Small and Medium-Sized Enterprises: An Empirical Study

Ismail Bakan and Bulent Yildiz

Abstract

Innovation may become the basis of all competition in the future. Therefore, organizational theorists and managers alike have long shown more interest in the role of innovation in organizations, primarily due to the crucial role innovation plays in securing sustained competitive advantage. As organizations attempt to get competitive advantage, they develop and/or adopt new products, processes, techniques, or procedures. The aim of the study is to investigate the innovation activities in Small and Medium-Sized Enterprises (SMEs). The survey collected information about product and process innovation as well as organizational and marketing innovation. The research data were collected by the questionnaires applied in the cities of Gaziantep and Kahramanmaras. The data were analyzed by using the SPSS program.

11.1 Introduction

Innovation—the introduction of new and/or improvement of products, services and production processes, or marketing methods is the driving force of a nation's economic growth and development, enhancing quality of life, and the improvement of competitiveness of its firms (Oerlemans et al. 2001).

Unfortunately, it seems necessary to point out to many companies around the world that the source of competitive advantage has changed. It is now very difficult to create differentiation in the marketplace from just technology, as companies did in the 1970s, or

N. Aydogan (ed.), *Innovation Policies, Business Creation and Economic Development,*   177
International Studies in Entrepreneurship 21, DOI 10.1007/978-0-387-79976-6_11,
© Springer Science+Business Media, LLC 2009

from high levels of quality, as was the case in the 1980s. To succeed in today's fast changing marketplace, companies must provide both through a process of innovating to match customers' needs. Now, this might seem blindingly obvious when spelled out, yet it only takes a quick look around at businesses to realize how many still get it completely wrong; many companies do not innovate to match customers' needs. Therefore, any processes, methods, or ideas that can help to facilitate more effective innovation within a company are extremely important (Lee-Mortimer 1995).

In today's fast-paced business environment and competitive marketplace, innovation is a prerequisite for success and perhaps even for survival. This is why innovation has found its way to the top of the agenda at organizations throughout the world. Once considered primarily an output of Research and Development (R&D) labs, innovation has become a corporate priority that touches every facet of, and indeed every employee in an organization (AMA 2006). The transformation of new ideas into commercial success requires equal attention to be paid, on the one hand, to the research and experimental development (R&D) and the technological factors of innovation, and on the other, to the social, institutional, and market factors that play a crucial role in innovation (South African Innovation Survey 2005). External constituents too—customers, academia, the government, vendors, even competitors—are playing a growing and an important role in companies' creative processes (AMA 2006). Therefore, there should be a growing awareness not only among entrepreneurs, but also among policy makers and scientists—innovation should be in the center of attention of business and policy strategies (Oerlemans et al. 2001)

As innovation drives growth and opportunity in the new markets, and breathes life into a mature industry, executives at all levels have a responsibility to lead and motivate innovative thinking across the entire enterprise. Stockholders, employees, and customers count on executives to create and develop a healthy, innovative work environment (AMA 2006).

The importance of innovation as a driver of sustainable development, performance, and competitive advantage is well covered in the literature (McEvily et al. 2004; Shoham and Fieganbaum 2002; Roberts 1999; Hitt e al. 1996; Banbury and Mitchell 1995). Kanter (1999) encapsulates the benefits of innovation by mentioning that "winning in business today demands innovation." However, existing studies on innovation focus largely on drivers of product development such as creativity, resource availability, mergers, acquisitions, divestitures, downsizing, and cost reduction as well as the firm size. More recently, attention has focused on the need to meet customer expectations and demands in shorter product cycles using flexible manufacturing systems (O'Regan and Ghobadian 2005).

There may be an abundance of literature on the topic of innovation, and innovation may be at the top of the agenda among global executives. Nevertheless, most organizations enjoy only moderate success in managing the innovation process (AMA 2006).Why are so many organizations struggling to master such a critical and important aspect of their business strategy? To answer this question and capture current thinking on innovation, and identify best practices, an extensive literature review was done and an empirical study was conducted for this chapter.

This chapter aims to focus attention toward innovation activities in the SMEs. There are only a small number of empirical studies in Turkey examining innovation activities. Accordingly, this study fills an important gap. This chapter is structured as follows: first, the word of "innovation" is defined and types of innovation are explained; second, the critical role of innovation in corporate success is mentioned; third, "innovation strategy" is explained; fourth, the findings of recent surveys on innovation are mentioned; fifth, factors for driving and curbing innovation are explained; sixth, characteristics of an innovative culture are described; seventh, the empirical study is evaluated, and analysis is depicted and interpreted; and finally, this chapter presents conclusions and recommendations for the future.

11.2 Definition of Innovation

In the innovation literature, there are different definitions of innovation. Innovation is defined as:

- Implementing new ideas that create value (Linder et al. 2003).
- The implementation of a new or significantly improved product (goods or services) or process, a new marketing method, or a new organizational method in business practices, workplace organization, or external relations (U.S. Census Bureau 2006).

- A new or significantly improved product (goods or services) introduced to the market or the introduction within your enterprise of a new or significantly improved process (Innovation Survey 2000–2009).
- The ability to define and create new products and services, and quickly bring them to market—an increasingly important source of competitive advantage (Terziovski 2004).

These definitions relate to the various forms that innovation can take, such as product development, the deployment of new process technologies, innovative management practices, new organizational methods, or new marketing methods (Zott 2003; Glynn 1996). In other words, innovation activities comprise the generation, use and diffusion of new knowledge, methods, processes, and products within organizations and in the market (South African Innovation Survey 2005).

Innovations of products, services, and production processes or marketing methods are the result of the development or the use of a completely new or recently developed technologies, like information technologies, technical sciences, or other technology related disciplines. These products, services, processes, and methods can be labeled as technologically new or strongly improved (Oerlemans et al. 2001). Therefore, it can be said that the innovation is based on the results of new technological developments, new combinations of existing technology, or utilization of other knowledge acquired by an enterprise (Innovation Survey 2000–2009).

However, one may describe innovation not as an essentially technological phenomenon, but rather as a phenomenon of a psychological and sociocultural nature because those are the keys to its success or failure. The adoption process for new products, processes, or methods varies from one individual to another according to characteristics such as demographics (age, place of residence, etc.), socioeconomics (salary, social class, etc.), psychographics (personality, open-mindedness, etc.), and culture (value system, ethnicity, etc.) (Daghfous et al. 1999).

Is there any difference between the words "invention" and "innovation?" In recent years, "innovative" has been increasingly used to make an important distinction from "mere invention." Invention is the first part where something new is created; innovation is getting an invention *all the way* to a product (Stefik and Stefik 2004); invention is having an idea; innovation is the remaining 99 percent of the work. From a business perspective, innovation is "taking new technology and realizing its economic potential." The creative insights of invention can happen in a flash. In contrast, innovation can take years (Stefik and Stefik 2004).

11.3 Types of Innovation

Over the last half century, the types of innovation that have been examined and the types of problems in which innovation scholars are interested have changed. The recent literature illustrates that there are various types of innovation (AMA 2006).

Innovation is the term used to describe how organizations create value by developing new knowledge and/or using existing knowledge in new ways. The term is often used to mean the development of new or significantly improved products or services, but organizations can also innovate in other ways, for example through new business models, management techniques, and organizational structures. The literature on innovation is very large and covers a wide range of topics (AMA 2006).

Innovation is defined as the implementation of a new or significantly improved product (goods or services) or process, new marketing methods, or a new organizational method in business practices, workplace organization, or external relations (U.S. Census Bureau 2006). As it is, in this definition, in recent innovation literature and the surveys on innovation indicate that there are four main types of innovations, namely (a) product, (b) process, (c) organizational, and (d) marketing.

11.3.1 Product (Goods or Service) Innovation

Product innovation—the development of new and improved products is crucial to the prosperity of the modern organization. As there is a strong connection between successful product development and business valuation (Strategic Direction 2004), improved and radically changed products are regarded as particularly important for long-term business growth (Hart 1996). The crucial power of product innovation in helping companies retain and grow to competitive position is indisputable. Products have to be updated and completely renewed for retaining strong market presence (Johne 1999).

Therefore, to survive in a demanding and turbulent competitive environment, companies are investing a growing amount of resources and managerial attention in product innovation. With pressures to decrease product development intervals and to increase the frequency of new product introductions, this attention is more and more continuous and the efforts involve partners outside the organizational boundaries, often on a global basis (Boer et al. 2001).

In the literature, there are different definitions of product innovation, but all definitions mention the same meaning with slightly different words. Product innovation is defined as:

- The market introduction of new goods or services, or a significantly improved goods or services with respect to its capabilities, such as improved software, user friendliness, components, or subsystems (The Fourth Community Innovation Survey CIS IV-2004).
- Introduction to the market of a new item of goods or service, of which buyers had not previously been aware, or the introduction of an improved version of an existing item of goods or service. This new version may include additional features or improved functionality (North Staffordshire UK DRIVE Partners 2006).
- Goods or services, which is either new or significantly improved with respect to its fundamental characteristics, technical specifications, incorporated software or other immaterial components, intended uses, or user friendliness (Innovation Survey 2000–2009).

The innovation (new or improved) must be new to an enterprise, but it does not need to be new to the sector or market. It does not matter if the innovation was originally developed by the enterprise or by other enterprises (The Fourth Community Innovation Survey CIS IV-2004). Changes of a solely aesthetically nature, and selling of innovations wholly produced and developed by other enterprises, shall not be included (Innovation Survey 2000–2009).

11.3.2 Process Innovation

Process innovation embraces quality function deployment and business process reengineering (Cumming 1998). It is a type of innovation which is not easy, but its aim is now well understood. An efficient supplier who keeps working on productivity gains can expect, over time, to develop products that provide the same performance at a lower cost. Such cost reductions may, or may not, be passed on to customers in the form of lower prices (Johne 1999). So, process innovation provides the means for safeguarding and improving quality and also for saving costs (Hart 1996).

A process innovation:

- Is the implementation of a new or significantly improved production process, distribution method, or support activity for goods or services (The Fourth Community Innovation Survey CIS IV-2004).
- Includes new and significantly improved production technology, new and significantly improved methods of supplying services and delivering products. The outcome should be significant with respect to the level of output, quality of products (goods/services) or costs of production and distribution (Innovation Survey 2000–2009).

11.3.3 Organizational Innovation

Innovation often means more than the creation of new or significantly improved products and services. It can mean innovation in terms of business models, management techniques and strategies, and organizational structures (Hamel 2006). The attempt to create new products and services may stimulate organizational, or what some term as "management innovation," or innovations such as new business models may arise to take advantage of the newly discovered market opportunities. One of the core reasons for organizational innovation is that established firms can lose not just their ability to innovate but also their insight into the necessity to innovate (AMA 2006).

An organizational innovation:

- Is the implementation of new or significant changes in firm structure or management methods that are intended to improve the firm's use of knowledge, the quality of its goods and services, or the efficiency of work flows? (The Fourth Community Innovation Survey CIS IV-2004).
- Includes new or significantly improved knowledge management systems; a major change to the organization of work; new or significant changes in a firm's relations with other firms or public

institutions such as through alliances, partnerships, outsourcing, or subcontracting (New in CIS IV).

The organizational innovation in the enterprise includes the:

- introduction of significantly changed organizational structures,
- implementation of advanced management techniques, and
- Implementation of new or substantially changed corporate strategic orientations (Innovation Survey 2000–2009).

11.3.4 Marketing Innovation

Marketing innovation is concerned with improving the mix of target markets and how chosen markets are best served. Its purpose is to identify better (new) potential markets and better (new) ways to serve target markets (Johne 1999).

Marketing innovation:

- Is the implementation of new or significantly improved designs or sales methods to increase the appeal of your goods and services, or to enter new markets? (The Fourth Community Innovation Survey CIS IV-2004).
- Includes significant changes to the design or packaging of goods or services; new or significant changes to sales or distribution methods such as internet sales, franchising, direct sales, or distribution licenses (New in CIS IV) (Jankowski 2006).

11.4 Innovation Is Critical to Corporate Success

Today's business environment is probably the most dynamic that any business has faced so far. Practically anything that can happen to business is happening to some company or other, as most attempt to minimize the fallout from price wars, continuous cost efficiency drives, and at the same time maximize new market opportunities (Amit and Zott 2001). In the literature, the critical role of innovation in corporate success is mentioned frequently with different statements. The following statements are as the examples:

- A business that is serious about competing in the fast changing markets with fast changing technology must make things happen;

it must innovate. If it does not innovate it risks being overtaken by competitors (Johne 1999).

- Top-performing global companies, much like their competitors, are banking on innovation to drive growth. But unlike their competitors, they are investing in the product development capabilities, the supply chain process infrastructure, and the sophisticated information systems needed to support and synchronize innovation across the value chain (Koudal and Coleman 2005).
- Clearly, we have to manage innovation, do innovation, and think innovation (Thompson 2004).

With the convergence of multiple discreet technologies and major changes in the competitive landscape transforming the market place, the potential for innovation is greater than ever (Prahalad and Ramaswamy 2003). By implication, failure to innovate or to be innovative is likely to result in reduced competitiveness. Others concur by stressing the importance of innovation as one of the primary means by which a firm can achieve sustainable development and growth (Senge and Carstedt 2001; McEvily et al. 2004), as well as address the key issues facing firms in today's dynamic competitive environment: greater cost efficiency and the provision of new products to meet customer's demands (O'Regan and Ghobadian 2005).

Innovation is at the heart of business development and competitiveness. The successful exploitation of new ideas, whether it results in new products and services, or new business processes and marketing methods, can give companies the competitive edge they are seeking. This is extremely critical if they are to survive the challenges and seize the opportunities that today's global market presents (MORI 2005).

In the Peters and Waterman study, a common thread among the successful firms is innovation. A common characteristic of excellently managed firms is that they tend to have a more flexible organization structure. In contrast to bureaucracies, the attributes of well-managed successful firms include informality, open communications, freedom of expressions, and participative decision-making. The flexible nature of organization led to a bias for quick action rather than inertia, and emphasis was placed on risk-taking and innovation (Mullins 1990).

When looking at management excellence itself, Peters and Waterman chose a double meaning for innovation (Mullins 1990). "In addition to what might normally be thought of—creative people developing marketable new product and services—... innovative companies are especially adroit at continually responding to change of any sort in their environments" (Peters and Waterman 1982).

When something changes in their environment, innovative firms change too. As a whole culture, they innovate to meet changes in the needs and expectations of their customers, the skills of competitors, the mood of the public, forces of international trade, or government regulations. The concept of innovation defined the task of the truly excellent manager or management team. Companies that appeared to achieve that type of innovative performance were the ones Peters and Waterman called as "excellent companies" (Mullins 1990).

Most chief executives fervently want their companies to be more and more competitive, not just on one or two dimensions but across the board. Yet, outstanding competitive performance remains an elusive goal. Although a few companies achieve it, most do not. What distinguishes the outstanding competitors from the rest? There are two basic principles:

- First, they understand that consistent innovation is the key to a company's survival and success. Being innovative some of the time, in one or two areas, just will not work.
- Second, they realize that the most powerful changes they can make are those that create value for their customers and potential customers.

What is the result? Competitive companies constantly try to find ways to change every aspect of their businesses. Then, when they are found, they make sure that they translate those changes into some sorts of advantages the customers will appreciate and act on (Pearson 2002).

The role of innovation and its importance as a driver of success, competitiveness, profitability, and productivity is well documented in the literature (Porter 1998). The key issue facing many SMEs relates to how they can create and foster effective innovation using organizational supporting mechanisms (McEvily et al. 2004). It is therefore no surprise that considerable research has been undertaken on the role and importance of innovation. However, the pattern of previous studies shows a strong focus on the effect of R&D, almost to the exclusion of aspects such as innovation and their various supporting mechanisms (O'Regan and Ghobadian 2005).

11.5 Innovation Strategy

An innovation strategy is only good and applicable for a finite amount of time. One of the worst mistakes an organization can make is to believe that because an innovation strategy was successful it will always be successful. The environment shifts, customers' expectations and needs change, competition gets smart, technologies improve, and the organization itself evolves (Schumann and Prestwood 1994). To develop an innovation strategy, the organization must:

- Understand needs and aspirations of people in the organization.
- Understand the market in which the business operates.
- Understand the needs of its stakeholders.
- Synthesize the needs of the market, stakeholders, and people into a vision.
- Establish a shared vision.
- Develop goals, mission, and strategic plans with the organization.
- Create an innovation strategy by interpreting the innovation opportunity through the business needs as stated in the vision, goals, and mission (Schumann and Prestwood 1994).

Innovative companies:

- have visionary leaders within small, flat organizations;
- have managers who set broad challenging goals for new programs;
- encourage and reward entrepreneurial fanatics;
- give easy access to development funds for good ideas;
- look to anticipate tomorrow's customers' values;
- ensure close interaction between technical and marketing people at all levels;
- accept the value of failure;
- pay attention to informal and formal communication routes;
- recognize and control the satisfiers (recognition of achievement) and dissatisfiers (company policy and administration);
- Value and motivate their staff (Lee-Mortimer 1995).

The most successful companies know that their competitive successes are built on a steady stream of improvements in production, finance, distribution, and every other function, not just a big hit in sales, or marketing, or R&D. Therefore, they look at innovation systematically. So they make sure they have got players who can deliver consistently. They create organizations that provide those players all the backup they need. That means:

- creating and sustaining a corporate environment that values better performance above everything else,
- structuring the organization to permit innovative ideas to rise above the demands of running the business,
- clearly defining a strategic focus that lets the company channel its innovative efforts realistically—in ways that will pay off in the market,
- knowing where to look for good ideas and how to leverage them once they are found,
- going after good ideas at full speed with all the company's resources brought to bear (Pearson 2002).

According to Deloitte Research (2001), there are some very decisive steps that companies can take to conquer the innovation paradox and generate profitable growth through innovation. The highlights are (Deloitte Research 2001, 2003; Koudal and Coleman 2005):

Step 1. Creating innovation: build an idea-generation machine.
Step 2. Exploit innovation where and when it matters.
Step 3. Invest in innovation capabilities: Behind the ability to create and exploit new ideas are four key capabilities that propel complexity masters to success:

- Get better visibility.
- Build flexibility into products and processes.
- Collaborate to innovate.
- Use advanced technologies and information systems.

11.6 Recent Surveys on Innovation

The European Union (EU) has initiated regular innovation surveys in the member countries. The European Community Innovation Survey (CIS) is a standardized survey focusing, among others, on R&D investment, technical personnel, training efforts, new product development, and market success of new products (Oerlemans et al. 2001).

The existing surveys on innovation (like the *CIS and The SISAMF-1996*) dealt primarily with inputs and outputs of the innovation activities in companies. The questionnaires of these surveys generally dealt with the following issues:

- General information (enterprise structure, turnover, employment, and innovation intent)
- Enterprise objectives of innovation (extension of product range, creation of new markets, lowering of production costs, etc.)
- Sources for innovation (internal sources, market/commercial sources, education/ research establishments, and information sources)
- Costs of innovation
- Recent innovations
- Impact of innovation activities (sales, exports, new products, etc.)
- R&D activity
- Factors hampering innovation (economic, enterprise, etc.) (Oerlemans et al. 2001).

The Boston Consulting Group (BCG) recently completed its third annual global survey of senior executives on innovation and the innovation-to-cash (ITC) process, which covers the many interrelated activities involved in turning ideas into financial returns. A total of 1,070 executives, representing 63 countries and all major industries, responded to the survey. Some of the key findings of the survey include the following:

- Innovation remains a top strategic focus for many companies.
- The majority of the respondents said their companies will increase spending on innovation in 2006.
- At the same time, nearly half of the executives surveyed remain unsatisfied with the financial returns on their companies' investments in innovation.
- Executives believe that Apple Computer, Google, 3M, Toyota Motor, and Microsoft are the world's most innovative companies, with Apple the clear leader.
- Globalization, organizational issues (such as metrics and measurement, structure, and people), and leadership are regarded as three of the biggest challenges facing companies that are seeking to become more innovative (BCG 2006).

According to 1,356 global respondents' opinions, The AMA/HRI Innovation Survey (2006) found that

- Innovation is either "extremely important" or "highly important" to their organizations today.
- Innovation is going to get considerably more important over the next decade.
- The biggest barriers to organizational innovation are insufficient resources and the absence of a formal strategy for innovation.
- There is no organizational consensus on how to evaluate ideas in organizations.
- Leaders can make or break innovation.
- Customer demand is viewed as the top reason for pursuing innovation.
- Creativity and innovation are inextricably linked to corporate cultures.
- In order to adapt to an uncertain future, companies need to become more resilient and agile in some areas, more disciplined in others (AMA 2006).

Another research was conducted by Market and Opinion Research International (MORI) on behalf of the Confederation of British Industry (CBI), and QINETIQ. The research data was collected from the CBI members in 2005. The study found that:

- Innovation is critical to corporate success.
- Business spends 12 percent of turnover on innovation.
- The single most important source of ideas for innovation is from within the company.
- Successful collaboration can enhance their innovation activity through access to additional knowledge, specialist skills, and fresh thinking.
- Supply chain management has worked best.
- Understanding the market is more important than pure research.
- Innovation seen as a success story.
- Government is an important influence on business innovation through its role as a major purchaser of goods and services, and through its legislative policies and business support initiatives (MORI 2005).

A survey of SMEs was conducted by the UK DRIVE partners. In liaison with the lead partners in the Republic of Ireland, the survey was designed to provide a base view of innovative activity and potentials for the North Staffordshire subregion, in parallel with similar work conducted in other partner regions. The survey analysis reveals a number of key features about innovative activity within the North Staffordshire subregion. In terms of the relevance to the UK DRIVE project, these can be summarized as follows:

- In over three-quarters of the survey, businesses introduced new or improved products or processes within the previous three years, although there is a sizeable minority of firms who have not developed products.
- Younger businesses within the sample tend to be more active in innovative product and process development.
- Around two-thirds of businesses have undertaken R&D in the past three years (North Staffordshire UK DRIVE Partners 2006).

Some of the findings of the *Permanent Innovation* Survey, conducted by InnovationLabs in November/December 2006, are as follows:

- Lots of room for improvement: Most respondents indicated that there is a lot of opportunity for improvement in the innovation practices of their firms.
- The linkage between strategy and innovation needs to be stronger.
- The willingness to take risks—appropriate risks—is critical to the success at innovation.
- The two biggest obstacles to innovations are resistance to change (51 percent) and lack of time for innovation (58 percent) (Permanent Innovation Survey 2007).

The South African Innovation Survey 2005 is the first official innovation survey to be conducted in the country. The survey found that:

- Nearly 52 percent of South African enterprises had technological innovation activities, comprising both product (goods and services) and process innovations.
- The majority (51 percent) of innovations was produced within the enterprises themselves, but this was more common in the industrial enterprises (70 percent) than in the services-oriented enterprises (35 percent).

- Although organizational and marketing innovations were common in enterprises with product innovations, it appears that businesses in the service sector were more likely to engage in such innovations.
- Nearly half of all innovative enterprises (49 percent) rated sources of information within the enterprise (or enterprise group) as highly important for innovation activities.
- The most often cited highly important effect of innovation was improved quality of goods or services.
- The national funding agencies (such as the National Research Foundation) appear to be having a stimulatory effect on innovation activities.
- The most important collaborative partnerships for innovation were between enterprises and their clients or customers.
- Innovative enterprises appear to be more export-orientated than noninnovative enterprises (South African Innovation Survey 2005).

11.7 Factors for Driving or Curbing Innovation Today

Various factors drive organizations and, indeed, whole societies to become more and more innovative, while other factors impede innovation. Some of these drivers stem from the business environment, while others stem from the larger social environment via patent laws, national cultures, educational systems, public spending on R&D, and other factors (AMA 2006).

Some of the drivers of innovation are the followings: Customer ("the customer always comes first"), technology, pace of change, talent, globalization, R&D spending, government influence, tax incentives, and patent laws among others (AMA 2006).

11.8 Characteristics of an Innovative Culture

The AMA/HRI Survey, combined with a literature review, clearly indicates that an innovative culture has various characteristics. There are many factors that play important roles in shaping innovation-friendly organizational cultures. Some of them are the followings (AMA 2006):

- Customer (focus on customer)
- Teamwork and collaboration

- The need for diversity: The most creative teams are drawn from diverse backgrounds where such teams bring diverse skills and knowledge to projects, offering many creative solutions to problems because they approach such problems with different perspectives (Glover and Smethurst 2003)
- Internal and external collaborations
- The right and enough resources
- Communication
- An ability to select the right ideas
- Creative people
- Freedom and risk-tolerance
- Ways of measuring results
- An ability to balance incremental and breakthrough innovations
- Leadership and accountability
- Motivation and reward systems.

11.9 International Comparison—Global Innovation Scoreboard

The "Global Innovation Scoreboard" report (GIS)17 compares the innovation performance of the EU25 to that of other major R&D spenders and emerging economies in the world: Argentina, Australia, Brazil, Canada, China, Hong Kong, India, Israel, Japan, New Zealand, Republic of Korea, Mexico, the Russian Federation, Singapore, South Africa, and the United States. Of the 25 indicators used to measure innovation performance in the European Innovation Scoreboard (EIS), GIS data were available for 12 of them. Based on the ranking of their Global Summary Innovation Index (GSII) scores, the countries analyzed can be divided into four groups:

- Finland, Sweden, Switzerland, Japan, the United States, Singapore, and Israel are the *global innovation leaders.*
- The group of *next-best performers* includes Germany, Denmark, Netherlands, Canada, the United Kingdom, Republic of Korea, France, Iceland, Norway, Belgium, Australia, Austria, Ireland, Luxembourg, and New Zealand.
- The group of *follower countries* includes Hong Kong, the Russian Federation, Slovenia, Italy, Spain, Czech Republic, Croatia, Estonia, Hungary, and Malta.

- The group of *lagging countries* includes Lithuania, Greece, China, Slovakia, South Africa, Portugal, Bulgaria, Turkey, Brazil, Latvia, Mexico, Poland, Argentina, India, Cyprus, and Romania.(European Innovation Scoreboard 2006).

11.10 The Evaluation of the Empirical Study

The aim of the study is to investigate the innovation activities in SMEs. The survey collects information about product and process innovation as well as organizational and marketing innovation. There is no proper empirical research examining the innovation activities in SMEs in Gaziantep and Kahramanmaras. Accordingly, this study fills an important gap and provides an example for the researchers in conducting innovation surveys in the Turkish cities and the region in which innovation surveys have not been conducted yet. This is a quantitative study where the data were gathered by using the questionnaire method. The unit of analysis is the individuals who responded to the questionnaire, and the study is cross sectional.

Sample: The population for the study consisted of SMEs based in the city of Gaziantep and Kahramanmaras. The survey covered enterprises with more than 10 and fewer than 250 employees, as the existing surveys (such as UK Second Innovation Survey, Thomas and Jones, 1998) regarded it as size criterion for innovation surveys at SMEs (European Commission size criterion of SMEs is the firms employing up to 250 staff—see O'Regan, 2004). The study has focused on SMEs as their importance is well documented in terms of innovation (SGS Consulting, 2002). One hundred questionnaires were distributed and a total of 49 returns were received—a response rate of 49.0 percent.

Data Collection: The data for the research was collected by using questionnaire. The questionnaire was prepared by conducting an extensive research on the existing surveys on innovation. The existing surveys provided crucial information and items for developing the questionnaire of this study. In other words, most of the questionnaire items were taken from the existing surveys on innovation (such as, The Fourth Community Innovation Survey—CIS IV-2004, BCG, 2006 AMA, 2006 Innovation Survey 2000–2009, MORI 2005, and Thunderbolt Thinking, ECIS). The questionnaire dealt with the following issues: General information about the respondents and the enterprises; the types of innovations (product, process, organization, and marketing); who developed the innovation activities; the importance of innovation; the reasons for pursuing innovation; the factors for developing an innovative culture; and barriers for pursuing innovation.

Analytic procedure (statistical analysis): Prior to statistical analysis, all questionnaire data were computer-coded for use with the Statistical Package for the Social Sciences (SPSS) for Windows. Frequency analysis was used to indicate the respondents' opinions for each questionnaire items.

11.10.1 Demographic Characteristics

As mentioned, the administration of the questionnaire resulted in 49 usable returns. Of the responses, when asked to specify their job status, the following was reported: senior manager (43.5 percent), middle manager (45.7 percent), lower ranked manager (4.3 percent), and others (6.5 percent). When asked to specify their personal characteristics, 91.8 percent were male and 8.2 percent were female. Regarding their age, 49.0 percent were between 20 and 30, 38.8 percent were between 31 and 40, and the remaining 12.2 percent were over 40-years old. When asked to specify their highest education level, the following was reported: completed primary school (10.2 percent), high school (16.3 percent), university (61.2 percent) masters or doctoral degree (12.2 percent).

Regarding their organizations, when asked "in which geographic markets did your enterprise sell goods or services," the following was reported: local/regional (23.9 percent), national (39.1 percent), and international (37.0 percent); 58.7 percent of the organizations export products, while the remaining 41.3 percent do not. To the question of "what is the size of your total organization's workforce," the following was reported: 10–49 employees (42.9 percent), 50–99 employees (26.5 percent), and 100–250 employees (30.6 percent).

11.10.2 Product Innovation

When respondents were asked "within last five years, did your organization produce a new or significantly improved goods," 58.7 percent

Table 11.1 Product innovation

Within the last five years, did your organization produce...	Yes	No	Total
New or significantly improved goods.	27 (58.7)	19 (41.3)	46 (100.0)
New or significantly improved services.	26 (59.1)	18 (40.9)	44 (100.0)

Table 11.2 Development of product innovations

Who developed these products (goods and/or services) innovations?	Frequency	%
Mainly our organization.	21	56.8
Our organization together with other enterprises or institutions.	15	40.5
Mainly other enterprises or institutions.	1	2.7
Total	37	100.0

stated "yes" while the remaining 41.3 percent stated "no"; 59.1 percent of the respondents reported that their organization produced new or significantly improved services within the last five years, while 40.9 percent of them reported that their organization did not produce these types of services during that period (Tables 11.1 and 11.2).

To the question of "who developed these products (goods and/or services) innovations," 56.8 percent of the respondents chose "mainly our organization" and 40.5 percent of them chose "our organization together with other enterprises or institutions." Only one respondent reported that these product innovations were developed mainly by other enterprises or institutions.

Briefly, the organizations, in which the research questionnaires were conducted, involved the activities of product innovations. These product innovations were developed mainly by their organization, or their organization together with other enterprises or institutions.

11.10.3 Process Innovation

Of the respondents, 59.6 percent stated that their organization developed "new or significantly improved methods of manufacturing or producing goods or services within the last five years," while the remaining 40.4 percent stated that their organization did not.

Table 11.3 Process innovations

Within the last five years, did your organization develop	Yes	No	Total
New or significantly improved methods of manufacturing or producing goods or services?	28 (59.6)	19 (40.4)	47 (100.0)
New or significantly improved supporting activities for your processes, such as maintenance systems or operations for purchasing, accounting, or computing?	39 (79.6)	10 (20.4)	49 (100.0)

Table 11.4 Development of process innovations

Who developed these process innovations?	Frequency	%
Mainly our organization.	23	56.1
Our organization together with other enterprises or institutions.	17	41.5
Mainly other enterprises or institutions.	1	2.4
Total	41	100.0

The majority of the respondents (79.6 percent) reported that their organization developed new or significantly improved supporting activities for their processes, such as maintenance systems or operations for purchasing, accounting, or computing, while only 20.4 percent reported that their organization did not (Tables 11.3 and 11.4).

The majority of the respondents (97.6 percent) were stated that these process innovations were developed by mainly their organization (56.1 percent) or by their organization together with other enterprises or institutions (41.5 percent). Only one respondent reported that these process innovations were developed by mainly other enterprises or institutions.

11.10.4 Organization Innovation

Of the respondents, 42.6 percent reported that "their organization developed/created new or significantly improved knowledge management systems; and/or created a major change to the organization of work within the last five years," while the remaining 57.4 percent

Table 11.5 Organization innovations

Within the last five years, did your organization develop/create	Yes	No	Total
New or significantly improved knowledge management systems and/or create a major change to the organization of work?	20 (42.6)	27 (57.4)	47 (100.0)
New or significant changes in your relations with other firms or public institutions such as through alliances, partnerships, outsourcing, or subcontracting?	20 (42.6)	27 (57.4)	47 (100.0)

Table 11.6 Development of organization innovations

Who developed these organization innovations?	Frequency	%
Mainly our organization.	10	32.3
Our organization together with other enterprises or institutions.	21	67.7
Mainly other enterprises or institutions.	–	–
Total	31	100.0

reported that their organization did not. When respondent were asked "within last five years, did your organization develop/create new or significant changes in your relations with other firms or public institutions such as through alliances, partnerships, outsourcing or sub-contracting," 42.6 percent stated "yes" while the remaining 57.4 percent stated "no" (Tables 11.5 and 11.6).

To the question of "who developed these organization innovations," 67.7 percent chose the option of "our organization together with other enterprises or institutions" while the remaining 32.3 percent chose the other option of "mainly our organization." One of the important points in here is that none of the respondents reported that these organization innovations were developed by mainly other enterprises or institutions.

11.10.5 Marketing Innovation

Nearly half of the respondents reported that within the last five years, their organization (a) had significant changes to the design or packaging of goods or services (52.1 percent), (b) developed new or significantly improved logistics, delivery or distribution methods for their inputs, goods, or services (55.1), 47.9 percent of the respondents reported that within last five years, their organization did not have significant changes to the design or packaging of goods or services, and 44.9 percent of them reported that during that five years period their organization did not develop new or significantly improved logistics, delivery or distribution methods for their inputs, goods or services (Tables 11.7–11.9).

Table 11.7 Marketing innovations

Within the last five years,	Yes	No	Total
Did your organization have significant changes to the design or packaging of goods or services?	25 (52.1)	23 (47.9)	48 (100.0)
Did your organization develop new or significantly improved logistics, delivery, or distribution methods for your inputs, goods, or services?	27 (55.1)	22 (44.9)	49 (100.0)

Table 11.8 Development of marketing innovations

Who developed these marketing innovations?	Frequency	%
Mainly our organization.	18	58.1
Our organization together with other enterprises or institutions.	13	41.9
Mainly other enterprises or institutions.	–	–
Total	31	100.0

Table 11.9 The focus of innovation

Thinking of this distinction in terms of your company, would you say that innovation is focused more on	Frequency	%
Product (new products/services) innovation	18	40.9
Process innovation	1	2.3
Organization innovation	4	9.1
Marketing innovation	6	13.6
Equal balance for all four types	15	34.1
Total	44	100.0

To the question of "who developed these marketing innovations," 58.1 percent of the respondents chose the option of "mainly our organization," while the remaining 41.9 percent chose the option of "our organization together with other enterprises or institutions." The organizations, in which the questionnaires were conducted, did not use the marketing innovations that were developed mainly by other enterprises or institutions.

11.10.6 The Focus of Innovation

So far, the research data indicated that the organizations, in which the questionnaires were conducted, have involved at least one type of innovation activities (product, process, organization, or marketing). These innovations were developed mainly by the organizations themselves, or the organizations together with other enterprises or institutions. At this point, as the organizations get involved with the innovation activities, the question to ask is which types of innovations (product, process, organization, or marketing) have they focused more on? In order to make that issue clear, the respondents were asked "thinking of this distinction in terms of your company, would you say that innovation is focused more on which types of innovations." To that question, 40.9 percent chose the option of "product (new products/services) innovation," 34.1 percent chose the option of "equal balance for the all four types" (product, process, organization, or marketing), 13.6 percent stated that their organization has focused more on "marketing innovation," 9.1 percent on "organizational innovation" and the remaining 2.3 percent on "process innovation."

11.10.7 The Rank of Innovation Among the Companies' Strategic Priorities

In order to find out the rank of innovation among the companies' strategic priorities, the respondents were asked the question of "where does innovation rank among your company's strategic priorities," 57.4 percent identified innovation as one of their company's top 3 (17.0 percent top priority and 40.4 percent top 2–3 priority) strategic priorities; 23.4 percent identified innovation as one of their company's top 4–10 strategic priorities. Only a small proportion of the

Table 11.10 Innovation rank among the company's strategic priorities

Where does innovation rank among your company's strategic priorities?	Frequency	%
Not a priority	9	19.1
Top 7–10 priority	3	6.4
Top 4–6 priority	8	17.0
Top 2–3 priority	19	40.4
Top priority	8	17.0
Total	47	100.0

respondents (19.1 percent) did not identify innovation activities as one of their company's top strategic priorities. From these data, it can be said that the companies regard innovation as one of their top strategic priorities (Table 11.10).

11.10.8 The Importance of Innovation

Regarding the importance of innovation in their organization, the respondents were asked, "How would you rank the importance of innovation in your organization for today?" To this question, the majority of the respondents (74.4 percent) chose "extremely important" (17.0 percent), "highly important" (31.9 percent), or "important" (25.5 percent); 12.8 percent regard the innovation as "somewhat important" in their organization. Only a small proportion does not think that innovation is important in their organization today (Tables 11.11 and 11.12).

Table 11.11 The importance of innovation

How would you rank the importance of innovation in your organization for today?	Frequency	%
Not important	6	12.8
Somewhat important	6	12.8
Important	12	25.5
Highly important	15	31.9
Extremely important	8	17.0
Total	47	100.0
Mean Value: 3.2		
Std. Deviation: 1.26		

Table 11.12 How will the importance of the innovation change?

In 10 years time, how will the importance of the innovation change in your organization?	Frequency	%
No change	3	6.4
A little change	4	8.5
Somewhat change	3	6.4
Important change	15	31.9
Highly important change	22	46.8
Total	47	100.0

Mean Value: 4.04
Std. Deviation: 1.22

To the question of "In 10 years time, how will the importance of the innovation change in your organization," the majority of the respondents (78.7 percent) chose the options of "highly important change" (46.8 percent) and "important change" (31.9 percent), 14.9 percent believe that somewhat (6.4 percent) or a little (8.5 percent) change will occur at the importance of innovation in their organization in 10 years time. However, only a small proportion report that in 10 years time the importance of the innovation will not change in their organization.

11.10.9 The Reasons for Pursuing Innovation in Organizations

When survey participants were asked about their reasons for pursuing innovation in their own organizations, their top reason was the need to "increase market share" (mean value = 4.42), followed by the need to "increase revenues or profit margins" (mean value = 4.36). Indeed, 84.4 percent of the respondents reported that the need to "increase market share" and "increase revenues or profit margins" were "extremely" or "highly" important reasons for pursuing innovation in their organization. In terms of the respondents' opinions, the importance levels of the following reasons for pursuing innovation were very close to each other: To define new market segments (mean value = 4.13), to better use new technologies (mean value = 4.11), to increase speed or time to market (mean value = 4.11), to respond to customer demands (mean value = 4.10), and to defend against job

Table 11.13 How important are the following reasons for pursuing innovation in your organization now?

	Not Important	Somewhat Important	Important	Highly Important	Extremely Important	Total	Mean/(St. Dev.)
To respond to customer demands	3 (6.3)	2 (4.2)	4 (8.3)	17 (35.4)	22 (45.8)	48 (100.0)	4.10 (1.13)
To increase operational efficiency	2 (4.3)	5 (10.9)	6 (13.0)	20 (43.5)	13 (28.3)	46 (100.0)	3.80 (1.11)
To increase revenues or profit margins	–	4 (8.9)	3 (6.7)	11 (24.4)	27 (60.0)	45 (100.0)	4.36 (0.96)
To develop new products/services	3 (6.4)	5 (10.6)	2 (4.3)	16 (34.0)	21 (44.7)	47 (100.0)	4.00 (1.23)
To increase market share	1 (2.2)	1 (2.2)	5 (11.1)	9 (20.0)	29 (64.4)	45 (100.0)	4.42 (0.94)
To better use new technologies	1 (2.1)	2 (4.3)	7 (14.9)	18 (38.3)	19 (40.4)	47 (100.0)	4.11 (0.96)
To increase speed or time to market	3 (6.8)	1 (2.3)	8 (18.2)	8 (18.2)	24 (54.5)	44 (100.0)	4.11 (1.20)
To define new market segments	2 (4.3)	3 (6.4)	6 (12.8)	12 (25.5)	24 (51.1)	47 (100.0)	4.13 (1.13)
To diversify revenue stream	4 (8.5)	3 (6.4)	7 (14.9)	12 (25.5)	21 (44.7)	47 (100.0)	3.91 (1.28)
To defend against job loss	3 (6.3)	1 (2.1)	7 (14.6)	14 (29.2)	23 (47.9)	48 (100.0)	4.10 (1.13)

loss (mean value = 4.10). Comparing with the importance levels of these reasons mentioned, "to develop new products/services," "to diversify revenue stream," and "to increase operational efficiency" were reported by the respondents as the less important reasons for pursuing innovation in their own organizations. But it should be mentioned that all the reasons shown in Table 11.13 are regarded by the respondents as the important reasons by pursuing innovation, as the lowest mean value among all the reasons was 3.80 ("To increase operational efficiency") out of 5.0 point scale. With the exception of two reasons ("To increase operational efficiency" and "To diversify revenue stream"), mean values for all reasons were 4.0 or higher out of 5.0 point scale.

11.10.10 Factors for Developing an Innovative Culture in Organizations

In order to find out the importance of the factors for developing an innovative culture in organizations, the respondents were asked "How important are the following factors for developing an innovative culture in your organization?" According to the survey data, "appropriate resources" (time and money) (mean value = 4.15) and "customer focus" (mean value = 3.93) were the two most important factors for developing an innovative culture in the organizations. Indeed, more that 70 percent of the respondents reported that "appropriate resources" (time and money) (80.4 percent) and "customer focus" (73.9 percent) were "extremely" or "highly" important factors for developing an innovative culture in their organization. These two factors were followed by the following factors in terms of their importance levels: Organizational communication (mean value = 3.88), teamwork/ collaboration with others (mean value = 3.83), ability to select right ideas for research (mean value = 3.71), and ability to identify creative people (mean value = 3.67). Compared with the importance levels of these factors mentioned, the following factors were reported by the respondents as the less important factors for developing an innovative culture in their organization: Encouraging small and big ideas, organizational structures, innovation accountability/goals, freedom to innovate, ability to measure results of innovation, culture of risk-tolerance, and diversity (Table 11.14).

Table 11.14 How important are the following factors for developing an innovative culture in your organization?

	Not Important	Somewhat Important	Important	Highly Important	Extremely Important	Total	Mean/(St. Dev.)
Customer focus	3 (6.5)	4 (8.7)	5 (10.9)	15 (32.6)	19 (41.3)	46 (100.0)	3.93 (1.22)
Teamwork/collaboration with others	2 (4.3)	5 (10.9)	10 (21.7)	11 (23.9)	18 (39.1)	46 (100.0)	3.83 (1.20)
Appropriate resources (time and money)	1 (2.2)	5 (10.9)	3 (6.5)	14 (30.4)	23 (50.0)	46 (100.0)	4.15 (1.09)
Organizational communication	1 (2.3)	3 (7.0)	8 (18.6)	19 (44.2)	12 (27.9)	43 (100.0)	3.88 (0.98)
Ability to select right ideas for research	1 (2.7)	7 (17.1)	7 (17.1)	14 (34.1)	12 (29.3)	41 (100.0)	3.71 (1.46)
Ability to identify creative people	3 (7.1)	3 (7.1)	11 (26.2)	13 (31.0)	12 (28.6)	42 (100.0)	3.67 (1.18)
Freedom to innovate	3 (7.1)	7 (16.7)	9 (21.4)	15 (35.7)	8 (19.0)	42 (100.0)	3.43 (1.19)
Ability to measure results of innovation	4 (10.0)	6 (15.0)	9 (22.5)	11 (27.5)	10 (25.0)	40 (100.0)	3.43 (1.30)
Encouraging both small and big ideas	3 (7.1)	8 (19.0)	9 (21.4)	9 (21.4)	13 (31.0)	42 (100.0)	3.50 (1.31)
Innovation accountability/goals	4 (8.9)	6 (13.3)	12 (26.7)	11 (24.4)	12 (26.7)	45 (100.0)	3.47 (1.27)
Culture of risk-tolerance	6 (14.3)	6 (14.3)	7 (16.7)	14 (33.3)	9 (21.4)	42 (100.0)	3.33 (1.36)
Organizational structures	6 (13.0)	3 (6.5)	12 (26.1)	13 (28.3)	12 (26.1)	46 (100.0)	3.48 (1.31)
Diversity	7 (15.6)	5 (11.1)	9 (20.0)	14 (31.1)	10 (22.2)	45 (100.0)	3.33 (1.37)

Table 11.15 How important are the following barriers for pursuing innovation in your organization?

	Not Important	Somewhat Important	Important	Highly Important	Extremely Important	Total	Mean/(St. Dev.)
Insufficient resources	1 (2.2)	9 (19.6)	5 (10.9)	15 (32.6)	16 (34.8)	46 (100.0)	3.78 (1.19)
No formal strategy for innovation	2 (4.3)	2 (4.3)	10 (21.7)	18 (39.1)	14 (30.4)	46 (100.0)	3.87 (1.05)
Lack of clear goals/priorities	1 (2.2)	5 (11.1)	6 (13.3)	23 (51.1)	10 (22.2)	45 (100.0)	3.80 (1.00)
Lack of leadership/management support	7 (15.2)	6 (13.0)	5 (10.9)	15 (32.6)	13 (28.3)	46 (100.0)	3.46 (1.43)
Short-term mindset	9 (19.6)	1 (2.2)	5 (10.9)	16 (34.8)	15 (32.6)	46 (100.0)	3.59 (1.47)
Structure not geared toward innovation	9 (20.0)	–	12 (26.7)	12 (26.7)	12 (26.7)	45 (100.0)	3.40 (1.42)
Organizational constraints such as policy	14 (30.4)	4 (8.7)	7 (15.2)	13 (28.3)	8 (17.4)	46 (100.0)	2.93 (1.53)
Too much management control	7 (14.9)	6 (12.8)	6 (12.8)	13 (27.7)	15 (31.9)	47 (100.0)	3.49 (1.44)
Culture of fear about failure	9 (20.0)	5 (11.1)	6 (13.3)	13 (28.9)	12 (26.7)	45 (100.0)	3.31 (1.49)
Lack of rewards for creative behaviors	6 (14.0)	4 (9.3)	7 (16.3)	15 (34.9)	11 (25.6)	43 (100.0)	3.49 (1.35)
New ideas threaten existing product lines	8 (17.8)	4 (8.9)	12 (26.7)	8 (17.8)	13 (28.9)	45 (100.0)	3.31 (1.44)
Economic risks (Cost-benefit analyses presented too many uncertainties)	2 (4.5)	4 (9.1)	8 (18.2)	18 (40.9)	12 (27.3)	44 (100.0)	3.77 (1.10)
Costs too high (Estimated innovation costs are too high for our firm)	4 (8.9)	3 (6.7)	10 (22.2)	20 (44.4)	8 (17.8)	45 (100.0)	3.56 (1.14)
Lack of qualified personnel	3 (6.5)	1 (2.2)	8 (17.4)	17 (37.0)	17 (37.0)	46 (100.0)	3.96 (1.11)
No time within the firm for innovative activities	6 (14.0)	4 (9.3)	9 (20.9)	15 (34.9)	9 (20.9)	43 (100.0)	3.40 (1.31)
Lack of appropriate external financial resources	5 (11.1)	2 (4.4)	10 (22.2)	15 (33.3)	13 (28.9)	45 (100.0)	3.64 (1.26)
Demand risks (Too many uncertainties on [future] product markets)	–	6 (13.3)	9 (20.0)	14 (31.1)	16 (35.6)	45 (100.0)	3.89 (1.05)
Lack of information on technology	4 (9.1)	3 (6.8)	7 (15.9)	14 (31.8)	16 (36.4)	44 (100.0)	3.80 (1.27)
Lack of information on markets	7 (15.6)	4 (8.9)	5 (11.1)	16 (35.6)	13 (28.9)	45 (100.0)	3.53 (1.41)
Insufficient flexibility of regulations or standards	6 (13.3)	5 (11.1)	8 (17.8)	17 (37.8)	9 (20.0)	45 (100.0)	3.40 (1.30)
Lack of customer responsiveness to new goods or services	7 (15.6)	3 (6.7)	4 (8.9)	16 (35.6)	15 (33.3)	45 (100.0)	3.64 (1.42)

11.10.11 The Barriers for Pursuing Innovation in Organizations

In order to find out the importance of the barriers for pursuing innovation in organizations, the respondents were asked "How important are the following barriers for pursuing innovation in your organization?" According to the survey data, "Lack of qualified personnel" (mean value = 3.96) was the most important barrier for pursuing innovation in the organizations; 74.0 percent of the respondents reported that "Lack of qualified personnel" was "extremely" or "highly" important barrier for pursuing innovation in their organization. This barrier was followed by the following barriers in terms of their importance levels: Demand risks (too many uncertainties on future product markets) (mean value = 3.89), no formal strategy for innovation (mean value = 3.87), lack of clear goals/priorities (mean value = 3.80), lack of information on technology (mean value = 3.80), insufficient resources (mean value = 3.78), and economic risks (cost-benefit analyses presented too many uncertainties) (mean value = 3.77) (Table 11.15).

Comparing with the importance levels of these barriers mentioned, the following barriers were reported by the respondents as the ones with lower important levels for pursuing innovation in organizations: Lack of appropriate external financial resources, lack of customer responsiveness to new goods or services, short-term mindset, costs too high (estimated innovation costs are too high for our firm), lack of information on markets, too much management control, lack of rewards for creative behaviors, lack of leadership/management support, structure not geared toward innovation, no time within the firm for innovative activities, and insufficient flexibility of regulations or standards. But the following three factors were the less important barriers for pursuing innovation in organizations: Organizational constraints such as policy, culture of fear about failure, and new ideas threaten existing product lines.

11.11 Conclusion

In today's fast changing and dynamic business environment, the organizations must innovate to be able to survive and compete. By implication, failure to innovate or to be innovative is likely to result in reduced competitiveness. Innovation is regarded as one of the primary means by which a firm can achieve sustainable development and growth. The successful exploitation of new ideas, whether it results in new products and services, or new business processes and marketing methods, can give companies the competitive edge they are seeking.

In order to investigate the innovation activities in SMEs, an empirical study was conducted. The survey collected information about product and process innovation as well as organizational and marketing innovation. The data were gathered by using the questionnaire method; the questionnaires were conducted in the cities of Gaziantep and Kahramanmaras.

The main findings of the empirical study are as follows:

- The organizations, in which the questionnaires were conducted, have involved at least one type of innovation activities (product, process, organization or marketing). These innovations were developed mainly by the organizations themselves or the organizations together with other enterprises or institutions.
- Innovation is identified as one of the companies' strategic priorities.
- It is believed that the innovation is very important for the success of the organizations, and its importance will increase in the future.
- The top reasons for pursuing innovation in organizations are "increasing market share" and "increasing revenues or profit margins."
- "Appropriate resources" (time and money) and "customer focus" are the two most important factors for developing an innovative culture in the organizations.
- "Lack of qualified personnel" is the most important barrier for pursuing innovation in the organizations.

It should be known that innovation is crucial for the organizational success and its importance will increase in the future. Therefore, organizations should be well aware of its importance and involve innovation activities properly. Otherwise, their competitive power can decrease and can come across lots of problems, such as loosing market share.

References

AMA (2006). *The Quest for Innovation, A Global Study of Innovation Management 2006–2016*, American Management Association: New York.

Amit, R. and Zott, C. (2001). Value creation in e-business. *Strategic Management Journal*, 22(6/7), 493–520.

Banbury, C. and Mitchell, W. (1995). The effect of introducing important incremental innovations on market share and business survival. *Strategic Management Journal*, 16, 161–82.

Barclay, I., Holroyd, P., and Poolton, J., (1994). A Sphenomorphic Model for the Management of Innovation in a Complex Environment. *Leadership & Organization Development Journal*, 15(7), 33–44.

BCG (2006). *The Boston Consulting Group 2006 Senior Management Innovation Survey*. Boston Consulting Group: Boston, USA.

Boer, H., Caffyn, S., Corso, M., Coughlan, P., Gieskes, J., Magnusson, M., Pavesi, S., and Ronchi, S. (2001). Knowledge and continuous innovation The CIMA methodology. *International Journal of Operations & Production Management*, 21(4), 490–503.

Cumming, B.S. (1998). Innovation overview and future challenges. *European Journal of Innovation Management*, 1(1), 21–9.

Daghfous, N., Petrof, J.V., and Pons, F. (1999). Values and adoption of innovations: a cross cultural study. *Journal of Consumer Marketing*, 16(4), 314–331.

Deloitte Research (2001). *Creating Unique Customer Experiences: The Next Stage of Integrated Product Development*. New York, NY: Deloitte Research.

Deloitte Research (2003). *Move over Barcodes: Consumer Goods Firms Eye Radio Frequency ID*. New York, NY: Deloitte Research.

ECIS (2001). *Eindhoven Centre for Innovation Studies, Research Design for the South African Innovation Survey*. Working Paper 01.02. (L.A.G. Oerlemans, A.J. Buys and M.W. Pretorius) The Netherlands: Faculty of Technology Management, Eindhowen University of Technology.

European Innovation Scoreboard (2006). Comparative Analysis Of Innovation Performance, http://www.proinno-europe.eu/inno-metrics.html.

Glover, C. and Smethurst S. (2003). Great Ideas Wanted. People Management Online (April 8). Retrieved from www.peoplemanagement.co.uk.

Glynn, M.A. (1996). Innovative genius: a framework for relating individual and organizational intelligences to innovation. *The Academy of Management Review*, 21(4), 1081–111.

Hamel, G. (2006). The Why, What and How of Management Innovation. *Harvard Business Review* (February) 72–84.

Hart, S. (1996). *New Product Development*. London: Dryden Press.

Herbig, P., Golden, J.E., and Dunphy, S. (1994). The Relationship of Structure to Entrepreneurial and Innovative Success. *Marketing Intelligence & Planning*, 12(9), 37–48.

Hitt, M., Hoskisson, E., Johnson, R., Richard, A., and Moesel, D.D. (1996). The market for corporate control and firm innovation. *Academy of Management Journal*, 39, 1084–119.

Innovation Survey (2000–2002). Statistical Service, 1444 Nicosia.

Jankowski, J.A. (2006). *National and International Context for Innovation-Related Statistics*. Arlington, Virginia: National Science Foundation Division of Science Resources Statistics.

Johne, A. (1999). Successful market innovation. European *Journal of Innovation Management* 2(1), 6–11.

Kanter, R.M. (1999). From spare change to real change: the social sector as Beta site for business innovation. *Harvard Business Review*, 77(3), 122–32.

Koudal, P. and Coleman,G.C. (2005). Coordinating operations to enhance innovation in the global corporation. *Strategy & Leadership*, 33(4), 20–32.

Lee-Mortimer, A. (1995). Managing innovation and risk. *World Class Design to Manufacture,* 2(5), 38–42.

Linder, J.C., Jarvenpaa, S., and Davenport, T.H. (2003). Towards an innovation sourcing strategy. *MIT Sloan Management Review*, 44(4), 43–9.

McEvily, S.K., Eisenhardt, K.M.M., and Prescott, J.E. (2004). The global acquisition, leverage, and protection of technological competencies. *Strategic Management Journal*, 25(8/9), 713–22.

MORI (2005). *Innovation Survey 2005*, Research Study Conducted for the CBI/Qinetiq, UK.

Mullins, L.J. (1990). *Management and Organizational Behavior* (2nd. Edition). London: Pitman Publishing.

North Staffordshire UK DRIVE Partners (2006). SME Innovation Survey Analysis – North Staffordshire (UK) Partners, UK.

O'Regan, N. (2004). Testing the homogeneity of SMEs. *European Business Review*, 16(1), 64–77.

O'Regan, N. and Ghobadian, A. (2005). Innovation in SMEs: the impact of strategic orientation and environmental perceptions. *International Journal of Productivity and Performance Management*, 54(2), 81–97.

Oerlemans, L.A.G., Buys, A.J., and Pretorius, M.W. (2001). *Research Design for the South African Innovation Survey 2001*, Working Paper 01.02, The Netherlands: Eindhoven Centre for Innovation Studies.

Pearson, A.E. (2002). Tough-Minded Ways to Get Innovative. *Harvard Business Review*.

Permanent Innovation Survey (2007). Results of the Permanent Innovation Survey Summary Report, InnovationLabs in November/December 2007. www.innovationlabs.com

Peters, T.J. and Waterman, R.H. (1982). *In Search of Excellence*. Harper and Row: USA

Porter, M.E. (1998). *On Competition*, Harvard Business School: Boston, MA.

Prahalad, C.K. and Ramaswamy, V. (2003). The new frontier of experience innovation. *MIT Sloan Management Review*, 44(4), 12–18.

Roberts, P.W. (1999). Product innovation, product-market competition and persistent profitability in the US pharmaceutical industry. *Strategic Management Journal*, 20(7), 655–70.

Rothwell, R. (1994). Towards the Fifth-generation Innovation Process. *International Marketing Review*, 11(1), 7–31.

Schumann, P. and Prestwood, D. (1994). *Innovate!*. USA: McGraw-Hill.

Senge, P.M. and Carstedt, G. (2001). Innovating our way to the next industrial revolution. *MIT Sloan Management Review*, 42(2), 24–38.

SGS Consulting (2002). *SMEs: a national survey*, March, SGS 5251/0302.

Shoham, A. and Fieganbaum, A. (2002). Competitive determinants of organizational risk-taking attitude: the role of strategic reference points. *Management Decision*, 40(2), 127–41.

Shrader, C., Mulford, C. and Blackburn, V. (1989). Strategic and operational planning, uncertainty, and performance in small firms. *Journal of Small Business Management*, 27(4), 45–60.

South African Innovation Survey (2005). *South African Innovation Survey 2005 Highlights*, Republic Of South Africa: Department Of Science And Technology.

Stefik, M. and Stefik, P. (2004). *Breakthrough Stories and Strategies of Radical Innovation*. The MIT Press: London

Strategic Direction (2004). Innovations: Innovation performance and the role of senior management. *Strategic Direction*, 20(5), 28–30.

Terziovski, M. (2004). *Assessment of Innovation Capability Models to Create Innovation Driven Companies*, Australian Research Council Discovery Project, The University of Melbourne, Australia.

The Fourth Community Innovation Survey (CIS IV) (2004) Statistik Austria.

Thomas, M. and Jones, P. (1998). *UK results from the 2nd Community Innovation Survey*. Department of Trade and Industry: London

Thompson, J. L. (2004). Innovation through people. *Management Decision*, 42(9), 1082–1094.

Thunderbolt Thinking, Innovation Survey, www.thunderboltthinking.com, 15.09.2007.

Thomas M. and Jones P. UK 2nd Community Innovation Survey. Department of Trade and Industry, London, and Office For National Statistics:Newport.

U.S. Census Bureau (2006). Measuring USA Innovative Activity, NSF/SRS Workshop on Advancing Measures of Innovations: Knowledge Flows, Business Metrics, and Measurement Strategies, Arlington, VA June 6–7, 2006.

West, G. (1994). Innovate to Accumulate. *World Class Design to Manufacture*, 1(3), 11–14.

Zott, C. (2003). Dynamic capabilities and the emergence of intra industry differential firm performance: insights from a simulation study. *Strategic Management Journal*, 24(2), 97–126.

12 Innovation Policies in Small and Medium-Sized Enterprises: A Comparison Between European Union and Turkey

Belgin Akçay and Başak Söylemez

Abstract

Recent developments in world economy have shown that small and medium-sized enterprises (SMEs) can import their own dynamics into the economic progress. Recognizing the importance of SMEs, most of the countries, especially the developed ones, have started implementing those regulations that will aid the promotion, development, and protection of the SMEs. Turkey, as a candidate member state of the European Union (EU), can use the advantages of SMEs to gain competitiveness in the EU markets and in the global markets as well. Today, the most effective method to reach this aim is to promote innovation, while investing in research and development (R&D). In this chapter, advantages and disadvantages of the Turkish SMEs during the transition period to EU membership will be examined after the importance of innovation in SMEs in the developing countries being discussed.

12.1 Introduction

Currently, technological progress and emergence of the information technology has shifted the dimension of the competition from having inexpensive labor and access to natural resources, to inventing

The views and opinions expressed in the chapter are those of the authors and do not reflect those of the Ankara University and TUSIAD, or its staff.

N. Aydogan (ed.), *Innovation Policies, Business Creation and Economic Development,*   213
International Studies in Entrepreneurship 21, DOI 10.1007/978-0-387-79976-6_12,
© Springer Science+Business Media, LLC 2009

new production technologies and original products that can compete successfully in the international markets. In this framework, to have a competitive industry that can survive in the international markets, it is important to have customer-oriented production, a full knowledge of the contemporary management to fulfill the necessities of the R&D activities, technological developments, and innovative studies.

In addition to establishing a competitive industry, the developments achieved through SMEs must be sustainable. In order to gain sustainable development, it is necessary for a shift in production over high value-added products while activating economic structure and social dynamics. At this point, technology is the key factor that determines the sustainable development and competitive advantage. Technology and innovation are not only important for gaining total factor productivity, but also for reaching sustainable long-term economic growth targets (World Bank 2006). Today, in order to have a technology and innovation-oriented economy, SMEs are the key elements. Therefore, in developed countries, the economy is mainly composed of SMEs. Also, SMEs are important for the competition for a stronger information technology. In countries like Turkey, where economy is mainly composed of SMEs, it is important to have appropriate circumstances for technological development and innovation, encourage cooperation between organizations, and to exhort firms and consumers to buy new products from domestic SMEs. This is the reason why it is important to develop technology and innovation-oriented firms that focus on new products, process, and services, while taking advantage of knowledge and risking their potential for R&D.

Because Turkey is somehow a part of the European single market for industrial goods, and since she established a customs union with the EU years ago, Turkish SMEs have to compete not only with their domestic rivals, but also with the rivals in the EU member states (Yücel 2006). It means Turkey has to reevaluate and review its regulations regarding SMEs. This necessity also forced SMEs to review their existing technology and innovation problems, and to think possible solutions for them. By solving these problems, new R&D projects can be planned, and Turkey can increase its long-term productivity and competitiveness.

In this chapter, Turkish and European SMEs are examined and their innovation policies evaluated. The main objective of this research is to participate in Turkey's EU harmonization process while emphasizing on the necessity of increasing the competitive powers of SMEs.

12.2 Definition of Small and Medium-Sized Enterprises

All around the world, national and international organizations adopt different definitions for SMEs, (e.g. in the United States, there are more than one definition of the SMEs). But most of the commonly used definitions consider the number of employees as a criterion. As shown in Table 12.1, the majority of these definitions consider enterprises that have less than 1,000 employees as an SMEs. However, these thresholds can be set at 500 employees for small-sized enterprises and 1,500 for medium-sized enterprises (Çelik and Akgemci 1998).

In the Organisation for Economic Co-operation and Development (OECD), SMEs are also categorized by staff headcounts (Müftüoğlu 1991). Regarding this definition, approximately 95 percent of the enterprises in the OECD countries have less then 100 employees. Also with the same thresholds, approximately 3 percent of the enterprises employ 100–500 staff (Basılgan 2003).

Likewise, EU has generated a common definition in order to improve SMEs' consistency and effectiveness, and to limit distortions of competition (Table 12.2). In spite of the usage of this definition being voluntary, the EU Commission urges member states, European Investment Bank (EIB), and European Investment Fund (EIF) to use

Table 12.1 Enterprise category for staff headcount in the United States and SME definition in the OECD (Ekinci 2003; Müftüoğlu 1998)

	Enterprise category	Staff headcount
USA	Small	1–99
	Medium-sized	100–1000
	Large-scale	1500 $^+$
OECD	Micro	1–19
	Small	20–99
	Medium-sized	100–499
	Large-scale	500 $^+$

Table 12.2 Former SME definition in EU (Commission Recommendation 1996)

Enterprise category	Headcount	Annual turnover	Annual balance sheet total
Medium-sized	< 250	≤ € 40 million	≤ € 27 million
Small	< 50	≤ € 7 million	≤ € 5 million

this common definition as widely as possible. The aim of this common definition is to lead all community policies, EIB and EIF activities regarding to SMEs (İKV 2005). Also this definition is used in member states as a big incentive concerning SMEs.

The common SMEs' definition, summarized in Table 12.2, is the first SMEs definition that was recommended in April 1996. This definition has been widely applied throughout the EU. However, taking into account of economic developments since 1996, the Commission adopted a new recommendation (Commission Recommendation 2003) on May 6, 2003. This new definition came into force on January 1, 2005 and will apply to all policies, programs, and measures that the Commission designates for SMEs (Table 12.3) (EUREKA 2003).

The new definition is more suitable to the different categories of SMEs and takes better account of the various types of relationships between enterprises. It also helps to promote innovation and foster partnerships, while ensuring that only those enterprises, which genuinely require support, are targeted by public schemes.

In the meantime, developments in price and productivity make it necessary to adjust the financial thresholds. Their significant increase will allow an important number of enterprises to maintain their SME status and at the same time ensure their eligibility for supportive measures. Likewise, with the new definition the autonomy of the SMEs gained importance. Moreover, clear instructions are given on how to treat particular relationships between an SME and other enterprises or

Table 12.3 The new thresholds (European Commission 2003)

Enterprise category	Headcount	Annual turnover	Annual balance sheet total
Medium-sized	< 250	≤ € 50 million	≤ € 43 million
Small	< 50	≤ € 10 million	≤ € 10 million
Micro	<10	≤ € 2 million	≤ € 2 million

investors when calculating the enterprise's financial and staff figures. In essence, the new definition takes into account an SME's ability to call on outside finance. However, the staff headcount thresholds remain at their previous levels, since to raise them would have diluted the measures tailored for SMEs.

As shown in Table 12.3, the category of micro-, small-, and medium-sized enterprises consists of enterprises that employ fewer than 250 persons that have either an annual turnover not exceeding € 50 million or an annual balance sheet with the total not exceeding € 43 million. By adapting this definition, precise financial specification for micro enterprises has been made for the first time. This definition should facilitate national and regional supportive schemes specifically designed for this category.

Also by this new definition, the scope of the SMEs is clearly marked out. Thus, the self-employed, family firms, partnerships, and associations regularly engaged in economic activity may be considered as enterprises. So, it is the economic activity that is the determining factor, not the legal form. With this definition, it is ensured that the supportive measures are granted only to those enterprises that genuinely need them. For this reason, it introduces methods to calculate the staff and financial thresholds to gain a more realistic picture of the economic situation of an enterprise. To this end, a distinction was introduced between different types of enterprises: autonomous, partnership, and linked. Each corresponds to a type of relationship, which an enterprise might have with another.

In addition, staff headcount is a crucial criterion for determining the category into which the SMEs fall. First, apprentices or students engaged in vocational training with apprenticeship or vocational training contracts are not included in the headcount. Anyone who worked full-time within the enterprise or on its behalf during the entire reference year is admitted as a member of the staff.

In Turkey, it is observed that different organizations interested in the activities of the SMEs use different SMEs definitions as far as it concerns the framework of their job descriptions, target groups, and resources allocated for their operations (Table 12.4). These definitions reflect differences between criteria selected for the identification of the definitions to be used and the limits determined within the extent of these criteria.

Table 12.4 SME definitions used in Turkey (State Planning Organization 2004)

Organization	Scope of definition	Criterion for definition	Micro-sized enterprise	Small-sized enterprise	Medium-sized enterprise
KOSGEB	Manufacturing Industry	Number of workers	–	1–50 workers	51–150 workers
Halkbank	Manufacturing Industry, Tourism, Software Development	Number of workers	–	–	1–250 workers
Undersecretariat of Treasury	Manufacturing Industry, Tourism, Agricultural Industry, Education, Health, Software Development	Fixed Investment Amount (Euro)	230,000	230,00	230,000
		Number of workers	1–9 workers	10–49 workers	50–250 workers
		Investment Amount, Amount of Investment Subject to SME Incentive Certificate (Euro)	350,000	350,000	350,000
Undersecretariat of Foreign Trade	Manufacturing Industry	Number of workers	–	–	1–200 workers
Eximbank	Manufacturing Industry	Fixed Investment (Euro) Number of workers	–	–	1,830,000 1–200 workers

Table 12.5 New SME regulation in Turkey (Regulation 2005)

Enterprise category	Headcount	Annual turnover or annual balance sheet total
Micro	< 10	≤ 1,000.000 YTL
Small	< 50	≤ 5,000.000 YTL
Medium-sized	< 250	≤ 25,000.000 YTL

That is why formulation of a common SMEs definition is needed in order to establish a standard in development policies for SMEs, to plan the programs to be implemented within the framework of these policies, and to conduct research in this field. Due to the discrepancy between SME definitions, companies are exposed to different assessments by separate institutions when demanding services. Therefore, on September 19, 2005, the Council of Ministers had released a regulation about definition, classification, and qualification of the SMEs. This common definition was issued in conformity with the SME definition of the EU (Table 12.5).

This common definition does not only set financial thresholds, but also puts emphasis upon the autonomy of the SMEs. Financial thresholds and autonomy criteria were determined in accordance with the EU's SME definition. But it sets significantly lower limits on the amounts of turnover and total assets than the EU.

Additionally, the definition takes the increasing number of micro enterprises into account by setting financial thresholds for them. This aims to encourage the adoption of measures addressing the specific problems that micro enterprises face, especially during the start-up stage. This definition was again modified, effective May 18, 2006, to eliminate differences between the SMEs definitions used by various institutions in Turkey (European Union Twinning Project for Turkey 2006).

12.3 Innovation Policies Regarding Small and Medium-Sized Enterprises in the European Union

Innovation holds the key in the confrontation with the most pressing socioeconomic and environmental challenges, such as global warming, globalization, and job creation. Therefore, the Commission

Vice-President Günter Verheugen who also heads the Enterprise and Industry DG, noted that: "Europe needs to become a truly knowledge-based and innovation friendly society, where innovation is not feared but welcomed, is not hindered but encouraged; where it is part of our society's core values and seen to work for the benefit of all citizens" (European Commission 2006e). As is well known, the concepts of innovation-friendly society and knowledge-based economy are the core elements of the Lisbon Strategy.

R&D Framework Programme (FP) is one of the Union's most powerful instruments to reach the aims of Lisbon Strategy. The new Framework Programme, FP7, which is planned to run from 2007 to 2013, refocuses its efforts to address the Lisbon Strategy. In fact, the instruments to be used and the research themes it will cover are very much in line with the FP6. Whilst the R&D Framework Programmes are well known across Europe after more than 20 years of their existence, the EU supports initiatives in other fields of business that are less well known. As mentioned in the Lisbon Strategy, Europe's development depend on improving competitiveness and innovation, and for that reason the Commission has put forward proposals for a new framework program focused on these two areas.

Approved by the Council and European Parliament, the Competitiveness and Innovation Framework Programme (CIP) will support innovation and growth covering the period from 2007to 2013. Its overall budget will be in different order, with the proposal calling for € 4.2 billion over the next 7 years. Out of the € 3.62 billion CIP budget, the largest part, worth € 2.17 billion, is earmarked for the Entrepreneurship and Innovation Programme (EIP) that targets SMEs in particular (European Commission 2006d). Many of the instruments of the EIP are built on earlier initiatives, successfully accomplished like the Innovation Relay Center (IRC), Innovation TrendChart, Gate2Growth, and PAXIS:

IRC: In 1995, the European Commission established the IRC network in order to facilitate the transfer of innovative technologies between European companies or research departments (IRC Network 2006). As a motivator of innovation with its 71 regional and 33 countrywide IRC network, it has become a leading European network for the promotion of technology partnerships and transfer, mainly between SMEs (Commission of the European Communities 2005).

- Innovation TrendChart: Since January 2000, it tracks innovation policy developments in the EU member states, Iceland, Israel, Liechtenstein, Norway, Switzerland, and Turkey (European Commission 2006b). It also provides a policy monitoring service for three North Atlantic Free Trade Agreement (NAFTA), Brazil, Asia, and the Euro-Mediterranean Partnership (MEDA) countries. Although tracking innovation, it also provides strength and weakness analysis that can make the screening process more effective.
- Gate2Growth: The prime objective of the Gate2Growth Initiative is to support innovative entrepreneurs in Europe (Entrepreneur Contact 2006). It also aims to assist entrepreneurs by fostering networking, and the exchange of experience and good practice at the European level. Therefore, it provides tools, infrastructure, and support services directed to innovative entrepreneurs as well as to their supporters.
- PAXIS: It was launched in 1999 to boost the transfer of local and regional excellence in innovation and to have an instrument for the cooperation, and the exchange of tactic knowledge, and learning among local innovation stakeholders (CORDIS 2006).

Moreover, within the EIP, € 430 million has been allocated to eco-innovation, which is a transversal theme for the whole CIP. Eco-innovation will ensure that innovative companies are supported in developing environmental technologies and services. The pull of eco-innovation can be enhanced by environmental policy, notably through a well-designed regulation and the development of market-oriented instruments. Eco-innovation can also be promoted by fostering cooperation between research and enterprises in promising areas, such as construction, water management, bio-industries, carbon capture, and storage or recycling. The Commission intends to implement this innovation-friendly lead-market initiative within the existing legal and institutional framework. Therefore, it will steer this process and foster cooperation toward a common agenda. The decisive step that will make a real difference is the full political commitment from all relevant actors to help identify and remove potential barriers to the emergence of innovation-friendly markets.

Also, Innovating Regions in Europe (IRE) network offers regions a joint platform for collaboration and exchange of ideas on the development of regional innovation policies. The IRE network aims at creating an interregional learning process for the implementation of regional innovation support actions, and it seeks to promote transregional innovation projects.

Another initiative is the 10-year lending plan started by the EIB, with the EIF as a trial in 2000—Innovation 2010 Initiative (i2i). With committed funds of at least € 50 billion to support innovation over the whole decade, i2i is the EIB Group's contribution to the Lisbon agenda.

In addition to the aforementioned initiatives, there are a number of incentive applications and regulations that support and encourage the innovation. For example, in cooperation with the EIB, the Commission will launch a Risk Sharing Finance Facility (RSFF), which will support investment in high-risk research, technological development, and demonstration projects through loans and guarantees. By reinforcing the financing capacity of the EIB in the area of research, the commission will mobilize the efforts of a large number of European banks and financial institutions into research and innovation, thus increasing private investment and funding in this area.

Although there are a number of incentives focused on improving innovation, the proportion of enterprises with innovation activity in small enterprises was 40 percent in the industrial sector and 36 percent in the service sector (European Communities 2004). There were proportionally more enterprises in the EU with innovation activity in industry than in services for each of the size-classes.

Regardless of the sector, EU enterprises with some form of innovation activity were 39 percent among small enterprises and 60 percent among medium-sized enterprises (European Communities 2004). In order to boost the economic development of member countries and, as a whole, of EU, definitely the proportion of enterprises with innovation activity should be increased.

Approximately half the medium-sized enterprises and a third of the small enterprises conduct innovation activities. In Switzerland, Luxemburg, Iceland, Belgium, and Germany local innovation activities are dominant. However, that proportion is less than 20 percent in Slovenia, Slovakia, Poland, Denmark, and Greece (Fig. 12.1).

In general, financial resources, knowledge, human capital, and management competences are the barriers to innovation and investment (European Commission 2006c); these areas are equally important.

Fig. 12.1 1998–2000,
Innovation activities of
SMES (OECD 2005)

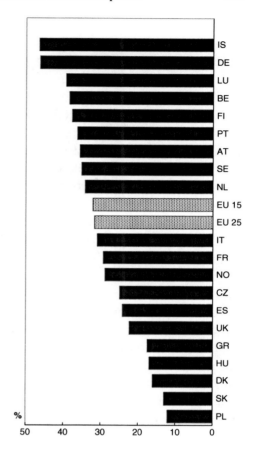

Specific types of SMEs have specific types of needs, and what may be available to meet these needs may depend more on the financing system within individual countries than on the characteristics of the firm such as size, sector, age, and profitability. Therefore, while developing SMEs oriented policies, divergence precautions should be adopted. At this point, the most effective tool that will beckon is eco-innovation.

12.4 Innovation Policies Regarding Small and Medium-Sized Enterprises in Turkey

Supreme Council for Science and Technology, which convenes at least twice a year pursuant to the law, held its 11th meeting on March 10, 2005. In this meeting, the Supreme Council decided to translate the Oslo Manual, which was originally prepared by OECD to define innovation, innovation activities, innovating firm, and all the related innovation concepts in a systematic manner, to the Turkish language and to use it as a reference in all the assessments.

The Oslo Manual describes technological product and process innovations as an implemented technologically new products and processes, and significant technological improvements in products and processes (OECD and Eurostat 2006). A technological product and process innovation is implemented if it was introduced on the market or used in a production process. Technological product and process innovations involve a series of scientific, technological, organizational, financial, and commercial activities.

This wide definition of innovation comprises an extended set of innovation. However, until today, there was no common definition for innovation or innovation activities; therefore, Oslo Manual is so important for Turkey in the path of innovation.

Parallel to the importance given by the Scientific and Technological Research Council of Turkey (TÜBİTAK) to the innovation, Supreme Council for Science and Technology discussed the topic from a different perspective in the meeting on September 12, 2006. In this meeting, it was concluded that Turkey needs a strategy and an action plan that is oriented to improve innovation activities in order to improve its innovation performance. Therefore, it was decided to prepare a "National Innovation Strategy and Action Plan" in collaboration with TÜBİTAK. National innovation system will cover the following areas (TÜBİTAK 2007):

- Enterprise, productivity and innovation
- Transfer of knowledge and technology to the firms
- Competitiveness
- Infrastructure and workplace
- International collaboration
- Governance and coordination

The necessity of innovation activities in SMEs is emphasized in enterprise, productivity, and innovation action area. The aforementioned strategy and action plan has not been concluded as yet.

Although Turkey does not have a uniform innovation policy, the subject gradually gained importance and started to be discussed in

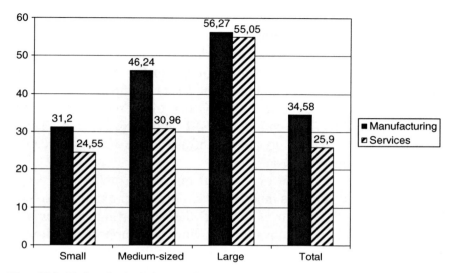

Fig. 12.2 Technological innovation in manufacturing and services sector (TURKSTAT 2006)

every platform. In Fig. 12.2, the innovation action of the manufacturing and service sector was given for the period from 2002 to 2004. Even though Turkey does not have a uniform innovation policy, it is interesting to note that the enterprises with more than 10 employees in the manufacturing and service sector achieved 34.58 percent and 25.90 percent of the technological innovation respectively. The extent of the technological innovation being directly proportional to the enterprise's size, large enterprises do more technological innovation than small enterprises.

In this context, in the Ninth Development Report (2007–2013), the importance of innovation was emphasized, and its essential role in increasing efficiency and competitive power was repeated (State Planning Organization 2006). Also, it is pointed out that all the necessary legal and institutional regulations should be done in order to boost the National Innovation System.

Innovation is one of the most important component of a competitive economy. This is the reason why it should be supported and its international transfer should be ensured. Therefore, in the harmonization period, with the scope of the Sixth R&D FP, Turkey has established IRCs. One of the IRC is located in the Aegean Area (IRC Ege) and the other in Anatolia.

Other than this, in the context of FP6, there has been an effort for some time to create the Regional Innovation Strategy (RIS) in Mersin. This project, undertaken by a consortium formed with the participation of Mersin University, Mersin Chamber of Commerce and Industry, Mersin Tarsus Organized Industrial Zone and Business Innovation Center of Epirus, is directed by the Office of Mersin Governor and coordinated by METU Techno Park (RIS Mersin News 2006). This is the first attempt in Turkey to support infrastructure and human capital to increase the innovation activities.

Turkey has no national or regional innovation policy nor a special program that supports innovation activities. For example, in SME Funding Program, which is one of the supporting programs of TÜBİTAK-TEYDED, innovation activities are supported indirectly while at the same time supporting R&D activities of SMEs.

12.5 Comparison Between European Union's and Turkey's Innovation Policies Regarding Small and Medium-Sized Enterprises

As always, goods and services should be different from their competitors if their producers are to be the winners of the race in the market. Innovation is the key to this differentiation. Consequently, innovation is gaining importance for the commercialization and the transfer of the knowledge.

Innovation activities may differ from each other. Although some of the enterprises carry on well-defined innovation activities such as product development, others may execute less common innovation activities like improving marketing and/or production process. Both these firms can be considered as innovating firms because innovating firm is the one that has implemented technologically new or significantly improved technological products or processes during the period under review. It should be mentioned that technology and knowledge to advance innovation activity needs collaboration between firms. During the process of diffusion, one firm's new or improved product may become another firm's intermediate goods, while producing new or improved products. Therefore, new technology, process management, and product development needs close coordination between firms. They are the foundation stones that form the national innovation system.

In 1995, innovation relay centers were established in the EU. These centers help incite innovation by stimulating technology transfer. There are 30 innovation relay centers all around the EU. But in Turkey, the establishment of these centers was a part of FP6 and was established in the year 2002. In the Turkish system, the effective coordination, and flow of knowledge and human resources between universities, firms, and research centers is performed by innovation relay centers that are insufficient considering the country's economic and demographic structure. There is limited communication between research institutions and firms due to the limited availability of inter-mediaries facilitating exchanges between the industry and research centers. Also in Turkey, there is a lack of incentives to stimulate collaboration between universities and enterprises, whereas there are some mechanisms that support cooperation and communication between research centers and business in the EU. But in Turkey, co-operation between the business and research communities is weak (European Commission 2006a).

In Turkey, regulation flows from government agencies to innovation organizations, and financial flows from the government to private sector are insufficient. The lack of regional and sectoral approaches in formulating and implementing innovation policy, the insufficient number and diversity of financial institutions for innovation, and the small number of financial and innovation intermediaries are the most important shortcomings of the system. Also, there is a cultural difference between EU and Turkey regarding innovation. In the EU, the importance of innovation has been understood earlier and a necessary infrastructure has been constructed. On the other hand, innovation being a new concept, financial structure to solely support innovation activities has not been developed in this country. That is why innovation-oriented funds are added to the existing support programs. But these funds are insufficient to support innovation activities. Hence, the current situation is too difficult for the SMEs to be duly involved in innovation activities in Turkey.

The increase of competition conditions, economic development, and EU negotiation process makes the innovation activities gain importance in Turkey. In this respect, systems, programs, and regulations

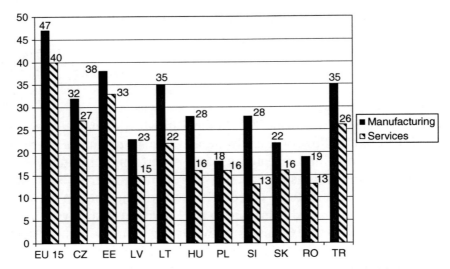

Fig. 12.3 Firms with innovation activities in 2004 (Crowley 2004, TURKSTAT 2006)

that support and encourage national innovation systems have been proposed, although a national innovation system has not yet been developed.

The most important aspect that supports the efforts on innovation activities is the enterprises that adopt innovation in all dimensions. As shown in Fig. 12.3, the percentage of firms that adopt innovation activities in the EU 15 is 44, while this percentage is 31 in Turkey. This figure also points out that Turkey is giving importance to innovation, but in general not all the firms adopt innovation activities.

Private sector organizations are a significant component of the national innovation system of Turkey. There are 1,720,598 enterprises (TURKSTAT 2006). However, investment in R&D and innovation by the private sector is unsatisfactory.

12.6 Conclusion

In order to support competitive powers of the SMEs, it is important to have SMEs-oriented regulations. These regulations will support the country's economic conditions while easing the way to doing business in the country.

Since the establishment of the EU, an ever growing importance was given to the SMEs. It has generated a number of regulations, action plans, and support programs. At every level, it gave importance to R&D activities regardless of the sector, and it has established technology and innovation-oriented SME policies.

However, the role and the importance of the SMEs in the economic and social life in Turkey is only recently being realized. Up to November 2005, the lack of a uniform definition of SMEs consistent with EU definitions hampered data collection and comparative policy/program development on SMEs. However, this new definition entered into force in May 2006. The new definition distinguishes between micro-, small-, and medium-sized enterprises, and sets limits on turnover and total assets. So, with this definition firms in the service sector gained the SMEs statute.

In the harmonization process, Turkish SMEs will be forced to compete with their rivals in awkward conditions. Therefore, in order to maintain its economic development and to gain advantage over its rivals, Turkey should focus on improving its innovation activities and should emphasis the conclusion to the "National Innovation Strategy and Action Plan" activities.

References

Basılgan, M. (2003). *Avrupa Birliği'nde ve Türkiye'de küçük ve orta boy işletmeler (KOBİ'ler)*. Bursa: Uludağ University Master Thesis.

Çelik, A., and Akgemci, T. (1998). *Girişimcilik kültürü ve KOBİ'ler*. Ankara: NOBEL Publications.

Commission of the European Communities (2005). *The activities of the European Union for small and medium-sized enterprises (SMEs) SME Envoy Report {COM (2005) 30 Final}* Belgium.

Commission Recommendation 96/280/EC of 3 April 1996 concerning the definition of small and medium-sized enterprises (30.04.1996). *EU Official Journal*, 107, 4–9.

Commission Recommendation 2003/361/EC of 6 May 2003 concerning the definition of micro, small and medium-sized enterprises (20.05.2003). *EU Official Journal*, 124, 36–41.

CORDIS (2006) What is the pilot action of excellence (PAXIS) on innovation start-ups. In: The Pilot Action of Excellence on Innovation Start-ups. Available via INTERNET. http:// cordis.europa.eu/paxis/src/about_paxis.htm. Cited 1 Nov 2006

Crowley, P. (2004). Innovation activity in the new member states and candidate countries. *Eurostat*, 2004(12).1.

Ekinci, B. M. (2003). *Türkiye'de KOBİ'lerin kurumsal gelişimi ve finansal sorunları*. Ankara: ASKON Research Reports.

Entrepreneur Contact (2006) About the Gate2Growth initiative. In: The pan-European Gateway to business and innovation. Available via INTERNET. http://www.gate2growth.com/g2g/ G2G_Initiative.asp. Cited 1 Nov 2006

EUREKA (2003) Commission redefines SMEs in order to boost competitiveness. In: A Network for Market Oriented R&D. Available via INTERNET. http://www.eureka.be/inaction/viewNews.do?docid=12677. Cited 20 March 2006

European Commission (2003). *The SME definition*. Brussels: Enterprise and Industry Publications.

European Commission (2006a) European trend chart on innovation annual innovation policy trends and appraisal report. In: Innovation Policy in Europe. Available via INTERNET. http://trendchart.cordis.lu/reports/documents/Country _Report_Turkey_2006.pdf. Cited 15 April 2006.

European Commission (2006b). *European innovation progress report 2006 Trend-Chart*. Belgium.

European Commission (2006c). *Reporting intellectual capital to augment research, development and innovation in SMEs*. Belgium.

European Commission (2006d). Entrepreneurship and innovation support firmed up. *European Innovation*, 2006(5), 26.

European Commission (2006e). A holistic blend for Europe's innovation pie. *European Innovation*, 2006(6), 3–4.

European Communities (2004). *Innovation in Europe (THEME 9 Science and Technology)*. Luxemburg.

European Union Twinning Project for Turkey (2006). *Toward Improving the Investment Climate in Turkey: Comments on the YOİKK Reform Process*. Ankara.

İKV (2005). *Avrupa Birliği'nde KOBİ Destek Mekanizmaları ve Türki ye*. İstanbul.

IRC Network (2006) What is an Innovation Relay Center? In: IRC public website. Available via INTERNET. http://irc.cordis.lu/ircnetwork/faq.cfm. Cited 1 Nov 2006

Müftüoğlu, T. (1991). *Türkiye'de küçük ve orta ölçekli işletmeler; sorunlar ve öneriler*. Ankara: Desen Ofset.

Müftüoğlu, T. (1998). *Türkiye'de küçük ve orta ölçekli işletmeler KOBİ'ler*. Ankara: Turhan Publications.

OECD (2005) OECD science, technology and industry scoreboard 2005 – towards a knowledge-based economy. In: Organization for Economic Co-Operation and Development. Available via INTERNER. http://puck.sourceoecd.org/ vl=13790462/cl=12/nw=1/rpsv/scoreboard/. Cited 25 Oct 2006

OECD and Eurostat (2006). *Oslo kılavuzu yenilik verilerinin toplanması ve yorumlanması için ilkeler*. Ankara.

Regulation 2005/9617 concerning the definition, classification and qualification of micro, small and medium-sized enterprises (18.11.2005). *Turkish Official Journal*, 25997.

RIS Mersin News (2006) İnovasyon forum. In: IRC-Anatolia. Available via INTERNET. http://www.irc-anatolia.org.tr/web/index.php?id=629. Cited 10 Nov 2006.

State Planning Organization (2004). *SME strategy and action plan.* Ankara.

State Planning Organization (2006). *Dokuzuncu kalkınma planı (2007–2013).* Ankara.

TURKSTAT (2006). *2002–2004 yılları sanayi ve hizmet sektörlerinde teknolojik yenilik.* Haber Bülteni, 2006(01), 1–30.

TÜBİTAK (2007). *Bilim ve Teknoloji Yüksek Kurulu onbeşinci toplantısı 07 Mart 2007; gelişmelere ilişkin değerlendirmeler ve kararlar.* Ankara.

Yücel, H. İ. (2006). *Türkiye'de bilim ve teknoloji politikaları ve iktisadi gelişmenin yönü.* Ankara: State Planning Organisation.

World Bank (2006). *Turkey Country Economic Memorandum Volume II.* Washington, DC.

13 Financing for Turkish Small and Medium-Sized Enterprises: SMEs Restructuring, Business Plans, and Value-Adding Chains as Tools

Klaus Jurgens

Abstract

Before debating the financing for Turkish small and medium-sized enterprises (SMEs), we must understand SMEs. Likewise, Turkish SMEs must learn to understand the concept behind "technical readiness." Their obstacles may be linked to not having enough money as reserve, not being able to offer collateral, not producing anything that has a "high value," not having a turnover or balance sheet that is convincing to the local bank manager, or in the case of start-ups, not having a product idea or the required own investment to get going. When talking about innovation, financing is the key obstacle. First, SMEs need to be trained about how to obtain funding and from where; the need for training about how to develop a sound and profitable product or service idea; and training about how to prepare a professional business plan.

The originality of this contribution is to link SMEs financing with company restructuring, as I argue that without a streamlined organization, even SMEs will not be able to make good use of the financing once obtained. I argue further that without the promise of restructuring, many lenders will be hesitant to give the funds. On top of that, every start-up must consider their venture as an organization, too. However, SME restructuring differs greatly from that of larger companies as will be explored in detail.

N. Aydogan (ed.), *Innovation Policies, Business Creation and Economic Development*, 233
International Studies in Entrepreneurship 21, DOI 10.1007/978-0-387-79976-6_13,
© Springer Science+Business Media, LLC 2009

13.1 The New SMEs Definition for the EU and for Turkey

SMEs, accounting for 99.8 percent of Turkish companies, form the backbone of the Turkish economy. Foreign investors and companies may come and go, the Turkish SMEs will stay. This chapter tries to, in the first instance, bridge the gap between Business Administrative-related research and problems encountered by SMEs (company restructuring as basis for SMEs Financing, which in turn is a tool to overcome obstacles as currently faced by the Turkish SMEs); it then takes a look at how SMEs in the European Union (EU) countries over time embraced Europeanization as a chance, rather than perceiving it as a threat (with Germany as a case in point); and moreover, analyzes the potential for a comparative approach as application in both the Turkish and European Enterprise policy-making domains.

SMEs matter to each economy, but in particular to Turkey. A comparative analysis is required to establish the state of the art with regards to research into SMEs. "Integrated approach" implies that research into SMEs must include the option for establishing best practices about how to support them. "Integrated approach" is a term used in a recent call for tenders about redesigning the network of European Info Centers (EIC). It refers to SMEs only.

Ultimately, integrated services for SMEs are a key to overcoming obstacles as currently experienced by Turkish companies. Integrated services are to be understood as the whole set of possible support mechanism that can be employed by SMEs to overcome these obstacles. Integrated services for SMEs will play a more crucial role in Turkey, once a network of Business Support Centers (BSC) has been set up (in continuation with the existing EIC). EIC is a network of support centers all across the EU, aimed at SMEs in particular.

As with clustering, support mechanism for SMEs must be where the enterprises are. We can incorporate Porter and his approach toward economic geography (Porter 2000). Reversely, one could argue that enterprises should be where their customers are. The debate about SMEs support mechanism is revisiting the argument (see Porter) about whether globalization has reinforced localization. We talk about whether clustering has become a key instrument to obtain more funding for SMEs. Not only is the proximity of SMEs support mechanism to the enterprises a success factor, but should clustering become a tool to help SME overcome their obstacles, we would also need to follow Porter in the introduction to his publication on *Clusters and the New Economics of Competition*:

> ... further explains how clusters foster high levels of productivity and innovation and lays out the implications for competitive strategy and economic policy. Economic geography in an era of global competition poses a paradox. In theory, location should no longer be a source of competitive advantage, (or disadvantage) for that matter.

Besides, Porter argues that "Competitive advantage lies increasingly in local things—knowledge, relationships, and motivation—that distant rivals cannot replicate (Porter 1998).

In other words, SMEs support mechanism including advice about clustering and financing must be tailor-made not only for a specific region and its problems (the "proximity"), but also for focusing on opportunities that are further afield.

My methodology is novel and innovative as it encourages SMEs to improve their technical readiness via company restructuring that requires financing. I argue that financing without a clear idea on how to add value does not yield any results.

It favors the setting up of organizational structures specifically designed for SMEs and opens the door to serious "innovation" financing thereafter (for SMEs: up to 250 staff), before embarking on expansion. It contradicts the assumption that 40 percent of the Turkish SMEs will go out of business due to globalization and EU harmonization—this chapter argues the case that on the contrary, more sustainable SMEs can be established if "competition" is understood and applied correctly, and adequate financing mechanism are put into place.

Family businesses and SMEs need to tackle their problems by increasing skills and upgrading knowledge including that of current employees, in particular about financing and export options. Turkish SMEs contributed only 26.5 percent to the overall value of the economy and 10 percent to total exports. They do amount to 99.8 percent of enterprises, though. This gap shows a number of problems that will be discussed now.

Whereas the headcount with regards to the current SMEs definition has been harmonized for Turkey and the EU (micro SMEs: less than 10 staff, small SMEs: less than 50, and medium-sized SMEs: up to 250 employees), the turnover threshold was capped at YTL 25 million for the medium-sized SMEs in Turkey, while € 50 million are acceptable for the medium-sized EU SMEs. Likewise, the maximum balance sheet limits are YTL 25 million for the Turkish SMEs, contrary to € 43 million for the EU SMEs (European Commission 2005a).

According to TURKSTAT, and as printed in the negotiating paper for the screening of Chapter 20, Enterprise and Industrial Policy, prepared by ABGS on May 4, 2006 (ABGS 2006), the 99.8 percent (the number of SMEs as percentage of total enterprises in Turkey) constitute for 76.7 percent of the total employment, 38.0 percent of the total investments, but only for 10 percent of the total exports. Additionally, Turkish SMEs only represent 26.5 percent of the total value that is added to the Turkish economy. The figures show a similarity when compared with the EU in so far as the 99.8 percentage apply there as well, with slight variations (when counting the number of SMEs as percentage of all enterprises in the EU = 25). However, the significant difference is the amount of value added by the EU SMEs to the EU = 25 economy, standing at 56.9 percent when compared to the 26.5 percent valid for the Turkish SMEs (European Commission 2005b). Bulgaria and Romania (EU = 27) are not yet included in this set of data.

Does this underline that SMEs in Turkey are feeder industry only? Can we derive information about the quality of Turkish products? What can we learn about the differing purchasing powers? Ultimately, the Turkish SMEs will be measured against the same EU SMEs definition thresholds, as even before a possible EU accession has taken place, the EU SMEs definition will be applied accordingly. Already today, Turkish SMEs are defined according to the EU definition for funding purposes under the Seventh Framework Program (FP7), which allows a far greater number of Turkish SMEs to benefit from funding. The acceptance of the EU SMEs definition, including turnover and balance sheet for the Turkish SMEs with regards to obtaining funding under the EU FP7, was confirmed by Berand Verachtert during an ITO Workshop in Istanbul. This will stimulate Turkish SMEs to participate more actively in FP7. SMEs will grow if they start managing growth (Verachtert and Niehoff, 2007). Coming back to one of my previously stated points, the acceptance of having to overcome obstacles, and the willingness to understand that markets will not disappear but grow, should be clearly explained to the SMEs.

13.2 Cooperatives in Turkey

Although nearly all cooperatives operate with a very small number of members and/or staff, we must distinguish them from the more general umbrella term: SMEs. In other words, cooperatives are in fact SMEs but are accounted for separately for various reasons. Let me briefly introduce the key cooperatives in Turkey. The data introduced here formed the basis for the screening process between the Republic of Turkey and the European Commission in May 2006 (ABGS 2007).

A Turkish cooperative needs at least seven individuals as founding members. A cooperative union may be opened with the same number, seven individual cooperatives. Turkey has nearly 85,000 cooperatives totaling 8.7 million individual partners. Whereas 27 percent of the co-operatives are active with regards to housing, 55 percent are engaged in activities linked to the agricultural sector. By sheer numbers the Turkish cooperatives form a serious part of the economy. Research into their inner workings and interrelationship with other parts of the economy has been somewhat overlooked. Cooperatives are a good example for the SMEs. In general, how important the concept of clustering can become when setting up business, expanding, or diversifying. This is in particular true with regards to obtaining financing on a scale that would be impossible for individual applicants. Joint purchasing power combined with joint distribution channels have worked well for the cooperatives, but were neglected by the SMEs. Turkish SMEs can therefore learn from experiences of the cooperatives.

We must understand that agriculture is a part of the economy and not as a side effect. Hence, Turkish cooperatives form a vital part of the economy and face similar problems. One of them is the fact that cooperatives do not contribute enough value to the economy. We measure this by counting the percentage of value added to an economy. The number of people employed in the agricultural sector does not correspond to the value added (or required to be added) to the economy. In 2004, these figures stood at 35.2 percent of employment and only 11.7 percent of value added (data provided by ISO; Turkish economic indicators for the year 2004). Assuming that cooperatives form the basis for most employment in the sector in Turkey, the approach toward restructuring is as imminent as when analyzing SME in general.

Two points need further debate. First, how can cooperatives become more professional? We need to introduce the concept of "cooperative management." Second, we have to count how many cooperatives are actually economically active. I will give precise suggestions for further case work toward the end the chapter.

13.3 Obstacles in Domestic and Cross-Border Ventures

The following selected obstacles, taken from a much longer list that is currently used as part of the first fully-fledged SMEs Module taught at a Turkish University, create problems for the Turkish SMEs. Bilkent University Faculty of Business Administration was the first Turkish University that offered a course about "SMEs and obstacles in cross-border ventures" to both its undergraduate and MBA students. The author's own research has shown that this was still valid at the time of this publication with regards to courses taught in the English language, with very few offerings at other Universities where Turkish is the language of instruction.

They include: a lack of skills with regards to staff including management; not enough knowledge about, and access to innovation; not understanding SME as an organization; lack of knowledge about, and access to financing; misinterpreting the concept behind "technical readiness"—which is not only about up-grading your company's laboratory; a wrong approach toward enhancing the product quality; being caught in the middle between acting as "feeder industry" or end-product manufacturer; not having understood globalization as no one explained it to the SMEs and their owners in due time; competition is seen as a threat instead of as a chance to be better; missing market entry data; and last but not least, not enough knowledge about the importance of Market Structure Surveys.

For the purpose of this chapter, I have chosen the lack of knowledge about, and access to financing as one of the key obstacles for the Turkish SMEs. I then continue arguing that obtaining money per se does not yield results; SMEs must align themselves with the twenty-first-century reality by restructuring and incorporating globalization and Europeanization, with or without the EU accession process (however, not ignoring it either).

The SMEs module at Bilkent focuses on the SMEs and their particular obstacles. It would of course be beneficial to have more Universities embarking onto the path toward 'research into the functionality of the Turkish SMEs." The Turkish SMEs are largely feeder industry, much less so end-product manufacturer. Further obstacles, besides not having enough access to finance as mentioned earlier, are environmental deficits and no advance preparation for the accession process with the EU. The dilemma here is that "with or without" EU accession (Arrow, 1996), domestic laws and regulations will change in line with the EU Acquis.

The problem for the SMEs in Turkey (and to a lesser extent to those in the 12 countries that joined the EU since 2004) is the fact that because EU accession was not perceived as happening in the immediate future, most industry sectors did not prepare for the eventual EU membership. It seems as if the Turkish industry wanted to wait until the actual start date of the negotiating process was announced. However, once it had been announced, industry and the SMEs in particular were left completely in the cold. This is not a dilemma SMEs can blame on the EU or the government. It is a homemade industry problem that can be summarized as "no foresight."

Even non-EU experts are aware of the fact that national laws have to change long before the membership is sealed as it is the prerequisite for, and not a follow-up result of it. Sector Impact Analysis (IA) and Regulatory Impact Analysis (RIA) about the costs and benefits of certain directives and decisions as well as regulations, should have been carried out in the early 1990s, not after having started the actual accession process.

IA has to be understood as Industry Sector Analysis, whereas RIA is carried out by the administration (Jurgens 2006). A recent much over-hyped topic, it is basically nothing more than analyzing the "before, during and after" phase—policy-making scenario impacts and effects. It should include a "before the before"—analyzing potential impacts long before the actual policy-making documents are prepared in its first version. The Turkish industries still have not understood the relevance of preparing their own industry-based IA to enter a policy-making dialogue. The Acquis Communautaire is in principle, nonnegotiable. Derogations are the exception, although not entirely impossible (Işik 2007). Of much greater importance is using sector-based IA to show policy makers why certain sectors would need more time to adjust. The government can then produce its own RIA, having taken sector IA into account. Working the other way round is very disadvantageous for industry, and in particular for the SMEs of a CC.

The topic introduced here points to an other problem: Turkish SMEs lack the strategic vision that the European SMEs have acquired over the decades. Europeanization and globalization simply forced European SMEs to adapt. Globalization is similar to the EU Acquis— it will not go away.

Of course, one has to defend Turkish companies up to a certain extent as the EU SMEs grew alongside the Acquis, but current CC SME must "swallow" 82,000+ pages at once. This further explains options and limitations for importing Best Practices to CC. For example, "best practices" form the backbone of the Twinning Scheme currently in place between Turkey as CC and selected EU MS. A Turkish Ministry asks for a response to a Fiche they circulate amongst the MS about a national policy-making item the CC has identified itself. Experts from the MS then work in the CC. The scheme is only applicable to Administrative Capacity Building. The term "administrative capacity building" refers to the ongoing Twinning Scheme/Program between the EU and the EU Candidate Countries. A future Public Policy Management module for Turkish Universities may aid this important skills and knowledge aggregation.

What Turkish SMEs need, however, is not copying practices employed in other countries, but a unique, tailor-made approach based on the present day Turkish (industry as well as administrative) reality. The exceptions to this rule as presented in this chapter are "competition" and "company restructuring."

It is expected that most SMEs relevant directives, decisions, and regulations will enter into force during the upcoming two to four years. Health and Safety or the Working Time Directive is two such examples (Pereira, 2006). The simple fact that many SMEs will have to double their transportation costs due to the required replacement of the present overloaded trucks is another case in point. Environmental concerns will come in as expensive.

However, while not all obstacles can be removed (the change in regulations concerning overland transport of goods for example), they may be deferred. SMEs can be given time to prepare for the changes. It cannot expect the Turkish SMEs to change overnight (and neither did European companies in other candidate countries). Other countries, other relevance: not only the speed of transposition of the EU Acquis as such is a benchmark for change, the general perception of family business and SMEs is, too. In Germany, for example, "Mittelstand" refers to business people who are situated in-between the single entrepreneur and larger companies. It is a word that originates in the German language, linking the middle class with their business activities. "Stand" refers to one's position in the societal hierarchy. "Mittelstand" includes nonentrepreneurs, while "mittelstaendische Wirtschaft" focuses on the middle-class (not big, not small) company owners and entrepreneurs. However, over the decades the German Mittelstand embraced competition: "Konkurrenz belebt das Geschaeft," meaning "Competition brings more business to your business"; a vital development the Turkish SMEs must learn about as quickly as possible. Europeanization was the driving force behind this development in Germany and other European countries.

SMEs support aims at keeping enterprises in business as well as guiding would-be entrepreneurs into the right, profit-making start-up direction. At this stage, I wish to introduce the UK Household Survey. The United Kingdom Department of Trade and Industry (DTI 2003) published a survey about attitudes in the public with regards to establishing their own business. All integrated services, paired with Business Administrative-related research, can only come to fruition when enough potential entrepreneurs exist in any given country. DTI separated the thinkers from the doers, and introduced the term "avoiders."

According to their findings from the year 2003, 24 percent are the combined number for thinkers and doers with 11 percent as thinkers, 13 percent as doers, and 76 percent as avoiders. Key considerations according to the DTI study are the following: Thinkers disagree that they are scared of being in debt, disagree that they avoid taking risks whenever possible, agree that they often see success stories about running a business in the media, and finally, disagree that they would not feel confident speaking to a bank manager about a loan. It shows that a relatively large number of the population hesitate to open up their own business. It seems that security concerns (job, income, and others) have outperformed entrepreneurial spirit. One of the initial tasks for a novel Turkish SME Research Center would be to analyze the level of intent (thinkers) in Turkey, and which enterprise policy-making areas could stimulate interest in establishing a company. Another focus could be whether self-employment and company ownership reduces unemployment in real terms or not. It is, however, wrong to only complain about the inflexibility of the SMEs. When policies change, they need to be explained to the business community. On top of that, SMEs owners and managers have serious concerns and demands that need to be channeled. Restructuring the Turkish SMEs means to give a perspective for initially the next six to seven years. This figure is based on the assumption that the Turkish industry will be ready for EU accession by the time the next EU budget is finalized (2012–2013). My argument is that Turkey, as far as her technical readiness is concerned, will be "EU ready" before the EU is ready to accommodate Turkey. A fast-track SMEs technical readiness could be achieved in even less time (three to five years, as long as the political willingness to financially support the SMEs continues to grow). Assuming that real birthrates of SMEs can only be measured after four years (two years until the break-even point is reached, one year to start making profit and another year to become a sustainable enterprise), we need to concentrate on two types of enterprises (i.e. companies that are already in business but face problems, and those that are potential or real start-ups). The average family business may have been set-up by a perfect entrepreneur who took calculated risks, but is not a long-term manager. SMEs need strategic vision that in most cases must be implanted making use of external advice.

13.4 Introducing the Value-Adding Chain for the Turkish SMEs

Any start-ups and all restructured SMEs need to fully understand the importance of the value-adding chain. From the original start of production to the final price including VAT, a precise calculation has to be made that weighs the options for each existing or new product, compares the maximum value scenarios, and helps SMEs go cross-border.

The most important tool to introduce serious forecasting from day (and product) one is using "the value-adding chain." Although it includes VAT at all relevant stages, it is not about VAT (CBI 2005). Each cost segment makes the product more expensive, and the costs must be offset in order to achieve a sustainable profit margin. However, as the product becomes more expensive ("costly"), it acquires more value. It does in fact add value threefold: first, the company producing the goods or delivering the service achieves a higher end price and hence turnover. Second, the economy benefits as SMEs add more value to it. Finally, the consumer benefits as the product will be of better quality and functionality. This model only works well if applied correctly. SMEs can not aim at achieving the highest price possible in markets where purchasing power is limited. In order to understand markets, SMEs must undertake a Market Structure Survey that can be very costly. SMEs must professionalize their approach toward pricing and costing. This can not be done by individual SMEs. Sector associations should take this role on board and furnish their members with annually updated (EU and further afield) market entry data. Each step requires a separate analysis as indicated in the following paragraph.

Once all steps have been carefully laid out, the crucial question of VAT comes into play. A zero rate VAT market (for example, for books in the United Kingdom) does not necessarily mean that paper is a good product to be sold into the UK market (EU Commission [d]/EU Commission [e]). Assuming no trade restrictions apply, we must analyze why there is no VAT on books. Is it because of a declining readership? Is it because the Government wants to encourage children to read more? Is it because the industry sector lobbied successfully to reduce the VAT rate? For how much can we sell our paper, or is the market saturated? For how much do end-users buy end-products, are books cheap or are they only cheaper in relative terms? What kind of paper quality is used in books in our zero-rate VAT market? The list is still not exhaustive. It underlines, however, that the average SMEs in Turkey will not have sufficient access to all relevant data. Even if they do, they would not be able to analyze them correctly.

What is introduced here as a threat, however, is ultimately the only option to go into, or stay in, business. A threat can become an opportunity. The keyword is "embracing the competition." Better and more varied products, quality assured and sold in a number of markets are one solution. Turkish SMEs must approach competition as a positive factor. Although competitors come to Turkey, Turkish SMEs can look and go cross-border. Not only restructured, but technically ready SMEs will also survive. Many classic sectors of the economy including micro business will benefit from a generally speaking stable economic climate. The aim is to bring as much knowledge to all the SMEs, including e-Commerce and e-Tendering.

Let us further introduce the value chain for tourism SMEs by adding the business administrative dimension. Tourism and Hotel Management training features varied topics and covers all aspects of how to run a successful business. However, emerging markets require a specific, more tailor-made syllabus. One such item on the syllabus is the introduction of the value chain to tourism operators. More specifically, the value chain for the tourism SMEs as nearly all operators in the industry are SMEs. SMEs owners and if applicable, their managers, very often will have learned about the short-term perspective with regards to opening a tourism or hospitality company. More often than not, they will not have been exposed to sound business administrative, cost-benefit analysis and strategic planning, and forecasting.

In line with the OECD Conference on Global Tourism Growth in Korea, September 6–7, 2005 (OECD 2005), I have added the following topics onto more cost-benefit oriented Tourism and Hotel Management:

How to become a successful tourism start-up in an emerging as well as mature market; How to successfully diversify your offer in a saturated market; How to analyze market trends and consumer preferences; How to maximize value; How to establish a value chain for each segment of your offer; How to start networking with other Tourism SMEs; How to make use of clustering as one such tool.

13.5 The SMEs Business Plan: How to Maximize the Value-Added to Both SME and the Economy; Exit Strategy as the SMEs Survival Kit

I shall elaborate on why the SMEs exit strategy should be the "SMEs Survival Kit." Finding funding for SMEs is a crucial step in staying in business and starting the required company restructuring process.

Not only existing companies will benefit from better access to money, but also potential start-ups as well. Although in most European countries a relatively solid pool of financing instruments for SMEs exist, in most CC including Turkey finding sufficient funding for the preparation (seed), the start-up phase, or the way to expansion and growth is difficult to say the least. When we combine this with reluctance in general to go into debt, we are faced with a combination of potentially problematic obstacles. Integrated services must bring knowledge about the available financing tools to the SMEs, while monetizable, business and administrative-based advice will help to establish links and draft the most important document in this chain—a business plan tailor-made for the needs and requirements of SMEs.

Why do SMEs business plans differ from other business plans, and which parts differ? SMEs have a breakeven point that kicks in relatively early (i.e. after only two years). Assuming that most SMEs do not have sufficient capital to survive after these 24 months, investors would be very hesitant to lend larger amounts of money if the breakeven point is forecast to be much later than the accepted two-year SMEs average. A business plan for SMEs must show that the first serious profit will be obtained after 24 months. The SMEs then has another 12–24 months to come to a sustainable profit margin. Most SMEs would be considered as sustainable having a profit margin of around 7–8 percent. Hence, we can measure the real birth rate of SMEs by giving them those 48 months to stabilize. The way to measure stabilization is by measuring the profit margin.

SME have to face greater volatility with one exception: in most instances, staff will have worked for the same entrepreneur for a considerable number of years (existing companies). In all other instances, SMEs depend on external factors, most often outside their own control. From inflation to exchange rates to corporate taxation to changes in VAT, as well as being dependent on a limited number of buyers who very often have an exclusive relation with their supplier SMEs.

Going into end-production or diversifying the product portfolio would help to ease the level of dependency, but would still not abolish the external factors. Less turnover means less assets, and less assets mean less security for potential investors. It is a vicious circle SMEs must break free of.

A critical point is that every good SMEs business plan requires a comment about the exit strategy. This is easily understood by the

second generation, but not necessarily fully embraced by the owner/
first generation. Even SMEs who have successfully restructured including a general manager position (required for all SMEs from 150
staff onwards), still depend on the owner/family. SMEs as parts of
larger multinational holdings form not part of my analysis. Although
they may have less than 250 staff, their headcount and balance sheet
will in most cases not fit in with the by now EU accepted SMEs
definition.

Exit strategy is the point in your company's history where you feel
it is ready to be sold or publicly listed. An exit strategy is a key tool
in convincing would-be investors that you as the company owner or
entrepreneur want to make as much equity as fast as possible in order
to reinvest. This in turn means the investor has a reduced risk level, as
you and the investor pull and move in the same direction.

Does this mean that streamlining the Turkish SMEs will lead to a
sellout of the Turkish SMEs once the exit strategy date has come? Do
we only restructure SMEs to ultimately sell them? Not really. The introduction of the exit strategy into concepts about advising the SMEs
has another purpose. It helps SMEs owners and managers to realize
that change is a constant factor. Change management is vital for any
successful entrepreneur and manager. Still, change is perceived as a
threat. SMEs must learn how to work with change and "manage" it.
This implies that 10 years from now, your product will no longer be
sold in the same format as it is today. Consumers will have changed
preferences (not about companies, but about products). New players
will have arrived in your market. You should become a new arrival in
someone else's market!

The 10 year perspective (at most, for the SMEs) including whether
to change direction, sell, expand, venture into a totally new prod-
uct/market or any other viable scenario, shows the would-be investor
that you have learned your lesson about "change." A missing exit strategy in your business plan will most likely lead to immediate rejection
by potential investors.

I have inserted a basic guideline about how to draft a successful
business plan for SMEs in the appendix. The original version has been
compiled by Courtney (2006) and adapted by the author for teaching
and SMEs advice purposes. The investor deal as well as the exit strategy feature in it.

13.6 Snapshot of the Turkish SMEs Reality

In order to understand the Turkish SMEs even better and without giving away any internal company details, let us take a brief look at three "fictitious" companies in three Turkish regions:

First, the so-called "Techno Triangle" between Istanbul, Bursa, and Kocaeli does not only offer vast production capacities, but also carries huge environmental risks. It does feature large numbers of job opportunities too. Nearly all companies assembled here are SMEs (not counting the subsidiaries of foreign multinationals, or those companies that form part of the Turkish family holdings). Many SMEs have located (or relocated) themselves to the fringes of Istanbul either near Atatürk Airport, or around Tuzla and Gebze.

The following example may help to explain the root of the problem: a 150 staff—SMEs in the parts production sector of the Turkish manufacturing industry totally relies on their main (or in this case, only) buyer and encounters periods of high and low production. Forecasting is very difficult, and dependency on one contractor makes changes to the product line impossible. Over time, problems arose and competition arrived. Production in Turkey became in many instances as expensive as in Spain. The location Turkey factor translated into an advantage does not support enough SMEs any more. In order to stay in business and to ultimately increase the profit margin, a restructuring is required that would help this SMEs to diversify its product portfolio by adding individual or collective research, and then diversifying the buyer/contractor structure. The key question in this case was "do we buy know-how" or "can we develop it in-house?" A combination is often the best solution. Phasing out the licensing, phasing in the R&D. Keeping the parts production, but adding capacity for new products. All this requires long-term forecasting and implementation of a management structure including a general manager. No change can be implemented without a change in the SMEs organizational structure first!

Second, Central Anatolia in comparison, and despite its image of a barren but beautiful landscape, has many areas where economic activity is of huge importance and success too. As a matter of fact, clever positioning has made location away from the centers possible. Here, another problem arose. Whereas 20 years ago local workforce was available in abundance, more recently an expansion where the hiring of extra staff is required is simply impossible. Although Turkey has a relatively high unemployment rate (with very positive trends in place), in many parts of the country skilled labor does not exist. As most SMEs were in the parts production, semiskilled workers filled most vacancies. Career planning was unheard of. Now, new product lines together with diversified business activities require better trained staff. Salaries, however, have not risen in line with these developments. Many Turkish SMEs face a paradox: high unemployment in general in the country, but a shortage of skilled labor in the regions. The dilemma here can be summarized as a "shortage of skills." This not only applies to the production floor, but also to junior and senior management levels too. SMEs need to acquire knowledge. Knowledge is the sum total of the knowledge of staff, and if required, external experts. It is a very difficult transition period for company owners, managers, and staff. Figures show that 80 percent (!) of SMEs owners in Turkey have no high school diploma. Urgent action is required. No change can be implemented without acquiring more and better knowledge. The knowledge-based economy needs knowledge-savvy SMEs.

A third example comes from within the tourism industry—an entrepreneur on the Aegean coast. This example shows how a misunderstanding about trends can lead to financial ruin. An hotelier explained to me that due to the fact that tourists opt to buy property instead of staying in his hotel, he wants to convert his business into apartments. Although tempting at first sight, I explained to him that gaining a certain amount of surplus cash in the short term does not mean that the selling of the hotel will have generated enough cash-flow to buy another hotel. Once all his money has been spent building and converting apartments, nothing is left until the day buyers have arrived and match his expectations (UK£ 55,000 per two bedroom flat at the time). My advice was to update services, refurbish the hotel, attract wealthier clients (not foreigners, but the new Ankara elite), and keep going until things really got bad, or as expected due to the wave pattern in tourism, got better again. The "wave pattern" implies that tourists change their preferences on a regular basis and a permanent increase in visitor numbers is highly unlikely.

A vital element is introducing economic forecasting to SMEs. Forecasting for the SMEs is a totally different matter when compared with larger companies or family businesses in general. Many family businesses have long outgrown the SMEs definition thresholds. Hence, I focus on SMEs only for the specific purpose of this analysis.

All this requires knowledge about where to get the funding from and, even more than that, what to do with it. In other words, it requires knowledge about financing and its value-adding usage.

13.7 Financing Demands as Expressed by the Turkish SMEs: Micro, Small and Medium-Sized Companies and Funding Opportunities for the Turkish SMEs

Different SMEs have varying financing demands. They must be matched with the supply side. Following are eight examples:

- Banks: perfect to rearrange existing loans if the collateral matches, easily up to YTL 10 million.
- Family: spreading the risk while staying in control; in most cases, not more than YTL 100,000.
- Own Resources: the "overdraft entrepreneur"; it is possible to set up a successful e-company with US$ 20,000.
- Business Angels: anything from UK£ 50,000 to UK£ 1 million.
- Venture Capitalists: anything on top of that amount.
- Government(s): KOSGEB.
- EU: tenders and research.
- Other: from increasing output to innovation with hardly any cost.

Turkish BAN and EBAN would require a separate analysis. Business Angel's networks can form a central part in the strategy to open up new sources for financing SMEs.

13.8 Case Study and Empirical Work: (A) How to Avoid Contaminated Case Data When Analyzing the Turkish SMEs; (B) An Introduction to SELP II

13.8.1 Avoiding Contaminated Case Data

Cheng and Chen (2006) have contributed significantly to the debate about how best to fit logistic regression models with regard to contaminated case–control data. My own approach toward RIA draws heavily on previous, as well as their more recent, findings on how best to avoid using contaminated data due to wrong set of samples. A regression model seems to be the best solution. What can we learn from Cheng and Chen with regards to case studies about the financing for the Turkish SMEs? Cheng and Chen argue that "errors in measurement frequently occur in observing responses." If case–control data are based on certain reported responses, which may not be true responses, then we have a contaminated case–control data. In this chapter, we first show that the ordinary logistic regression analysis based on contaminated case–control data can lead to very serious biased conclusions (Cheng and Chen 2006).

- What can we derive from these findings that will add value to the Turkish research about SMEs.
- What do I suggest to analyze first: real birth rates of the Turkish SMEs according to my criteria introduced earlier on in this chapter; sustainable increased profit margins for existing and expanding SMEs.
- What will be the expected outcome: benchmarking SMEs performance against investors' willingness to invest.
- Which logical framework do I employ: matching expected outcomes with assumptions about commercialization of innovative concepts.
- Which impacts do I expect: keeping Turkish SME in business while at the same time increasing the number of real birth rates.

13.8.2 SELP II

The Turkish Central Finance and Contracts Unit (CFCU) is about to carry out the implementation of SELP II. SELP I was a project about technical assistance for small enterprises, and how to achieve better access to loan facilities.

SELP I, and probably SELP II, underline my assumption that support for the Turkish SMEs has to come in the form of technical assistance as well as administrative help. Hence, I employed the term "technical readiness" as the benchmark to evaluate whether integrated support mechanism actually work.

My conclusion is that we can only measure two things: the "real birth rate" of successful SMEs start-ups, and the success rate of expansion or diversification for the existing SMEs. The first one can be measured by evaluating whether the start-up has become profitable after 36 months on a sustainable basis (i.e. having achieved its breakeven point after a maximum of 24 months). SMEs breakeven points greatly differ from those of larger companies. The second one can be measured by having established a net growth in the volume of the profit margin as percentage of the total turnover.

SELP II is a good indicator about the desire to develop better statistics with regards to financing needs for SMEs, and then continue to measure them against their success ratios. I call it part of the integrated approach toward SMEs support mechanism.

Two points need further debate. First, how can cooperatives become more professional—we need to introduce the concept of "cooperative's management." Second, we have to count how many cooperatives are actually economically active.

All my previous comments and suggestions rely on improved data collection and analysis in Turkey. Although the approach to statistics has greatly improved over the last couple of years, much remains to be done. SMEs restructuring is based on forecasting. Forecasting must be based on noncontaminated case data, as well as serious economic analysis. Employment statistics must go hand-in-hand with tax and income projections. Even "how much knowledge" we need is based on facts and figures. In other words, SMEs and policy makers need better empirical, less hypothetical data.

Universities, and in particular Faculties and Departments of Business Administration and Management, are best suited to act as interface between industry and policy-makers. They may even be well placed to add training and teaching (of course, based on both research as well as an understanding of administrative realities) about Public Policy Management. Once SMEs restructuring and improved PPM are in place, SMEs and the Turkish as well as European economy as a whole could benefit.

Abbreviations

ABGS	The Secretariat General for European Affairs for the Republic of Turkey
Acquis Communautaire	The body of EU legal documents and law-making (currently more than 82,000 pages)
BAN	Business Angels Network
CC	Candidate Country to the European Union
DTI	Department of Trade and Industry (United Kingdom)
EBAN	European Business Angels Network
EIC	European Info Centre
FICHE	Official Document (here, with regards to asking for Proposals by EU MS for EU-CC Twinning Projects)
FP7	Seventh Framework Program of the EU for R&D
IA	Impact Analysis (sectoral)
ISO	Istanbul Sanayi Odasi (Istanbul Chamber of Industry)
ITO	Istanbul Ticaret Odasi (Istanbul Chamber of Commerce)
KOSGEB	Small and Medium Industry Development Organisation (Turkey)
MS	Member State of the European Union
NMS	New Member State to the European Union (12 including Bulgaria and Romania since 2004)
OECD	Organisation for Economic Cooperation and Development
PPM	Public Policy Management
RIA	Regulatory Impact Analysis
R&D	Research and Development (AR-GE in the Turkish language)
SEA	Single European Act
SELP	Technical Assistance for Small Enterprises Loan Program, 2nd Phase (Turkey)

SME	Small and Medium sized Enterprise (KOBI in the Turkish language)
SWOT	Strength, Weaknesses, Opportunities, Threats
THM	Tourism and Hotel Management
TURKSTAT	Turkish Statistical Institute
VAT	Value Added Tax

Appendix

Business Plan chapters as suggested by John Courtney (2006) and adapted for the purpose of MAN 473 by the author of this chapter:

Executive Summary
History and Background
Product/Services
The Market
People
Financial Analysis
Investor Deal
Appendices

Note by the author of this chapter: it has to be stressed that in particular the knowledge about how to formulate a feasible investor deal, as well as understanding the importance of the exit strategy for SMEs, is most often overlooked when SMEs ultimately do prepare a business plan. A situation that requires urgent attention.

References

ABGS (2006), Screening Chapter 20: Enterprise and Industrial Policy, Agenda Item III: SME and Enterprise Policies, Country Session: The Republic of Turkey, May 4–5, 2006, p. 32.

ABGS (2007), EU Accession Negotiations, Screening Process (as published on the ABGS website www.abgs.gov.tr, English version, Turkey – EU Relations, Screening Process), March 13, 2007.

Arrow, K. J. (1996) The Ten Arrow Principles, in: Kovacsy, Z., and Orban, K., Regulatory Impact Analysis – A Comprehensive Approach – Summary, (November 18, 2005), Ministry of Justice, Department of Impact Analysis, Deregulation and Registration of Law, Republic of Hungary, p. 4.

Clark, G. L., Feldman, M. P., Gertler, M. S. (2000). The Oxford Handbook of Economic Geography, Oxford University Press, Oxford.

CBI (2005), Center for the promotion of imports from developing countries of The Netherlands, EU Market Survey 2005, Organic Food Products, p. 111.

Cheng K. F., Chen, L.C. (2006), Fitting logistic regression models with contaminated case–control data, *Journal of Statistical Planning and Inference*, 136(12), 4147–4160.

Courtney, J. (2006), Introduction to Business Plan Drafting, Beer and Partners, www.beerandpartners.co.uk.

DTI (Department of Trade and Industry), Small Business Service, NOP Social & Political, Household Survey of Entrepreneurship 2003, Executive Summary.

European Commission (1985), White Paper: Completing the Internal Market, COM (85)310.

European Commission (2002), Descriptive Report on the simplification and modernization of VAT obligations for the European Commission, PriceWaterhouse-Coopers.

European Commission (2005a), The new SME definition – User Guide and model declaration, Enterprise and Industry Publications, European Commission, www.europa.eu, in effect as from January 1, 2005.

European Commission (2005b), Commission Staff Working Paper, The activities of the European Union for small and medium-sized enterprises: SME Envoy Report, SEC(2005)170, February 8, 2005, p. 8.

European Commission (2006), VAT Rates applied in the Member States of the European Community, Situation February 1, 2006, DOC/1803/2006-EN, DG Taxation and Customs Union, Tax Policy, VAT and other turnover taxes.

Işik, S. (2007), Guest Lecture at Bilkent University (MAN 473), April 19, 2007.

Jurgens, K. (2006), Why Regulatory Impact Analysis can Overcome Obstacles Turkey Faces on her Way to Europe?, *Insight Turkey* 8(3), 121–125.

OECD (2005), OECD Conference on Global Tourism Growth, Korea, September 6–7, 2005.

Pereira, F. (2006), Analytical examination of the Acquis Communautaire, Working Time Directive, DG Employment, Social Affairs and Equal Opportunities, Unit D2 – Labor Law and Work Organization, European Commission.

Porter, M. E. (1998), Clusters and the New Economics of Competition, *Harvard Business Review*, November–December.

Porter, M. E. (2000), Location, Competition and Economic Development: Local Clusters in a Global Economy, *Economic Development Quarterly*, Vol 14(1), 15–34.

Verachtert, B., Niehoff, J. (2007), Research for the benefit of SME, EU Commission Brussels, as presented at a KOBI Workshop organized by TUBITAK at ITO, Istanbul on February 14, 2007.

14 Innovation and Restructuring: The Conceptual Dilemma in the Continuous Process Improvement

Uğur Zel

Abstract

The relationship between "continuous improvement," "reengineering," and "innovation" has been a heavily debated topic in recent years. However, these concepts (approaches) have interlaced characteristics, but strongly differ in focus. Processes and systems have parts that perform the work of the system and relations among the parts that define how the work should be performed. In the frame of "System Theory," changes in the relations of the system represent the largest potential for improvement as the relations provide the structure in which the system functions.

This chapter examines the differences between the meanings and applications of the concepts innovation and reengineering by using different researchers' views. Articles and books written on these concepts are used to collect data to form the theoretical background of the chapter. As a conclusion, some evolutions are made to reveal the differences between the concepts in the frame of case studies.

14.1 Introduction

Based on the system theory, changes in a system's relations represent the largest potential of the process improvement. The "structure," in which the system functions, is formed thanks to these relations. The changes in this system are expressed in different forms. The relations between the concepts of reengineering and innovation, which are used frequently in the philosophy of continuous improvement, are among the issues often discussed and misused. These concepts are actually

N. Aydogan (ed.), *Innovation Policies, Business Creation and Economic Development*, International Studies in Entrepreneurship 21, DOI 10.1007/978-0-387-79976-6_14, © Springer Science+Business Media, LLC 2009

similar in nature and they have resembling relations with each other. They only differ in the "themes" they focus on.

14.2 Differences in the Meanings of the Concepts

The concept of "restructuring" in certain parts of the literature is utilized in lieu of reengineering. In addition, restructuring and "reorganization" are used in the same meanings. Even the "lean organization" and "downsizing" falls into this category.

Restructuring is to provide doing fewer jobs with less resource that are aimed for in downsizing theories by interfering with the organization structure (Peppard 1999:312). In contrast, in reengineering the aim is to achieve more with less resource and to increase customer satisfaction (MacDonald 1996:65; King 1996:22). While doing this, the target is to run the process as fast as possible and purify it from unnecessary procedures (Bushnell 1995:49). Hammer's generally accepted following definition of reengineering that expresses these aspects comprehensively can be given as an example: *fundamental rethinking and radical redesign of business processes to achieve dramatic improvements* (Hammer 1995:3).

Reengineering should not be confused with concepts such as reorganization, decreasing the management levels, and lean organization because it would be correct to look for the problem not in the organizational but in the progressive structures. At the same time, in this form of reengineering, which targets deeper innovations and redesigns the existing processes with new approaches, is alienated from the "Total Quality Management" approach.

14.3 The Concept of "Innovation"

Innovation is a concept that entered our lives in the 1940s and which is currently used together with "competitiveness." Between 1994 and 1995, the number of books that involved innovation in its title was more than 300. Innovation that can be recognized as a technological variable in economic terms is closely related with technical discoveries and invention. Innovation in relation with invention is defined as "starting some new activities and making certain changes in the current situation." Loke expressed innovation as "a change in human behavior or a process, which produces change and indicated that the innovations altogether would be an evolution" (Loke 1978:21).

Another approach is that innovation is a change process. However, any change is not an innovation. Change caused by innovation is original, meaning there has not been any change like this before. It is a positive and special change, and is aimed at achieving the purposes of its system more effectively and economically. From this point of view, innovation is narrower than change.

At this point, it would be useful to mention briefly the relation between innovation and creativity. These two concepts are described differently. Creativity is related with producing ideas. It is the creation of new ideas out of already existing ideas. Nevertheless, innovation should not make use of an idea created for the solution of a problem. However, each new idea produced as a result of creativity may not have the capability to be applicable in the solution of the problem. Yet the solution of the problem requires the realization of the idea gained by creativity and there is a creative idea in the heart of each innovation (Webber 1975:653).

In the policy document of the European Commission issued in 1995, the vital importance of innovation is defined as follows:

> Innovation ensures the satisfaction of individual and social needs in an effective way. Innovation is also the basis for the spirit of the entrepreneur. After all each new initiative is born at the end of a process launched to bring about an innovation. Moreover, all initiatives need continuous innovation to sustain their competitiveness. These are all valid for nations. Nations must immediately turn new ideas into technical and commercial success in order to maintain their economic growth, competitiveness and employment potential.

Definitions of innovation and its types are comprehensively included in the Oslo Manual (OECD 1996), which is taken as a basis by the European Commission and Eurostat. As it was lucidly expressed in the definitions, the two basic categories of innovation are "technologic products innovations" and "technologic process innovations." According to the Oslo Manual, "new" may be "new in the world," "new for the business," and at the same time may be "new for the world." The key activity of the innovation process is the production and acquisition of the knowledge that is new to the business (Oslo Manual 1998:3).

14.3.1 Deming's Innovation Concept

Deming considers innovation as a concept beyond improvement and expresses this in the first of his 14 principles (Deming 1996:21):

> One prerequisite of innovation is to believe in future. If the top management does not utter its unshakable loyalty to quality and productivity, innovation, which is the foundation of future, cannot improve. Without the institutionalization of this policy middle management and other staff in the firm suspect the effectiveness of their efforts.
>
> Prior to this, Deming observed that innovation must be included in the "planning" process and enumerates as follows the topics that should be included in planning in the scope of "innovation":

1. New products and services that may provide people with better standards and that may gain foothold in the market,
2. Probable costs of new materials to be utilized,
3. Production methods,
4. New skill to be necessary,
5. Training of the personnel,
6. Training of the supervisors,
7. Production cost,
8. Marketing cost,
9. Usage performance,
10. Customer satisfaction.

As can be understood from the order, the concepts that Deming has established have a direct connection with innovation as product/service, input, cost, and customer satisfaction. "In general, it is possible to classify these concepts in two categories: process and "output. "In other words, "design of new product/service" to be realized in the light of the demands of the customer and planned in the organization in order to maximize customer satisfaction constitutes the theme of the notion of innovation. Reemphasizing this theme in his book *The New Economics*, Deming expresses marketing new products and innovation by exactly coinciding them with one another (Deming 1993:9).

> Deming underlines that innovation is completely an administrative responsibility and implies that it has four important dimensions (Deming 1996:135):

1. Innovation in product/service
2. Innovation in the process
3. Improvement in the product/service produced
4. Improvement in the process applied.

Deming says that the Japanese steal other people's ideas in the name of innovation, and adds that the cars they manufactured have the qualities of the previously produced Western cars. But in spite of this, he never neglects to say that the Japanese always do better than the Westerners. That the less fuel consuming, more secure, more powerful, and more beautifully designed cars are manufactured by the Japanese are displayed in the surveys made by the "consumer magazines" in the last decade in order to prove this fact.

14.3.2 Imai's "Innovation" Concept

Masaaki Imai dwelled upon innovation in detail in his book titled *Kaizen*. He gives this example to underline the difference between the Kaizen and innovation concepts: Kaizen is like a fruitful nursery that feeds small and continues changes, but innovation is like a magma, which occurs sometimes with a sudden outburst (Imai 1999:25). As can be understood from this example and from the comparison given in Table 14.1, Imai's concept of innovation is similar to reengineering. At this point, it can be said that each innovation attempt should be followed by the continuous process improvement (Kaizen) (Yeomans 1996:9).

According to Imai, in a system created as a result of innovation, when an uninterrupted effort is not made primarily to protect and then to improve, it will continuously regress. Once established, all

Table 14.1

Dimension	Kaizen	Innovation
1. Effect	Long term, long period but not exciting	Short term, exciting
2. Improvement	With short steps	With big steps
3. Tempo	Improving continuously and regularly	Improving with intervals and irregularly
4. Change	Gradual and continuous	Sudden and temporary
5. Participation	Everybody	Limited number of "champions"
6. Spark	Conventional knowledge, contemporary	Technological progresses, new inventions, and new theories
7. Effort inclination	Human	Technology

systems tend to retrogress. One of the famous Parkinson Laws says that "... once an organization forms its structure it starts to move backward." In other words, a continuous improvement effort is necessary for the preservation of the current situation (Imai 1999:26). Some researchers, such as Tushman and Nadler, also emphasized this statement (1996). It was also pointed out that "innovation management" is one of the most important functions of the organization, and that the organization's "creativity" and "learning" potential is closely related with innovation and continuous improvement practices (Martensen 1999:627).

Masaaki Imai introduced an other vision of innovation. Imai graphically explains the differences in approaches of the Western and Japanese managers regarding "continuous improvement" as shown at Fig. 14.1. The difference observed in these graphics is innovation and defined as "wide scope change" (Imai 1986:25–27). In this definition,

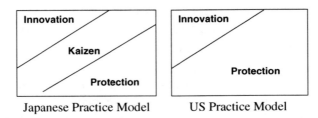

Japanese Practice Model   US Practice Model

Fig. 14.1 Japanese and US quality management practice models

"radical structural change" is meant to be and therefore carries a closer meaning to reengineering. However, Deming's definition of innovation is more related with process and product as regards the scope and differs from Imai's definition at this point.

14.4 The Concept of "Reengineering"

Reengineering means starting from scratch. The important thing is how we organize the business, taking the demands of today's market and technologies into account. In the heart of reengineering there lies interrupted thinking, which means defining and putting aside old rules and basic hypotheses that lead current business operations.

One of the concepts in the basis of reengineering is the concept of process. The organizational design of the companies in the last two centuries was affected by the mission-oriented system of thought, which means the disintegration of the work into the simplest forms and allocation of these parts to the specialized employees. Transition to the process-oriented system of thought started with the understanding of reengineering (Hammer 1995:32).

These are the common features seen in the business processes where reengineering is applied (Hammer 1995:46):

- Several works are integrated as a single work
- Employees make the decision
- The steps in the process are developed in a natural order
- Processes have many versions
- Work is performed in the most reasonable place
- Controls and inspections are reduced
- Understanding is minimized. The only point of contact is the case manager
- Centralized and decentralized procedures spread.

The difference between the concept of reengineering from Deming's innovation concept can be underlined as follows: Deming says that the organizations must ask these two questions about making innovations: (1) What are we doing? (2) Which product or service can help our customers in a better way than now? (Deming 1993:7–9). What is meant in innovation here is to reveal the customers' demands by analyzing their processes and design new products/services in this context.

14.4.1 Reengineering Practices of Western and Japanese Administrators

In the last two decades, one of the techniques that the organizations use commonly in the struggle against change is the "Total Quality Management." This expression does not exactly define the methods used by the organizations. When the practice forms are reviewed in detail, it is possible to see that it has different features. The existence of such variations in each method, understanding, or philosophy transferred from various cultures to ours is possible and obligatory. The most evident example of this is Japan, which does not call what they apply in their organizations as Total Quality Management. It is quite difficult to find this expression in the books of Japanese writers. The Japanese named this management philosophy "Kai-Zen" meaning "continuous improvement." Kai-Zen is the name of a "philosophy," which has peculiar specialties and cultural norms within its body that is reflected in the social and private life of the individuals. Of course, Japanese culture played a great role in spreading this philosophy throughout the country. The synthesis of the characteristic features of the Far East people and the Total Quality Management produced Kai-Zen.

In order to understand Kai-Zen, it would be useful to clarify its difference from the US Total Quality Management. This difference as a general scope is shown in Fig. 14.1.

Although the Americans try to maintain the level reached owing to innovations until the next innovation process, the Japanese try increasing this level through their Kai-Zen practices until the following innovation process. The point reached is considered to be standard, which is both protected and continuously improved by "Plan, Do, Check, Act" (PDCA). The graphic comparison of these two understandings is shown in Figs. 14.2 and 14.3.

When numerous but limited developments provided through continuous improvement is added to the radical developments realized through reengineering, considerable advances can be achieved. Although there is not a definite distinction, it is obvious that radical change is to be accomplished by the management that has the authority to manage the basic functions and organization of the establishment (Kavrakoglu 1998:54).

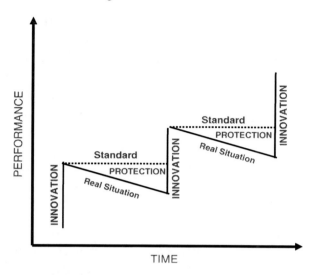

Fig. 14.2 US way of "quality management"

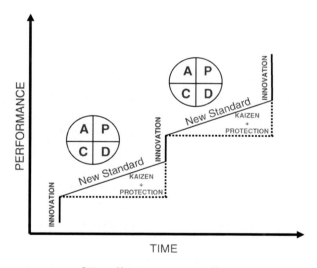

Fig. 14.3 Japanese way of "quality management"

From an other point of view, Japanese researcher Tsuchiya evaluates the success of the continuous improvement practices of the
Japanese organizations as unfavorable. To him, this achievement con-
ceals the need of the managers to practice "reengineering" and this, in
the long term, will result disadvantageously for the Japanese organizations (Tsuchiya 1998:403). Champy examined this issue in general

scope and stressed that there is a big mistake in the application of the continuous improvement process that must be in the following process of reengineering. This mistake is not to behave ambitiously or assertively. Consenting to assertive targets and insignificant changes instead of radical changes, or overextending the improvement process without any "jump" are the situations that interrupt change process (Champy 1995).

14.5 Conclusion

The common feature between the concepts of innovation or reengineering and continuous improvement is "change" (Boyd 1998:48). In fact, both reengineering and continuous improvement aims at processes and process improvement in common. The evident difference between them is that reengineering improves processes "fundamentally and radically," whereas continuous improvement (Kaizen) improves processes "gradually and in small parts."

No matter what word is used, in conclusion what must be believed in is the inevitability of change, and for this purpose effective use of certain mechanisms in the organization is compulsory. Change is a concept about future. In his book on this subject, Joel Barker underlines the importance of "paradigm converter" and states that we must get rid of the "paradigms" in our mind to seize the future (Barker 1992).

Improvement, regardless of its nature and content, is a journey over time. As the environment changes, so the external dynamics must be matched as far as possible by internal change. There is a need to evolve constantly.

Any process or system is composed of individual parts that perform the work of the system, and relations that describe how the work should be accomplished. In complex systems, which contain many parts and relations, the relations typically determine the system's performance. Therefore, improvement efforts that seek drastic improvements should focus on the relations. This is typically called business process reengineering. If small improvements are desired in a complex system, then the efforts should focus on improving the system's individual parts. This is typically called continuous process improvement. If the system is simple, the only way to achieve improvement is to focus primarily on the individual parts because very few relations exist.

References

Barker, J. A. (1992). *The Future Edge*, New York: William Morrow and Co.

Boyd, J. (1998). The Middle Way, *Computing Japan*, Vol. 5, Issue 6, p. 48.

Bushnell, R. (1995) When Do You Improve; When Do You Reengineer, *Automatic I.D. News*, Vol. 11, Issue 13, p. 49.

Champy, J. (1995). *Reengineering Management*, Glasgow: Harper Collins.

Deming, E. (1993). *The New Economics for Industry Government and Education*, Cambridge: MA: MIT Press.

Deming, E. (1996). *Out of Crises*, MA: The MIT Press.

Hammer, M. (1995). *Reengineering Revolution; A Handbook*, New York: Harper Collins.

Hammer, M. Champy, J. (1995). *Reengineering the Corporation*, New York: Harper Collins.

Imai, M. (1986). *Kaizen; The Key to Japan's Competitive Success*, New York: McGraw-Hill.

Kavrakoglu, İ. (1998). *Total Quality Management*, İstanbul: Kalder Pub.

King, I. (1996). The Road to Continuous Improvement: BPR and Project Management, *IIE Solutions*, Vol. 28, Issue 10, p. 22, October.

MacDonald B. (1996). Successful Reengineering. *Corporate Report*, Vol. 27, Issue 5, p. 64, May.

Martensen, A. (1999). Integrating Business Excellence and Innovation Management, *Total Quality Management*, July, p. 627.

OECD Oslo Manual. (1998). Measuring Knowledge Management; A New Indicator Of Innovation In Enterprises, *CPROST Report*, June.

Peppard, J. (1999). Benchmarking, Process Re-engineering and Strategy: Some Focusing Frameworks, *Human Systems Management*, Vol. 18, Issue 3/4, p. 297.

Tsuchiya, S. (1998). Simulation/Gaming as an Essential Enabler of Organizational Change, *Simulation and Gaming*, Vol. 29, Issue 4, p. 400.

Tushman, M., Nadler, D. (1996). Organizing for Innovation, (Ed) K. Starkey, *How Organizations Learn*, London: International Thomson Business Press.

Webber, R. (1975). *Management, Basic Elements of Managing Organizations*, Chicago, IL: Richard Irwin Inc.

Yeomans, M. (1996). Achieving Breakthrough Improvement Through BPR, *Armed Forces Comptroller*, Vol. 41, Issue 1, p. 7.

15 How to Address the Turkish Paradox of Innovation to Build a Competitive Economy?

Lale Gumusluoglu and Şirin Elçi

Abstract

The ability to innovate has become a crucial prerequisite of strong organizations as well as economies. Theoretical and empirical evidence demonstrates that developing countries with effective innovation policies and well-functioning national innovation systems are better positioned to close the development gap and improve their competitiveness. Turkey started discussing the innovation subject from the policy perspective in the mid-1990s, during the same time as the EU, where—at that time—a wide-ranging debate was stimulated by the "Green Paper on Innovation," and the government defined its main objective in this topic as "the establishment of the National Innovation System that would enable systematic operation of the whole institutions and mechanisms required to carry out scientific and technological research and development activities and to transform the results of those activities into economic and social benefit." However, until today, this goal has not been fully achieved and the innovation performance remained below the desired level. Although innovation performance is low, demand for innovative products/services, one of the prime drivers of innovation, is very high in Turkey. Departing from this paradox, this chapter discusses how to increase the innovative capabilities of the Turkish firms in favor of a competitive economy.

15.1 Introduction

The innovation literature dates back to the Schumpeterian times, early 1990s. Joseph Schumpeter, founder of the modern growth theory, was the first to emphasize the importance of new products as

N. Aydogan (ed.), *Innovation Policies, Business Creation and Economic Development,*
International Studies in Entrepreneurship 21, DOI 10.1007/978-0-387-79976-6_15,
© Springer Science+Business Media, LLC 2009

a stimulus to economic growth. He argued that with their innovator roles, entrepreneurs destroy the equilibrium in the market and lead to a continuous dynamism in an economy. To him, the entrepreneur brings in something new. It might be a new idea, product, or service, a new technology, or the entrepreneur finds new ways of using factors of production (Schumpeter 1990). In the contemporary literature, 1980s, we see Drucker as an advocate of innovative entrepreneurship. To him, "innovation is the specific tool of entrepreneurs, the means by which they exploit change as an opportunity for a different business or a different service" (Drucker 1985). Similar to Schumpeter, he focuses on the wealth creation character of innovation, and argues that businesses and societies who can organize and manage for innovation can prosper.

Innovation can be defined as the successful implementation of creative ideas within an organization (Amabile 1983). In spite of the varying definitions of innovation provided in the literature, most studies agree with its important contributions to economies. That is why this topic has recently attracted a considerable amount of interest from policy-makers, academicians, and practitioners. It is a well-established fact today that innovation is essential for the success and competitive advantage of organizations as well as for strong economies in the twenty-first century. A significant body of international theoretical and empirical evidence demonstrates links between technology, innovation and skills (the knowledge factors), total factor productivity (TFP) and economic growth (World Bank 2006). The OECD study (OECD 2001) that investigates the patterns of economic growth in the 1990s, and the role of innovation and information technology in growth reveals that levels of GDP per capita are no longer converging across OECD countries: Growth is higher in high-income countries and in those who continue to catch-up using technological innovation, like Ireland and South Korea. Countries with higher per capita growth rates maintain or even increase employment, while employment stagnate or fall in those experiencing a slowdown in growth. The reason is largely due to the fact that some countries were able to both increase the number of people working and increase their productivity through technological developments and innovation.

Developing countries with effective science, technology and innovation policies, and well-functioning national innovation systems

(NIS) (Lundvall 2000) are better positioned to close the development gap and mitigate inequalities. In this respect, based on effective policies, government intervention is necessary to develop human capital, to increase absorptive capacity of firms, and to create an environment conducive to innovation. The importance of such interventions is evident in the success cases of East Asian countries that achieve high growth and decline in inequality at the same time (World Bank 1993). These countries enjoyed fast catch-up by mastering sophisticated technological and managerial skills (Hobday 1995), and as a result of the ability to learn (Stiglitz 1996). In line with this, they provide lessons to developing countries like Turkey, who urgently need to make reforms in building an innovative economy.

In this short chapter, we do not aim to go into much detail regarding the innovation and innovation policy issues in Turkey. There is a growing amount of studies on the subject, most notably by the European Commission and the World Bank. Here, we limit ourselves to a brief overview of the situation with respect to innovation and the key challenges to address for increasing the innovation performance of the country.

15.2 Innovation in Turkey: An Overview

15.2.1 Private Sector Development and Entrepreneurship in Turkey

The short history of liberalization of her markets for Turkey began only after the 1980s. Before then, little room had been left to the private sector. After the 1930s, state-owned enterprises were established to compensate for the lack of a bourgeoisie who could otherwise replace the shortcomings of scarce resources and low productivity. The liberalization efforts after the 1980s, as well as the export-led growth strategy adopted, helped to develop a private sector of small and medium-sized businesses where social institutions supporting business development were established. Financial backups in the form of subsidies, tax exemptions, or cheap credits to business owners were provided. However, the slow pace of privatization, lack of regulatory institutions, high taxation, the inadequate technological infrastructure coupled with an inflation-prone and highly volatile macroeconomic environment remained impediments to private business development. In spite of all these drawbacks, the number of entrepreneurs kept increasing. With the membership to the Customs Union after 1995, there started a gradual shift from low value-added sectors such as textile and clothing to higher value-added sectors such as electronics, consumer durables, vehicles, and transport equipment (Cakmakci 2005). Furthermore, in 2000, the share of SMEs (1–250 workers) in the Turkish market reached 99.8 percent of total enterprises, which created 76.7 percent employment, but however accounted for only 26.5 percent of the value-added sectors and 10 percent of the exports (OECD 2004).

There are several studies about the profile of entrepreneurship in Turkey. A recent one (Gurel et al. 2003), based on the Household Labor Force Survey data collected by the State Institute of Statistics of Turkey, reports that entrepreneurship in Turkey falls short in the EU in terms of: (1) the share of women entrepreneurship (11 percent in Turkey, 22 percent in the EU), (2) and sectoral composition, where the shift from agriculture to nonagriculture in entrepreneurship has been much faster in the EU (share of entrepreneurship in agriculture in Turkey: 50 percent, the EU: 19 percent). Most studies also show that Turkish SMEs are below the EU-OECD average in terms of know-how and financing. These findings point out that to boost the innovativeness of Turkish firms and build a stronger economy, they need to be supported.

It was in mid-1990s that Turkey started discussing the innovation subject from the policy perspective during the same time with the EU where—at that time—a wide-ranging debate was stimulated by the "Green Paper on Innovation," and the Turkish government defined its main objective in this topic as "the establishment of the National Innovation System that would enable systematic operation of the whole institutions and mechanisms required to carry out scientific and technological research and development activities and to transform the results of those activities into economic and social benefit." However, until today, this goal has not been fully achieved and the innovation performance remained below the desired level. Although innovation performance is low, demand for innovative products/services, one of the prime drivers of innovation, is very high in Turkey. This is referred to as the "Turkish paradox of innovation" in this chapter and will be discussed in the next section. However, in order to better understand the innovation context Turkish firms are operating in, the preceding part presents the innovation climate and the National Innovation System in Turkey.

15.3 Innovation Climate in Turkey in the 2000s

The innovation climate in a country is determined by the political, macroeconomic, and institutional set-ups, and the demand conditions. Well-functioning financial and product markets, clearly defined and affordable intellectual property rights (IPR), favorable conditions for creation and growth of enterprises, and openness and ability of economy to engage in international trade and foreign direct investments are among the main framework conditions to enhance innovation in the private sector.

In spite of the timely initiation of political debate on innovation in Turkey in the mid-1990s, insufficient political commitment, weak economic environment, ineffective governance of NIS, and unfavorable framework conditions have been the major obstacles in development of a climate conducive to innovation in Turkey (Elci 2004).

Public sector imbalances, crises in Asia and Russia, the Marmara earthquake in the 1990s, and the economic crises in the early 2000s negatively affected Turkey's economic performance. However, a new economic program for restructuring the economy and achieving long-term stability, and structural reforms initiated led to a remarkable economic recovery. Inflation fell to single digits after 30 years. Gross Domestic Products (GDP) growth in 2004 reached 9 percent, followed by approximately 5 percent in 2005, and 6 percent in 2006, more than double of the EU-27 average. Foreign Direct Investment (FDI), which has been traditionally low, has started to rise; and particularly large-scale acquisitions in services, mainly in telecommunications and banking, increased FDI inflows to Turkey. The pace of privatization picks up and privatization sales reached nearly US$ 20 billion.

The reform programs continue to improve the business environment. The "Doing Business 2008" issued by the World Bank and International Finance Corporation provides information about the quality of the business environment, which is a key element influencing innovation climate. In the "ease of doing business," Turkey ranks 57 in 178 economies. The key indicator "starting a business," which is also a stimulating factor for innovative entrepreneurship, has been remarkably improved compared to the first "Doing Business" report issued in 2004, in terms of number of procedures and days. On the other hand, further actions are required in some areas like "closing a business." In an article on innovation called "Lessons from Apple" in *The Economist* 2007, the writer draws a wider conclusion from a lesson from Apple (which is what they call "fail wisely"). The wider lesson is phrased as "not to stigmatize failure but to tolerate it and learn from it." This argument is supported with the fact that "Europe's inability to create a rival to Silicon Valley owes much to its tougher bankruptcy laws" (*The Economist* 2007). The same issue remains as an obstacle in the creation of a favorable innovation climate in Turkey. According to "Doing Business 2008," the time and cost required to resolve bankruptcies are 3.3 years and 15 percent of income per capita, respectively. Both figures are comparable to the economies in the region, but nearly 2.5 times higher than the OECD average.

15.3.1 National Innovation System and Innovation Policy in Turkey

NIS is a network of organizations, individuals, and institutions that determine and shape the generation, diffusion and use of technology and knowledge, which in turn explains the pattern, pace, and the rate and economic success of innovation. Effectiveness of the NIS is determined by the quality and intensity of linkages, interactions, and flows between them: NIS is dynamic due to the "financial flows between government and private organizations...human flows between universities, firms, and government laboratories, regulation flows emanating from government agencies toward innovation organizations, and knowledge flows (spillovers) among these institutions" (Niosi 2002). Thus, public policies seek to facilitate and promote interactions between the different elements of the NIS, and to remove barriers to the flows.

The innovation system in Turkey is formed by the government bodies, implementing agencies of support programs, private sector establishments, knowledge and skill providers, innovation intermediaries, and other stakeholders such as technology parks, venture capital companies, incubators, and research centers. It has a relatively well structured government institutions in the NIS at national level. The Supreme Council of Science and Technology is the highest level policy coordination body for science, technology, and innovation in Turkey. It is chaired by the Prime Minister and is composed of re-lated ministries, high level representatives of the government bodies, universities, and nongovernmental organizations. On the enterprise side, there are approximately 1.8 million firms, majority of which are SMEs; nearly 15 percent of the enterprises are manufacturing industry companies; on the knowledge and skills providers' side, universities are the most important research performers; 67.9 percent of the coun-try's R&D spending is performed; and 61.9 percent of the researchers are employed by universities. R&D and innovation support programs are implemented by central agencies.

There is a remarkable effort for intensifying connections between the enterprises and the university system by innovation intermediaries and support programs. Technological support services and infrastruc-ture (in particular accreditation, metrology, quality control, and stan-dards) are in place, and their effectiveness is being improved in the process of the EU accession.

An important aspect of the Turkish innovation system is the large number of dynamic private and nongovernmental organizations that act as innovation intermediaries. These organizations are highly ef-fective in creating awareness on innovation, and thanks to them, inno-vation is a hot topic for discussion, and innovation policy in Turkey is driven by a broader public awareness (two examples of such efforts are provided in Box 1 and Box 2 in Section 15.4.1).

15.3.2 The Case of an Innovation Intermediary: IRC-EGE

Aegean Innovation Relay Centre (IRC-Ege) was established in April 2004 under the auspices of Ege University Science and Technology Centre (EBİLTEM), Aegean Region Chamber of Industry (EBSO), Izmir Ataturk Organized Industrial Zone (IAOSB), and Small and Medium Industry Development Organization (KOSGEB) as one of the two IRCs in Turkey. The primary objective of the center is to in-crease technical and commercial relationship between the Turkish and other European SMEs, with the help of IRC Network of the EU. In the long run, IRC-Ege aims to increase the level of competitiveness of the local SMEs by providing guidance and assistance in their own R&D projects. IRC-Ege serves SMEs in 14 provinces in Western Anatolia and employs 6 full-time staff.

IRC-Ege has been very active in promoting its services, and creating awareness on R&D and innovation among the regional SMEs. They use a proactive approach in this respect. In addition to conferences, road shows, TV programs, and the like, 568 companies were visited and 97 technology audits were conducted since the date of establishment. During the visits and technology audits, 75 new technologies were brought into daylight. In order to promote these new technologies developed by the Turkish SMEs in the region, the center organized and/or participated in 97 brokerage events throughout Europe. They also introduced technology requests by the regional SMEs. Some 1,608 bilateral meetings were organized during these events between Turkish and European SMEs with the assistance of the center.

As a result of these activities, 48 transnational technology transfers (TTT) were achieved between SMEs in Turkey and in other European companies. Twenty-five were from Turkish companies and the rest from Greece, Italy, Bulgaria, Israel, Finland, and the Czech Republic; and 23 were from European companies into Turkish companies. Apart from these 48 technology transfers, 5 Turkish companies established business collaborations with other European companies with the help of IRC-Ege.

The value created to the Turkish economy through these technology transfers is estimated to be around € 30 million. Ten SMEs, which made technology transfer, had not contacted any foreign companies for whatever reason until IRC-Ege approached them; 15 SMEs do not have any foreign language speaker in the company. Two technology-based start-ups were created after an inward technology transfer and started to produce new products and services that were new to their local market. Nearly 100 new jobs were created in the region as a result of the TTT activities. In addition, some SMEs started to employ staff to follow up new technologies in the IRC Network and participate actively in IRC-Ege activities.

The innovation system and policy in a country influence innovation process and performance in enterprises. In this respect, public intervention does not only aim to reduce or overcome "market failures," but also to systemic problems that can arise from failures of institutions in the innovation system. In Turkey, actions have been taken since the

1990s to address both problems. For example, improving intellectual property rights legislation and its enforcement, and increasing institutional capacity by the creation of the Turkish Research Area (TARAL) that, as one of its key objectives, aims to increase institutional capacity for innovation and support public–private cooperation in this area. On the other hand, there are still weaknesses within the innovation system that are mainly related to the issues of coordinating, linking, or addressing various systemic needs.

Although science and technology policy-making practices date back to the early 1960s in Turkey, innovation policy has not been handled explicitly. Innovation has become an integral part of science and technology policies between the mid-1990s and 2000s. In those documents, there were implications of diffusion of innovation and knowledge from an innovation systems perspective. Overemphasis on research activities, scientist and research institutions are observed in the science and technology strategies, developed and issued in 2005. These strategies are based on the linear view of innovation. The first stand-alone innovation strategy document issued in 2007 again does not attach sufficient emphasis on the systemic nature of innovation.

The innovation policy mix in Turkey focuses on four main categories (Elci Forthcoming report) : (1) Increase rates of expenditure on research and technological innovation in enterprises, (2) intensifying cooperation between public or higher education research organizations and enterprises on R&D activities, (3) increase the number of new innovation intensive enterprises created and their survival, and (4) increase the rate of commercialization/marketing of the results of R&D activities by research and higher education organizations.

Although there is still a need for more balanced policy mix, the measures introduced in late 2006 and 2007 contributed to the enrichment of the policy mix. Considering the categories covered by the existing policy mix, one can conclude that there are a large number of areas that are not addressed by these measures. For example, innovation policy measures/programs to foster an innovation friendly environment, and those aiming to develop future skills base, innovation intermediaries, and nontechnological innovation, to optimize financial regulations, and to exploit new market opportunities are among the important areas that need to be addressed by policy measures. Additionally, much work also remains to be done to create framework conditions that are conducive to innovation.

From the financial point of view, funds allocated by the government for R&D and innovation have remarkably been increased since the issuance of the new science and technology strategies in 2005. The main target of the strategies has been fixed to increase the level of gross domestic expenditure for R&D as percentage of GDP from around 0.8 percent in 2005 to 2.0 percent by 2010. Accordingly, the total amount of funds put aside by the government for new and ongoing R&D programs for the last 3 years is € 2.2 billion while it was € 1 billion during 2000–2004.

15.3.3 Innovation Demand and Performance in Turkey

Demand is an important driver for innovation. First, companies can consider the needs and tastes of the customers and use a demand/pull model in producing new or improved products/services. Second, demand for innovative products or services can be of crucial importance to the commercial success of innovation. In other words, as Porter (1990) states, home demand pressure local firms to innovate faster and achieve more sophisticated competitive advantages compared to their foreign rivals.

The 2005 Innobarometer (EC 2005) provides a measure of innovation demand based on a survey of 30,000 Europeans in the 25 member states plus Bulgaria, Romania, Croatia, the Turkish Republic of Northern Cyprus, and Turkey. Interviews were conducted face-to-face where a set of questions was asked in order to identify to which extent citizens feel attracted by innovative products or services. The survey findings show that 57 percent of the EU citizens feel attracted toward innovative products or services. Turkey got one of the highest scores in the EU where 71 percent declared that they are drawn to innovative products or services. The receptiveness of the Turkish people is notable, with 63 percent responding that they "quickly try the innovative one at least once." Furthermore, 35 percent declared that they would replace what they already use by an innovative one "even if they have to pay a certain premium."

In the study, there is also a typology analysis that revealed four groups that can be distinguished in terms of their attitudes toward innovation: the "anti-innovation" group (opposed to innovative products or services), the "reluctant" group (not yet ready to embrace

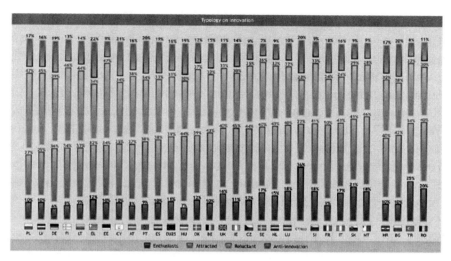

Fig. 15.1 Innobarometer 2005: typology on innovation

Source: Innobarometer, European Commission, 2006

innovative products or services), the "attracted" group (drawn toward innovative products or services), and the "enthusiasts" (calling out for innovation). Figure 15.1 shows the proportion of each of these groups in each country.

The survey findings revealed that in terms of enthusiasts, Turkish Republic of Northern Cyprus and Turkey can be distinguished with the highest proportions of 36 and 25 percent respectively. Romania, Slovakia, Malta, and Slovenia follow behind with the enthusiasts representing 11 percent of the EU-25 average. In terms of the "pro-innovation citizens" (i.e. either enthusiasts or the attracted group), Malta and Slovakia are the member states with the highest proportions—64 percent and 62 percent. Romania (60 percent) and Turkey (59 percent) follow very closely behind. The pro-innovation group represents 50 percent of the EU-25. Regarding the anti-innovation group, the highest proportions belong to Greece (22 percent) and Cyprus (21 percent). The anti-innovation group represents 16 percent of the EU-25 sample. For this group, Turkey ranks the second lowest with only 8 percent declaring that they are opposed to innovative products or services after Sweden (7 percent). Hence, all the findings indicate that citizens in Turkey are among the most ready to embrace innovation.

One example lending support to the high level of demand by the
Turkish people to innovative products/services is the mobile phone
usage rate in Turkey. The number of people using mobile phones has
grown by over 200 percent over the past 6 years. According to the
European Information Technologies Observatory, Turkey ranks the
10th among the frequent mobile phone user countries (*Turkish Daily
News* 2007). Telecommunication Board (TK) President Mr. Acarer
stated that the number of active subscribers exceeded 54 million in
Turkey (*Financial News* 2007). This corresponds to around 80 percent
of the whole population, similar to that of Russia (83 percent), and
more than that of the United States (70 percent) (UN 2006).

Another form of demand can be observed in a country's imports of
high technology. In this respect, Turkey is a net importer of high-tech
products. By the end of the 1990s, 10 percent of Turkish imports
were high-tech (of which 30 percent belonged to telecommunication equipment and 22 percent to chemicals), but the technological content of its exports were very low (2 percent) (Lemoine and
Ünal-Kesenci 2003). Indeed, the high-tech intensity of exports during 2000–2004 decreased by 15.9 percent, and the average annual
growth rate of the Turkish share in world high-tech exports during 2000–2005 decreased by 10 percent (EC 2007). These observations show that Turkish companies have declining competitiveness
in world markets. In other words, while the technological intensity
of world trade has increased over the past decade (OECD 2005),
the ability of Turkey to develop new knowledge and use it in the
production of technology goods has declined. These observations
also lend support to the Turkish paradox of innovation in that the
supply (exports) of high-tech products fall very short of demand
(imports).

In spite of the high demand to innovative products/services in
Turkey, the innovation performance of the country is low. Turkey faces
several important challenges in overcoming this paradox. These challenges as well as policy recommendations will be provided in the next
section. Before that, its innovation performance with respect to the
EU countries as well as to the globe is discussed in the following
paragraph.

From the innovation performance viewpoint, we refer to the data
provided by the EC: The European Innovation Scoreboard (EIS) is an

instrument developed at the initiative of the European Commission under the Lisbon Strategy, to evaluate and compare the innovation performance of the EU member states. The EIS 2006 includes innovation indicators and trend analyses for the EU25 member states, plus the two new member states: Bulgaria and Romania, as well as for Croatia, Turkey, Iceland, Norway, Switzerland, the United States, and Japan (EC 2006). The 2006 results of the EIS for Turkey show the country's weak innovation performance. However, the poor availability of data continues to be a problem for the evaluation of Turkey's innovation performance, as seen in Fig. 15.2.

Although at low levels compared to the EU average, positive trends are observed in all innovation drivers indicators (S&E graduates, population with tertiary education, broadband penetration rate, participation in life-long learning, and youth education attainment level).

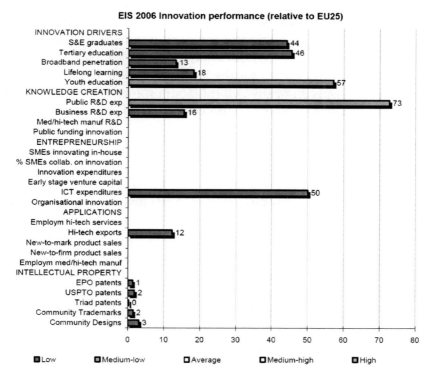

Fig. 15.2 Innovation performance of Turkey relative to EU25

Source: European Innovation Scoreboard, European Commission, 2006

Positive trends in public R&D continue with respect to knowledge creation. However, there is a decline in business R&D expenditures. Only one indicator is available in each of the "innovation and entrepreneurship" and "application categories," (ICT expenditures and exports of high technology products, respectively) and both show declines. Trend results suggest improvements in intellectual property (Elci Forthcoming report).

The 2006 EIS also compares the innovation performance of the EU25 to that of the candidate countries, and other major R&D spenders and emerging economies in the world (so-called "Global Innovation Scoreboard" [GIS]): Argentina, Australia, Brazil, Canada, China, Hong Kong, India, Israel, Japan, New Zealand, Republic of Korea, Mexico, the Russian Federation, Singapore, South Africa, and the United States. Of the 25 indicators used to measure innovation performance in the EIS, GIS data were available for 12 of them. GIS measures innovation performance by use of a composite indicator, the Global Summary Innovation Index (GSII) decomposed into five composite indices measuring five key innovation dimensions: innovation drivers, knowledge creation, diffusion, applications, and intellectual property (EC 2006). Based on the ranking of their GSII scores, the countries analyzed can be divided into four groups: Global innovation leaders, next-best performers, follower countries, and lagging countries. Figure 15.3 shows countries classified according to these groups.

Although Turkey is among the group of lagging countries, its performance is better than the four EU member states (Latvia, Poland, Cyprus, and Romania).

The results of the innovation performance analysis for Turkey suggest that it needs to focus on input innovation drivers and knowledge creation to be able to create an innovative private sector. R&D expenditure as percentage of Gross Domestic Products (GDP) remains at a low level (0.79 percent in 2004), with a slight increase since the mid-1990s. In spite of an increase in private R&D since the 1990s, firm-financed gross domestic expenditure in R&D was still low at 43.31 percent of the total in 2005. From the human capital and knowledge creation perspective, Turkey has low levels in new science and engineering graduates, population with tertiary education, participation in life-long learning, and youth education attainment level (more detailed analysis is presented in Section 15.4).

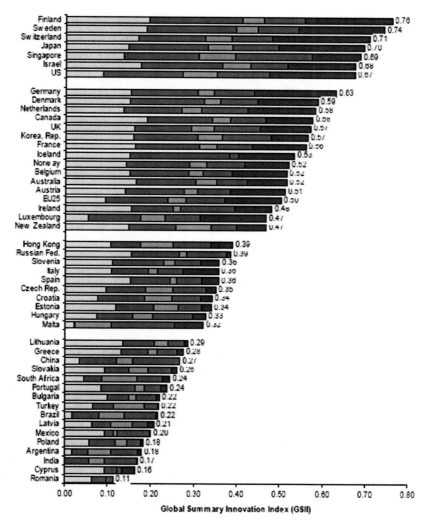

Fig. 15.3 Global innovation index

Source: European Innovation Scoreboard, European Commission, 2006

15.4 Challenges and Recommendations

The most recent indicators presented in the preceding paragraph, demonstrate that Turkey can only generate higher levels of innovation outputs only if it can improve its inputs. The public intervention for increasing the innovation performance of enterprises with a view to improving competitiveness for economic growth and social well-being can seek to address longer-term drivers such as the investment in human capital for innovation, and relatively short term and direct needs of entrepreneurs and firms, like funding early stage start-ups. To this end, strategically focused interventions are needed to address both the short-term needs and longer-term drivers to increase the innovation performance of the country. This section provides an overview and recommendations for the main challenges that Turkey should focus on to improve its innovativeness.

15.4.1 Investing in Longer-Term Drivers for Innovation

Although looking at the longer-term drivers, we limit our focus on two main areas: Human capital, and knowledge creation and diffusion. As argued by Porter (1990), these advanced factors (human and knowledge resources) are integral to a firm's capacity to innovate, and without their presence firms may lack the ability to respond to the demanding home buyers.

The World Bank defines a knowledge economy as one where organizations and people acquire, create, disseminate, and use knowledge more effectively for greater economic and social development. Human capital is the most important foundation to a knowledge economy where countries abundant in human capital are at an advantage in producing and disseminating new knowledge. Countries such as South Korea and Ireland have built knowledge economies by investing heavily in education and training, and boosting innovation through intensive R&D.

One benchmark of countries' abilities to compete in the knowledge-based economy is provided by the World Bank—Knowledge Economy Index (KEI). This index is based on four pillars related to the knowledge economy: economic incentive regime, education, innovation, and ICT. According to the most recent study, Turkey has improved its ranking in the world from 60 in 1995 to 53 in 2007, basically due to its improvement of its score in the innovation pillar (World Bank 2007), However, 2007 scores show that Turkey still ranks (5.56) below both the world average (5.93) and the averages of Western Europe (8.70), and Europe and Central Asia (ECA) (6.30). Although Turkey scores better than the ECA countries with respect to

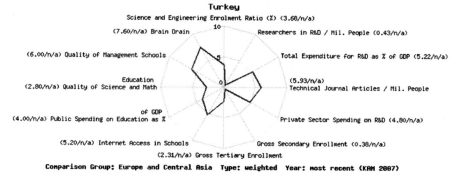

Fig. 15.4 Strengths and weaknesses of Turkey against the ECA region

Source: World Bank, KAM, 2007

its economic incentive and institutional regime, it performs worse in the education and the innovation pillars. Specifically, Fig. 15.4 show that Turkey has several strengths and weaknesses against the ECA region.

The indicators of the education pillar that Turkey has a weaker performance than the ECA average are gross secondary and tertiary enrolment, public spending on education as % of GDP, quality of science and math education, and the brain drain. As far as the knowledge creation is concerned, science and engineering enrolment, and researchers in R&D per million are some of the weaknesses whereas technical journal articles per million is a strength.

These findings are in line with those provided in ECA Knowledge Economy Study (Goldberg et al. 2006). By using KEI indicators from the World Bank's knowledge assessment methodology, this study provides a grouping of ECA countries according to their readiness for various innovation instruments. Similar to the World Bank methodology, it uses four pillars to calculate KEI—the composite index. Accordingly, countries are suggested to critically evaluate their scores for each pillar and consider reforming first those that have low scores. The rationale in doing so is that for a well-functioning NIS, problematic pillars need to be given a priori, as they create a bottleneck for government intervention; without reforming them, high performance on other pillars will not translate into an effective innovation system. Accordingly, Turkey ranks 21 out of 30 countries with its education pillar scoring the lowest (Education rank: 29, Economic Incentives

Rank: 16, Innovation Rank: 23, Information Infrastructure Rank: 18). In other words, the bottleneck in the Turkish NIS can be identified as education.

One other important benchmark study is provided by the European Innovation Scoreboard (EIS) mentioned in Section 15.3. According to the most recent EIS (2006) (EC 2006), although Turkish scores in the groups of innovation drivers and knowledge creation have experienced a slight increase, still they are notably below the EU-25 average.

Overall, the comparative statistics demonstrate that Turkey faces an urgent need to reform and improve its educational and knowledge creation capacity. First, there is the need to increase public spending on education where most of the total spending, 7 percent, comes from the private sector (WEF 2006–2007). Second, the quality of education should also be improved. In 2003, some important steps had been taken to modernizing the basic education curriculum to encourage creative thinking by the students. In fact, a notable progress along this line was realized as of fall 2006 where the national compulsory education curricula included innovation and innovative entrepreneurship as a subject to be taught in a three-year course entitled "Technology and Design." This was a success for Project Ekin "Triggering a Cultural Change for Innovation," which was launched by a civil organization. These modernization studies should continue and be evaluated periodically. Second, enrolment in secondary education should be increased. Although enrolment in secondary education (gross percentage) is 79 percent, only 27 percent of the Turkish children complete secondary education, as compared with 65 percent in the EU32 (Eighth Five Year Development Plan 2000). This raises the importance of making secondary education compulsory. It has been recognized by the Turkish policy-makers as a long run goal in the Eighth Five Year Development Plan (2000).

Reforms are also needed to increase both the quantity and the quality of graduates from higher education institutions. Only 10 out of a 100 in Turkey have tertiary education whereas it is 22.8 in the EU-25 (EC 2006). The first step for this is to redesign the university entrance examination (OSS) to include modern assessments aligned with the objectives of the revised curriculum. Recently, the OSS was revised to include some moderate levels of creativity measurement. Oral (2006) investigated whether four dimensions of creativity (fluency, flexibility, originality, and elaboration) were accounted for at OSS to select prospective teachers in Turkey. The results showed that all dimensions of creativity have been included in the verbal test though not in the numerical one. Although she states that although this shift at the OSS is a sign of an educational innovation, it is not sufficient to produce an educational reform for a creative, developed society. Increasing the number of universities, particularly science and engineering faculties, but at the same time assuring that they provide quality education can be another solution. Besides, the current curricula should be redesigned to include courses about the needs of the private sector. As a matter of fact, some universities have started to offer courses on entrepreneurship, innovation and technology management. More such courses should be offered and the curricula of science and engineering faculties should be more flexible to include such courses from social science faculties.

Apart from these schooling issues, participation in life-long learning should be encouraged throughout the society. Life-long learning is one crucial input to a knowledge economy and can be through many means such as post-graduate programs, corporate training, courses for adults, and online learning. Unfortunately, participation in life-long learning in Turkey is very low (2 per 100 population aged 25–64) compared to the EU-25 average (11 per 100 population) (EC 2006). In fact, EU provides many opportunities in this respect through programs such as Erasmus, Leonardo da Vinci, and so on. Already, these programs have attracted many Turkish students and teaching staff. However, awareness about the importance of life-long learning should be created in the society at large. The support of media and civil organizations for this purpose can be very crucial at this point.

15.4.2 Triggering a Cultural Change for Innovation: Project Ekin

The project called "Triggering a Cultural Change for Innovation" (Project Ekin) was launched by the Technology Management Association (TYD) in cooperation with Technopolis Group, Bilkent University, Turkish Informatics Association, METU Technology Park, and Referans Daily. This project was one of the winning proposals of the World Bank's Turkey Development Marketplace Competition in the category—"Social Inclusion and Progress on the way to Europe." Involving the cooperation of a large group of stakeholders from the private sector, academia, nongovernmental organizations, public organizations, and the media, the project intended to create awareness about the concept and importance of innovation-based entrepreneurship in educational institutions as well as the society at large. To this end, it aimed at training teachers and students in innovation and innovative entrepreneurship during June 2005–June 2006.

Three schools, two in a developed region and one in a less developed region of Turkey, participated in the pilot phase, carried out in two stages. In the first stage, the curriculum was defined, a book was produced, and the teachers were trained. In the second stage, the pupils were trained by their teachers in accordance with the content prepared. As well as the lectures, the students also experienced real life examples of innovation and innovative entrepreneurship as they visited several innovative companies located in the science parks. Then, in teams, they developed their own innovative ideas, established virtual companies, and prepared business plans. A group of university students trained on the subject coached these 12 virtual companies throughout the business planning process.

The pilot project ended with an event and award ceremony. In this final event, the teams presented their innovation ideas and business plans. Participants were invited to visit the virtual companies established by the students and become their "business angels" by buying virtual shares from those they preferred to invest in. The three companies that received most of the investments were presented with an award.

This project has been a big success as the main goal of "integrating innovation and innovative entrepreneurship in the national education curricula" was achieved (TrendChart Newsletter 2006). Following the project, and as of fall 2006, innovation is taught in schools throughout the country in a course entitled "Technology and Design."

As the knowledge creation and diffusion dimension of innovation is concerned, the main issues are to increase public and private R&D expenditures, the number patents filed by researchers and firms, and to intensify the linkages between firms and knowledge producers. As noted in Section 15.2.3, total spending on R&D, although increased from 0.67 (percentage of the GDP) in 2004 to 0.79 today, it is still below the EU-25 average, and R&D activities are mainly conducted by universities. Despite the important role played by the Turkish universities in the field of research, applied knowledge is hardly transformed in innovation. Although no data are available on the commercialization of research results (the number of spin-offs and patents by university researchers, etc.), when we compare the increase in the number of publications with that of the patents registered by the residents, there is a significant increase in the scientific output in terms of publications. But the increase in the patent registration is quite low. The number of publications by scientists in Turkey increased from 2,333 in 1995 to 17,717 in 2005. Turkey's world ranking accordingly improved from 34th to 19th. However, the number of patent registration by residents increased from 58 in 1995 to 95 in 2005. The main reason is the lack of incentives and measures for universities that stimulates commercialization of research results and cooperation with the private sector. Although policy initiatives are implemented to encourage patenting by researchers and firms, further actions are required to create the culture of and develop human resources on the IPR, and building intellectual property units/technology transfer offices at universities.

Structures like technology transfer offices facilitate knowledge diffusion as well. Although there are 115 universities in Turkey, only a few of them have special units organized for this purpose.

Clusters and networks are important for knowledge creation and diffusion between knowledge producers and enterprises. According to the results of 2006 Innobarometer survey by the EC (2006), apart from the Nordic countries (Finland, Sweden, Denmark, and Norway), Turkey is the only country with the highest level—and intensity—of networking. The majority of cluster companies actively participate at least in two business networks, and about 9 out of 10 cluster companies take a meaningful part in at least one such network. With this strength in mind, the challenge is to ensure that enterprises and universities as well as other actors in the networks specifically collaborate for joint innovation activities and knowledge exchange. This requires designing and implementing policy initiatives to foster further development of clusters and increase their economic benefits through innovation.

15.5 Addressing Short-Term Needs for Innovation

Addressing the short term and direct needs of entrepreneurs and firms for increasing the innovation performance requires policy measures, both to increase investments to improve capabilities for innovation in existing firms, and to stimulate creation of new innovative enterprises. It also necessitates the improvement of innovation policy governance. This can be achieved by developing a more coherent approach to policy-making, implementation, and evaluation, as well as by building effective coordination mechanisms.

Current policy initiatives encourage innovation in manufacturing firms and software companies, and mainly aim at cofinancing their R&D and technological innovation activities as well as stimulating cooperation with research community. Particular attention is needed to design and implement measures encouraging nontechnological innovation as well (marketing and organizational innovation), and specifically addressing innovation in the service sector and in traditional industries (agro-food, textile and apparel, tourism, etc., which are the most important sectors in the Turkish economy in terms of GDP, employment, and exports).

One can suggest that the main reasons for the Turkish paradox are that enterprises in general are not aware of the imperativeness of innovation, and most of them do not have the knowledge and capabilities to use the demand factor as a means to enhance their competitiveness. Not surprisingly, there are no policy initiatives designed so far specifically targeting raising awareness on innovation and developing innovation management skills in enterprises. As mentioned in Section 15.2.3, efforts on these issues have been taken by nongovernmental and private organizations. On the other hand, public intervention in these areas is needed to create a broad and sustainable impact.

The underdeveloped venture capital and business angels market is a crucial impediment for the creation and development of innovative businesses. Only a few of the existing venture capital companies prefer to invest in small and medium companies, and almost none chose to make early stage investments. Similarly, business angel investments are low and the very low number of business angels' networks prevents entrepreneurs' access to such finance options.

Existing venture capital firms do not prefer to invest in start-ups due to several reasons (Elci 2007): They do not want to invest in high-risk businesses, largely because of the traditionally risk averse culture they have as subsidiaries of banks; they do not have special expertise and experience in high-tech fields; they see investing in small deals as a problem, both due to heavy due diligence requirements and the requirement of the current venture capital legislation that foresees investment of 50 percent of the funds in a short period of time. On the demand side, there is an increasing interest from young entrepreneurs who are either new graduates from universities or students attending undergraduate and graduate programs. The fund-of-funds (FOF) programs have proved to be important tools in the development of seed and early stage venture capital industry. Successfully experienced in Israel through the Yozma program[1], the FOF program requires the government to act as a catalyst in the creation of venture capital industry by stimulating and preparing the conditions for private sector and foreign investors to set up new venture capital funds, and securing an obligation of the new venture capital funds to invest in start-up companies. The government's role in the FOF is temporary and ends with the privatization of the fund. The Turkish government could play an important role by learning from the FOF experience and adopting a program similar to Yozma.

Business angels are important sources of financing for seed, start-up and early stage ventures, and the potential for the growth of business angels' investments is high in Turkey due to the high volume of entrepreneurs looking for finance as well as that of individual savings. Stimulation of business angels' investments requires public

---

[1] The Israeli Government set up the Yozma venture capital company in 1993 to act as a catalyst for an emerging venture capital industry, and allocated US$ 100 million for that purpose. Under this program, a fund of funds—Yozma (initiative in Hebrew) was established. Under the Yozma initiative, 10 venture capital funds were formed in partnership with leading foreign venture investors. The total capital of each fund was US$ 20 to US$ 25 million of which the government's share was 40 percent and the foreign investors' was 60 percent. The major attraction of the Yozma program was the foreign investors' option to buy out the government's share at a pre-agreed price for a period of five years. In addition, Yozma was allowed to invest a certain portion of its capital directly. The government-owned Yozma fund was privatized in 1997 (Israel Venture Association, www.iva.co.il).

intervention. It is important to intensively promote the concept, raise awareness, and provide training and education both for the supply and demand sides. Equally important is to provide incentives to encourage investments in innovative businesses at early stages, for example through tax incentives.

Improving the innovation policy governance is another crucial issue to be dealt with in the short term. This requires the introduction of a more coherent policy-making approach. For instance, policies need to be developed involving consultation of key stakeholders at all stages, a well organized coherent system of policy coordination at government and agency levels should be in place, and policy mix need to be strategically focused on priorities. The evaluation of the programs and initiatives should be regularly exercised to support transparency, accountability, and the justification of funding decisions, and be a vital part of the policy-making process.

A change of culture is required at the policy level: The systemic view of innovation where innovation is not primarily a result of a science and R&D need to be recognized, and an innovation strategy that places innovation at the heart of all economic, and social development (including science and technology) policies should be adopted.

From the policy-making perspective, it is also important to recognize that given the size of the country and the economic, social, and geographical diversity of its regions, a fully centralized NIS is a barrier to addressing regional and local challenges. Regional and local strategies and institutions should be established to ensure that all regions are reached. It is worth to mention that such efforts have recently been initiated again in a bottom-up approach by the private sector and nongovernmental organizations.

15.6 Conclusion

Addressing the Turkish paradox of innovation is a critical part of achieving a sustainable, long-term economic growth, and social welfare. Most of the barriers on the way to reaching this goal could be overcome by taking the advantages of the demand for innovation in the society. Exploiting these advantages requires a good understanding of innovation, and its role in business and economy.

In that respect, it is important not to view innovation policy as a part of science and technology policy, but as a horizontal policy area: to ensure that the NIS functions properly and dynamically, policies are designed and implemented effectively and consistently, and that the challenges are satisfactorily addressed by suitable policy actions.

A firm commitment by the NIS actors to address the paradox will not only help Turkey to close the gap with the developed nations but also ensure that it reaps the social benefits of increased productivity and sustainable economic growth.

References

Schumpeter J. A. (1990) The Theory of Economic Development: An Inquiry into Profits, Capital, Credit, Interest and the Business Cycle. In: Casson M. (ed) Entrepreneurship, Edward Elgar Publishing, Hants.

Drucker P. F. (1985) Innovation and Entrepreneurship. Harper & Row, Publishers, Inc., New York.

Amabile T. M. (1983) The Social Psychology of Creativity. Springer-Verlag, New York.

World Bank (2006) Turkey Country Economic Memorandum Promoting Sustained Growth and Convergence with the European Union http://www.worldbank.org.tr/cem2006 Cited 10 Sep 2007.

OECD (2001) A New Economy? The Changing Role of Innovation and Information Technology in Growth. OECD, Paris http://www.oecd.org/document/62/0,3343,en_2649_33703_2675198_1_1_1_1,00.html.

Lundvall B. A. (2000) Systems of Innovation: Growth, Competitiveness and Employment. In: Edquist C and M McKelvey (Eds), Edward Elgar Publishing, Cheltenham.

World Bank (1993) The making of the East Asia miracle http://www.worldbank.org/html/dec/Publications/Bulletins/PRBvol4no4.html. Cited 10 Sep 2007.

Hobday M. (1995) Innovation in East Asia: The Challenge to Japan. Edward Elgar Publishing, Hants.

Stiglitz J. (1996) Some Lessons from the East Asian Miracle. http://wbro.oxfordjournals.org/cgi/content/abstract/11/2/151 Cited 10 Sep 2007.

Cakmakci U. M. (2005) The context of innovation and the role of the state. In: Trott P. (ed) Innovation Management and New Product Development, 3rd edn. Pearson Education Limited, England.

OECD (2004) Small and Medium-Sized Enterprises in Turkey: Issues and Policies. Small and Medium Enterprises Outlook, OECD, Paris. http://www.oecd.org/dataoecd/5/11/31932173.pdf. Cited 10 Sep 2007.

Gurel E., Gumuşluoglu L., Guney S. (2003) An Analysis of Entrepreneurship by Demographics and Sectoral Composition in Turkey and A Comparison with the European Union. Boğaziçi Journal 17(1): 75–104.

Elci, S. (2004) European Trend Chart on Innovation: Annual Innovation Policy for Turkey, September 2003-August 2004. European Commission. http://www. proinno-europe.eu/docs/reports/documents/Country_Report_Turkey_2006.pdf Cited 10 Sep 2007.

The Economist, June 7, 2007 http://www.economist.com/opinion/displaystory.cfm? story_id=9302662. Cited 5 August 2007.

Niosi, J. (2002) National systems of innovations are "x-efficient" (and x-effective): Why some are slow learners. Research Policy 31: 291–302.

Elci, S. (Forthcoming report) INNO-Policy TrendChart - Policy Trends and Appraisal Report: Turkey, 2007. European Commission http://www.proinno-europe.eu/index.cfm?fuseaction=country.showCountry&topicID=263&parent ID=52&ID=41.

Porter M. E. (1990) The Competitive Advantage of Nations. The Free Press, New York.

EC (2005) Population Innovation Readiness Study: Innobarometer http://www. eurosfaire.prd.fr/7pc/doc/1125061030_innovation_readiness_final_2005.pdf. Cited 10 August 2007.

Turkish Daily News, October 13, 2007 http://www.turkishdailynews.com.tr. Cited 16 Oct 2007.

Turkey Financial News, April 13, 2007 http://www.turkeyfinancial.com/news/2007. Cited 20 Sep 2007.

UN (2006) Information Economy Report. United Nations Conference on Trade and Development http://www.unctad.org/en/docs/sdteecb20061_en.pdf. Cited 11 Oct 2007.

Lemoine F., Ünal-Kesenci D (2003) Trade and Technology Transfers: A Comparative Study of Turkey, India and China. CEPII, Working Paper, No. 2003–16 http://www.cepii.fr/anglaisgraph/workpap/pdf/2003/wp03-16.pdf. Cited 9 Sep 2007.

EC (2007) Key Figures 2007 On Science, Technology and Innovation: Towards A European Knowledge Area. http://ec.europa.eu/invest-in-research/pdf/kf_2007_prepub_en.pdf. Cited 15 Sep 2007.

OECD (2005) Science, Technology and Industry Scoreboard 2005. OECD, Paris. http://www.oecd.org/sti/scoreboard. Cited 12 Sep 2007.

EC (2006) European Innovation Scoreboard 2006: Comparative Analysis of Innovation Performance Pro Inno Europe Inno Metrics. http://www.proinno-europe.eu/doc/EIS2006_final.pdf. Cited 1 Sep 2007.

World Bank (2007) Knowledge Assessment Methodology (KAM). http://www. worldbank.org/kam. Cited 10 Sep 2007.

Goldberg I., Trajtenberg M., Jaffe A. et al (2006) Public Financial Support For Commercial Innovation: Europe and Central Asia Knowledge Economy Study Part I. Europe and Central Asia Chief Economist's Regional Working Paper Series vol 1, no.1 http://siteresources.worldbank.org/INTECA/Resources/KE_Study_Final.pdf. Cited 3 Sep 2007.

WEF (2006–2007) Global Competitiveness Index, 2006–2007, World Economic Forum   http://www.weforum.org/en/initiatives/gcp/Global%20Competitiveness %20Report/PastReports /index.htm.

8th Five Year Development Plan of Turkey. The State Planning Organization, June 2000 http://ekutup.dpt.gov.tr/plan/viii/plan8.pdf. Cited 5 Oct 2007.

Oral G. (2006) Creativity of Turkish Prospective Teachers. Creativity Research Journal 18(1): 65–73.

TrendChart Newsletter, June 2006, European Commission http://www.proinno-europe.eu/index.cfm?fuseaction=wiw.informations&page=detail&ID=1646 Cited 10 Oct 2007.

EC (2006) 2006 Innobarometer on clusters' role in facilitating innovation in Europe: Analytical Report. http://cordis.europa.eu/innovation-policy/studies/gen_study17.htm. Cited 8 August 2007.

Elci S. (2007) Assessment of Venture Capital Environment in Turkey. Report to the World Bank.

Conclusion

The book tackles a wide range of issues on the developing world's race to move ahead in the innovation game. Ranging from theoretical issues of macro nature in an effort to understand growth to the significance of the information technology and the importance of competition in this market to technology development zones and National Innovation Systems are analyzed. In doing this, a rich set of empirical observation is provided in an attempt to offer the reader a more tangible account. Moreover, the issues are also provided with in-depth theoretical discussions with the hope of enriching the scope of our analysis.

The next step in this journey is to provide the readers with wider array of empirical research on a variety of countries with the attempt to understand the unique challenges that are faced by the developing countries on their road to sustainable growth. Bearing this in mind, the importance of innovation should stay as the unifying theme of all such studies.

Index

Lightning Source UK Ltd.
Milton Keynes UK

171971UK00006B/25/P